Action Research

*An Educational Leader's
Guide to School Improvement*

— Second Edition —

Action Research

An Educational Leader's Guide to School Improvement

— Second Edition —

Jeffrey Glanz
Wagner College

Christopher-Gordon Publishers, Inc.
Norwood, Massachusetts

Copyright Acknowledgments

Every effort has been made to contact copyright holders for permission to reproduce borrowed material where necessary. We apologize for any oversights and would be happy to rectify them in future printings.

Excerpt from *School Administrator's I Public Speaking Portfolio* by Susan Mamchak and Steven Mamchak. Copyright © 1983. Reprinted with permission of the Center for Applied Research in Educational/Prentice-Hall.

Excerpt from *Tracking Your School's Success: A Guide to Sensible Evaluation*, "Hints for Creating Useful Reports," reprinted with permission of Corwin Press. Sage Publications.

Excerpt from page 162 of Thomas K. Crowl, *Fundamentals of Educational Research*, 2nd edition, used with permission of the McCraw-Hill Companies.

All Students work used with permission.

Excerpt from *Education and Urban Society*, "Good Intentions, Questionable Results: Implications for the Professional Development of Teachers," reprinted with permission of Corwin Press, Sage Publications.

Olivero, J. (1982). "Principals and Their Inservice Needs," *Educational Leadership 43, (5); 343–344.* Reprinted with permission of the Association for Supervision and Curriculum Development. Copyright © 1982 by ASCD. All rights reserved.

Christopher-Gordon Publishers, Inc.
Bridging Theory and Practice

1420 Providence Highway, Suite 120
Norwood, MA 02062

800-934-8322 / 781-762-5577

www.Christopher-Gordon.com
Printed in Canada

10 9 8 7 6 5

12 11 10 09 08

ISBN 13: 978-1-929024-54-4
Library of Congress Catalogue Number: 2002113085

Activity 1.   Setting the Stage

Before you begin reading, answer these five questions (feel free to record your responses on this sheet):

1.   Why are you interested in learning about action research?

_____

_____

_____

_____

2.   What does the term *action research* mean to you?

_____

_____

_____

_____

3.   In what way might action research differ from traditional research?

_____

_____

_____

_____

4.   What do you hope to learn from this book?

_____

_____

_____

_____

5.   Do you have some idea that you would like to research? Explain.

_____

_____

_____

_____

Contents

List of Figures

List of Tables

List of Activities

Preface

There is no research without action,
and there is no action without research.

—Kurt Lewin

I have written the second edition of *Action Research: An Educational Leader's Guide to School Improvement* to provide educational leaders with the knowledge base and practical ideas they need to plan and implement an action research project. Educational leaders are confronted daily with a plethora of challenges that demand an immediate response or at least serious consideration in the near future. Armed with techniques and strategies of action research, these leaders can make thoughtful, reasoned, and intelligent decisions to benefit individual constituents in the school or the entire school or district. As Kurt Lewin's quote above implies, no action can or should take place without some sort of disciplined inquiry. Educators are, above all else, reflective practitioners (Breidenstein, 2001; Schon, 1987) who constantly seek ways of improving their classroom, school, or district.

Quality education in the schools requires excellence in its leaders.

—Linda Lambert

Schools are more complex than ever and demand more "sophisticated sets of skills and understandings than ever before" (Lambert,1998, p. 24). For these and other reasons, it is imperative that educational leaders possess competencies deemed necessary for success in the field (Calabrese, Short, & Zepeda,

1996). The literature recognizes that the role of the leader has three interrelated domains: educational leadership, managerial competency, and political leadership. Each of these domains involves philosophical, social, and psychological perspectives as well as technical competencies. Unprecedented changes in our communities and our society at large are adding to the complexity of these dimensions. Although managerial competency and political leadership are necessary, educational leadership is most crucial (Ubben, Norris, & Hughes, 2000) for leaders in the 21st century. Educational leadership requires expertise in the following areas:

- Foundations and Philosophy
- Learning
- Teaching
- Curriculum
- Research
- Teacher supervision
- Instructional evaluation
- Staff development
- Program evaluation

Action Research attempts to provide the knowledge and skills to address the research and program evaluation components. Educational leaders must be able to do the following:

- Study relevant research for school improvement
- Interpret educational data, issues, and trends
- Know about research, applied theory, informed practice, the recommendations of learned societies, and state and federal policies and mandates relating to curriculum and instruction
- Assess progress using a variety of appropriate techniques
- Understand program evaluation techniques and procedures
- Know how to conduct needs assessments
- Use qualitative and quantitative data to inform decisions
- Resolve problems using appropriate problem-solving techniques and decision-making skills

Informed dynamic educational leaders who use action research achieve excellence in their roles and thus ensure quality education in their school district.

I am gratified that the first edition of *Action Research: An Educational Leader's Guide to School Improvement* has been warmly received in the educational community. Users of the text indicated that its greatest strength was its clarity of expression, especially in explaining difficult concepts. Users also appreciated the step-by-step approach and valued the way that ideas in each chapter built on what the reader had learned in the previous chapters. Reviewers in particular noted the organization of the text as beneficial, and appreciated the friendly writing style, appropriate for both university readers and inservice practitioners.

The second edition of this book continues to incorporate these strengths. Several revisions, however, were made to enhance and improve the overall quality of the text. The following salient changes in this edition are as follows:

- Separate chapters introduce quantitative and qualitative research approaches to the reader.

- Separate chapters are also included for quantitative and qualitative data analyses.

- A separate chapter is included to help the reader get started with an action research project.

- Sample action research projects are provided.

- New pedagogical features are included at the beginning (focus questions) and end of each chapter (activities in the form of tear-outs) to review important information and to activate readers for what they are about to encounter.

In addition to these salient changes, the following minor changes have been made throughout the text:

- All references and Web sites have been updated.

- Some exercises in several chapters have been relocated.

- Sentences and paragraphs have been rewritten to enhance clarification.

- One or two more concrete examples have been provided to make a point stronger.

- The mathematical approach in the quantitative chapter has been minimized.

- Some of the material in the quantitative chapter has been condensed.

- A new appendix has been added that includes a sample cover letter.

These changes will, I hope, substantially improve *Action Research.* I continue to strive to make this book readable and user-friendly. I use a casual writing style throughout most of the chapters, while fully covering the content required for how to do action research.

I am eager to hear your reactions to the new edition. Please feel free to e-mail me your reactions and suggestions for future editions, offer some advice, or ask a question. You may contact me at jglanz@wagner.edu. If you wish, I will include your e-mail address in an e-mail chat group on action research. I wish you continued success in all your professional endeavors.

References

Breidenstein, A. (2001). Outcomes of preservice teachers' qualitative research. *Clearing House, 74* (3), 141–144.

Calabrese, R. L., Short, G., & Zepeda, S. J. (1996). *Hands-on leadership tools for principals.* Princeton, NJ: Eye on Education.

Lambert, L. (1998). *Building leadership capacity in schools.* Alexandria, VA: Association for Supervision and Curriculum Development.

Schon, D. A. (1987). *Educating the reflective practitioner: Toward a new design for thinking and learning in the professional.* San Francisco: Jossey-Bass.

Ubben, G. C., Norris, C. J., & Hughes, L. W. (2000). *The principal: Creative leadership for effective schools.* Boston: Allyn & Bacon.

Acknowledgments

I wish to acknowledge my new students at Wagner College and my former students at Kean University and the College of Staten Island, City University of New York, who have helped to revise this volume into a more useful and practical guide to action research. Special acknowledgment is offered to the following three reviewers, whose thoughtful and extensive comments helped to frame this new edition: Ken Lince, Dr. Janice Eckmier, and Marsha Beard. I wish to acknowledge the following individuals who have particularly inspired or assisted me in completing this second edition: Leonard Elovitz, Javier Velazquez, and my wife, Lisa, for her continuous moral and spiritual support. Any misrepresentations and inaccuracies are, of course, my sole responsibility.

Introduction

The reason everyone goes into education is to have a powerful influence on the educational lives of students. Action research helps reinforce and cement the belief that together [teachers and administrators] can make a difference.

—Glickman,1995

Brief Description

This book is intended as a practical guide to conducting action research in schools. Although it offers neither a cookbook nor a quick-fix approach, this book does outline the process of designing and reporting an action research project. Useful as a classroom text and self-teaching tool, *Action Research: An Educational Leader's Guide to School Improvement* is a comprehensive training manual. It can be used by practitioners in the field, by graduate students enrolled in leadership and/or master's thesis courses, or by anyone interested in learning how to conduct action research projects.

The underlying assumption of this work is that research is not a domain only for academics, it is also a powerful approach that can be used by practitioners to contribute to school renewal and instructional improvement. Rather than being merely a philosophical treatise or theoretical analysis, *Action Research* provides you with concrete strategies and techniques for conducting action research in schools.

Uniqueness

Action Research differs dramatically from other works on the subject. In this book, action research is more broadly conceived than it is in previous works. Many works on the subject describe the process simply as one in which a problem is identified by the practitioner, some questions are framed, data are collected from some sources, conclusions are drawn, and some action is then taken. Although these are the basic steps in action research, this approach simplifies the process to the point that it renders the project insignificant or as capable of making only minimal contributions at best. Action research, as described and explained in this book, places more faith in practitioners as professional educators who can be trained and expected to utilize elaborate, thoughtful, and significant approaches to solving problems in school settings. Hence, in *Action Research* attention is devoted to specific strategies and techniques that have traditionally been reserved only for the more advanced practice of educational research.

Action research, then, is not merely a type of research reserved for individuals with little if any formal training in educational research. Rather, action research is a viable tool used by professional and skilled educators who incorporate a wide variety of methodologies, designs, and approaches when conducting research. This underlying assumption makes this book unique.

Moreover, as will be explained later, action research is not a separate method of research (along with descriptive, historical, correlational, and evaluation research). Rather, it is a type of research that may utilize and incorporate many different methods of research. Hence, this book is also unique because it considers action research as a process that may include various methods to suit its purpose(s).

Audience

Action Research is designed primarily for three groups of practitioners (Walling, 1994):

1. Graduate students, usually teachers, enrolled in a research seminar or course as part of a program leading to a master's degree in administration or supervision and/or state or city certification as a school administrator or supervisor

2. Practicing administrators and supervisors such as principals, vice principals, department chairpeople, curriculum directors, and supervisors of instruction

3. Teachers in leadership positions

Three other groups may also find this book useful:

1. Teachers who want more information about action research

2. Parents involved in collaborative research projects in site-based managed schools

3. Staff developers who conduct workshops on action research

Rationale

Many fine textbooks present a general overview of educational research. Most of these books, however, go far beyond what practitioners (e.g., teachers, school administrators, or supervisors) may need to know in conducting on-site research. Having taught research techniques to teachers and supervisor-trainees for many years, I have found that my students do not need, or rarely use, many of the research techniques described in more traditional textbooks. Statistical procedures such as factor, multivariate, discriminant, path, and meta-analysis have marginal value, at best, for the teacher-practitioner or the practicing school administrator. Students have frequently asked for a text that encapsulates the essence of research in a straightforward and understandable way, emphasizing strategies and techniques of research that have practical value. *Action Research* is an attempt to fill this perceived need.

Although discussion of advanced statistical analysis goes beyond the purview of this text, action research can and does utilize both qualitative and quantitative approaches. I will argue that although action research is a process that can be simply applied to improve schools, it is by no means a simple approach to research. Action research, as described in this volume, can involve some rather sophisticated methods and approaches to research. This latter point is often neglected or underemphasized by many individuals who write about and advocate action research.

Action Research is not designed, however, to treat all the fundamental research strategies and techniques that students who are writing doctoral dissertations (for example) may require. The student interested in a more comprehensive text on research should consult Charles (1997), Creswell (2002), Crowl (1996), Gay (1999), McMillan and Schumacher (1997), Tuckman (1999), and Wiersma (1999), among others. This book is designed to introduce those research strategies that are likely to be used by practicing supervisors and teachers in their attempt to improve school practices on a daily basis. As such, this book might also be a valuable guidebook for conducting action research at the master's and doctoral levels.

The field of action research has a number of useful introductory books that give the reader a general overview (Greenwood & Levin, 1998; McLean, 1995; McNiff, 1995; Mills, 2000; Reason & Bradbury, 2001; Sager, 1992; Stringer, 1999). Although a few books exist that deal specifically with action research, many of them are not very user-friendly, do not provide enough techniques, are often too technical and brief, and are not geared at all to practicing school administrators. The value of this book is that specific, easy-to-use techniques and strategies are discussed, so that practitioners in the supervision field can apply action research for school improvement more judiciously and comprehensively.

Assumptions

Action Research: An Educational Leader's Guide to School Improvement was written with the following assumptions in mind:

1. Most students reading this textbook have had little if any exposure to research methodology and design.

2. School administrators, supervisors, and teachers do not have enough time to engage in lengthy, complicated research. As such, they need to be acquainted with practical and useful research techniques and strategies in order to gather sufficient data before making decisions.

3. Many textbooks on educational research are far too technical to have much practical value for administrators, supervisors, and teachers.

4. School administrators, supervisors, and teachers need training in conducting action research.

5. Action research is an invaluable tool for simultaneously improving instruction at the classroom level and rejuvenating the overall health of the school organization.

Goals

After completing *Action Research,* you should be familiar with the basic elements of research design and be equipped with a number of effective research and evaluative strategies. You will better understand the importance of research, feel more confident about implementing an action research project, and realize how applying these strategies and techniques can help you to become a better decision maker and problem solver. The organizational health of your school depends, to a large extent, on the degree to which you are committed to an inquiry-oriented approach toward instructional excellence. In sum, the three main goals of this book are as follows:

1. To familiarize you with the steps necessary to carry out action research and evaluation in educational settings

2. To provide you with a method for making intelligent and informed decisions about educational problems or concerns

3. To encourage you to appreciate the art of disciplined inquiry

Organization and Content

Action Research is meant to be interactive in the sense that you are encouraged to complete the sample review exercises provided in each chapter to reinforce newly learned concepts. Readers are encouraged to complete the activity sheets that are included as tear-outs. These activities prepare readers for what lies ahead and reinforces previously learned material. A general pretest (which can serve as a posttest as well) is presented in Appendix A. I suggest that you assess your knowledge of research by taking this test before starting chapter 1. Please note that you are not expected to know many of the answers to the questions on this pretest. The pretest serves to assess your knowledge of some areas of research. After completing the book, you will certainly have an increased knowledge of research. Don't get frustrated when taking the pretest; just try to do your best.

I have tried to make this book as user-friendly as possible. Examples are drawn from everyday school experiences and situations that those concerned with supervision and teaching are likely to encounter. Exercises are provided, in most chapters, to help you think of meaningful ways to use and apply research in your position as a supervisor or teacher. The book will serve as a reference guide and handy manual as you continue to undertake a research-oriented approach to school improvement.

I start with a basic introduction to research in chapter 1, "An Introduction to Action Research: It's Not All That Complicated." This chapter takes you through some concepts and principles of research in general and then explains the meaning and value of action research. Steps are provided for conducting action research, and exercises are introduced to help you think through some of the ways action research may be incorporated. The chapter suggests that action research is a viable, useful, and relatively easy-to-use means of promoting school improvement, as well as an approach that can certainly enhance your personal professional development.

In chapter 2, "Teaching and Doing Action Research Through General Semantics," I introduce a multidimensional model that is integral to understanding and planning any sort of action research project. Drawing briefly on general semantics (the study of the relationship among language, thought, and human behavior) the chapter challenges you to gain a varied perspective when confronting an educational problem. This multidimensional view limits potential bias because a multitude of data sources is utilized. The concept of *triangulation* is introduced as a powerful tool for conducting research.

Chapter 3, "Getting Started on an Action Research Project," discusses the first steps that action researchers must take. This chapter provides an overview of the research plan and lists a set of questions to clarify the purpose and plan of your research project. Alerting you to logistical concerns, the chapter concludes with several suggestions for getting started.

Chapter 4, "Quantitative Approaches to Action Research," opens by suggesting that both quantitative and qualitative approaches are desirable. Once an approach (or several approaches) has been identified, selection of a suitable method and type of research is considered. Then the importance of designing the research to suit the area of investigation is emphasized. You will also be introduced to some basic principles and elements of research that form the foundation for being able to select an appropriate research strategy. You will read about situations in which educational leaders make decisions and solve problems as they refine their research designs. You will learn several practical quantitative research designs that can be used by practitioners in almost any school setting.

Chapter 5, "Qualitative Approaches to Action Research," accomplishes the same goals as the previous chapter by focusing on historical, ethnographic, and case study research.

In chapter 6, "Easy Steps to Program Development and Evaluation Research," I discuss the most common form of action research for educational leaders. Developing programs and evaluating their effectiveness assume great importance among educational leaders. This chapter includes a discussion of eight steps in program development and five steps in program evaluation, as well as examples and applications.

In chapter 7, "Data Collection Techniques That Work," I discuss various methods for collecting data that can be readily used by practitioners. Various data collection instruments for conducting both quantitative and qualitative research are explained in depth.

Chapter 8, "How to Analyze Quantitative Data Easily," explains what to do once all the data have been collected. Various quantitative methods for analyzing data are presented, and basic statistical procedures are discussed.

Chapter 9, "How to Analyze Qualitative Data Easily," accomplishes the same goals as the previous chapter by focusing on nonstatistical, qualitative procedures.

Chapter 10, "Putting It All Together: What Does It All Mean?", discusses concrete ways of interpreting and reporting findings generated from action research projects. Suggested guidelines for writing action research reports are also offered.

In chapter 11, "Completing Your Action Research Master's Degree Thesis Project," five easy steps are outlined to help you successfully complete a thesis or research project. Detailed descriptions of steps for quantitative and qualitative studies are provided. Parts of sample thesis projects are included.

Chapter 12, "Action Research in Action," discusses ways to implement action research in your school by providing concrete strategies. It argues that action research, as a form of inquiry, is most welcome in a school or a district that is framed as a learning community.

Chapter 13 summarizes the action research approach advocated in this book and provides seven final suggestions or caveats for conducting action research while briefly discussing some ethical issues related to conducting action research.

A glossary of key terms is also provided. Although many terms are explained in the text where they occur, some terms are discussed anew and at length in the glossary. Use it interactively as you read the text. Words that are defined in the glossary are printed in boldface on first (major) usage. Annotated references of selected key works are provided as a guide for further reading, and the appendixes include materials to supplement and reinforce your newfound knowledge and to provide information necessary to conduct and report action research. In each chapter, the references that are asterisked can be found in the annotated references at the end of the book.

I hope you will find the research techniques described in this book to be useful. As you seek better ways to improve your school, you will appreciate action research as a user-friendly process for making more intelligent decisions about various educational problems. Follow the guidelines suggested in this book, especially the ones outlined in chapter 13. Feel free to share your experiences and seek advice. If you would like to continue dialogue about school improvement through action research and/or offer suggestions for future editions of this book, please e-mail me at jglanz@wagner.edu. I wish you continued success in all your professional and personal endeavors.

References

Charles, C. M. (1997). *Introduction to educational research.* New York: Addison-Wesley Longman.

Creswell, J. W. (2002). *Educational research.* Upper Saddle River, NJ: Merrill Prentice-Hall.

Crowl, T. K. (1996). *Fundamentals of educational research* (2nd ed.). Madison, WI: Brown & Benchmark.

Gay, L. R. (1999). *Educational research: Competencies for analysis and application* (6th ed.). Englewood Cliffs, NJ: Prentice-Hall.

*Glickman, C. D. (1995). *Action research: Inquiry, reflection, and decision-making.* [Video]. Alexandria, VA: Association for Supervision and Curriculum Development.

Greenwood, D. J., & Levin, M. (1998). *Introduction to action research: Social research for social change.* Thousand Oaks, CA: Sage.

*McLean, J. E. (1995). *Improving education through action research: A guide for administrators and teachers.* Thousand Oaks, CA: Corwin Press.

McMillan, J. H., & Schumacher, S. (1997). *Research in education: A conceptual introduction.* New York: Longman.

*McNiff, J. (1995). *Action research: Principles and practice.* London: Routledge.

Mills, G. E. (2000). *Action research: A guide for the teacher researcher.* Upper Saddle River, NJ: Merrill Prentice-Hall.

Reason P., & Bradbury, H. (2001). *Handbook of action research: Participative inquiry and practice.* Thousand Oaks, CA: Sage.

*Sagor, R. (1992). *How to conduct collaborative action research.* Alexandria, VA: Association for Supervision and Curriculum Development.

*Stringer, E. T. (1999). *Action research: A handbook for practitioners.* Thousand Oaks, CA: Sage.

Tuckman, B. (1999). *Conducting educational research* (5th ed.). New York: Harcourt.

Walling, D. R. (Ed.). (1994). *Teachers as leaders: Perspectives on the professional development of teachers.* Bloomington, IN: Phi Delta Kappa.

Wiersma, W. (1999). *Research methods in education: An introduction* (7th ed.). Boston: Allyn & Bacon.

Activity 2. Goal Setting

1. React to the list of assumptions on page xxiv. Can you attest to the validity of those statements?

_____

_____

_____

_____

_____

_____

_____

_____

_____

_____

_____

_____

2. Compare your learning objectives, as stated in the answer to the fourth question in Activity 1, to the goals on page xxv and to the content outlined on pages xxv–xxvii. Do the goals and contents of this book match your expectations?

_____

_____

_____

_____

_____

_____

_____

_____

_____

_____

_____

_____

Cut here

An Introduction to Action Research: It's Not All That Complicated

Focus Questions

1. What comes to mind when you think of the word *research*?

2. What does an "action researcher" do?

3. Have you ever participated in an action research project?

4. Why do you think evaluation research is the most common use of action research among educational leaders?

5. How might action research improve practice?

Although action research is not a quick fix for all school problems, it represents a process that...can focus the brain-power of the entire instructional staff on maximizing learning.

—McLean, 1995

Mentioning *research* to almost anyone conjures up images of some scientist conducting experiments in a distant and secluded laboratory. Mention *educational research* and reactions may include recollections of one's master's thesis project or less complimentary thoughts of some eccentric professor engaging in some inane study unrelated to practice. To many educators—teachers and supervisors alike—the value of research is marginal at best. Educators who work in public and private schools remain unconvinced of the efficacy of most of what gets published in professional and scholarly journals in the field of education.

Debating the efficacy and relevance of much of this type of educational research is not my intended purpose, although I could cite some strong reasons for its value and utility for practicing school people. It seems to me that the inclination to avoid research of any sort is shortsighted, provincial, and possibly deleterious. A fundamental premise of this book is that proper utilization of research is not only beneficial but necessary and urgent in order to renew our schools as well as empower both teachers and supervisors.

What Is Research?

The word *research* is derived, etymologically, from the French word *rechercher,* meaning to travel through or to survey. As such, research can be thought of as an investigation "to discover or establish facts and relationships" (Charles, 1997, p. 5). Research, at its most basic level, is a process of gathering information. All of us have conducted research in many ways. As teachers we find ways of gathering information in order to assess our students' achievement and social development. Observing Sarah interact in a cooperative learning group, for instance, gives us much information about the degree to which she cooperates with her peers. As educational leaders we may informally observe a teacher working with a group of students during a reading lesson. As we observe, we collect information. We may note, for instance, that the teacher is asking her male students more thought-provoking questions than she is asking the female students. We may also note that she allows more wait-time for boys than for girls. As we continue to observe, we begin to better understand the nature of the interaction between this teacher and her students.

Research, in a sense, is also a way of knowing. At times we come to know something intuitively. Educational leaders, as specially trained observers, are often able to see aspects of a particular situation that are unknown to the "unenlightened eye" (Eisner, 1991). They can gather information, at times, instinctively. Relying on instinct alone, however, is certainly insufficient as a way to fully appreciate the complexity involved in a teaching and learning situation. I'm reminded of the impressionistic and imprecise methods employed by supervisors of the 19th century. James M. Greenwood (1891), a prominent city school superintendent from Kansas, for example, described the skilled supervisor as someone who could simply walk into a classroom and "judge from a compound sensation of the disease at work among the inmates" (p. 227). Not a very appealing metaphor, wouldn't you agree?

Although there are different ways of knowing, research is essentially a more disciplined and scientific, if you will, approach. Although I hesitate to use the word *scientific* so early in this book—for fear that the word may conjure up some unpleasant memories or negative associations—research, nevertheless, is a systematic approach of applying the **scientific method,** a four-step approach to disciplined inquiry. We apply the scientific method by defining a problem, stating a hypothesis, collecting and analyzing data, and confirming or rejecting the hypothesis. Through this method we begin to get a more accurate understanding of a specific situation.

Situation: Dr. Bea Williams, middle school principal, institutes a pilot literature-based reading program in selected classes in grades 6 through 8. After a 6-month period, the principal wishes to assess the impact of this literature-based program on reading comprehension achievement.

Analysis: Dr. Williams essentially wants to know whether this new program is successfully meeting the academic needs of students. She may "know" that the impact of the program is a positive one through the following means of assessment:

1. Informally observing classes and speaking with one or two teachers

2. Being informed by others of the program's success

3. Surmising that the program is very successful

4. Logically deducing that because instances of reports of misbehavior have declined dramatically since the implementation of the program, it is likely that students are learning

5. Assessing posttest scores on a reading comprehension examination of two comparable classes per grade, one of which was exposed to literature-based reading while the other was taught by traditional basal readers

Obviously, a research-oriented approach would favor the fifth, more "scientific," method. We may very well be suspicious of an approach that seems to rely on informal, haphazard, and perhaps biased observations. Conclusions drawn from observations based only on information derived by others and from observations based on intuition or presumed logical reasoning may be equally suspicious.

Research, as disciplined inquiry, can contribute enormously to the work of educational leaders. Research is not some esoteric activity reserved for Ph.D.s and research scientists. Research is something we all can do to help us understand, if not solve, some of the urgent issues we confront on a daily basis in schools. To do so thoughtfully, comprehensively, and intelligently is what research is all about.

Ignorance About the Utility of Research

Many teachers, administrators, and other educational leaders have not been adequately prepared to understand how research can positively affect their work. More disturbing is that many educational leaders eschew research as being impractical and simply "not worth the effort." This apparent dichotomy between research and practice is troublesome and unfortunate. As a former practicing school administrator, supervisor, and teacher, I can personally attest to the lack of interest in or ignorance about educational research among many practitioners. Yet I have seen significant numbers of educational leaders who successfully incorporated research as a viable means for promoting effective schooling and enhancing student achievement.

Research as a Professional Responsibility

An essential characteristic of any profession is the expertise of its members. In order to question and evaluate effectively, the professional educational leader must have knowledge of research methodology. The leader is confronted on a daily basis by a plethora of problems that demand careful consideration and analysis. The decision-making ability of an educational leader is greatly hindered without the scrutiny of evaluation and research. An educational expert is required to test the validity of various proposals. In other words, he or she is a hypothesis maker and tester. The leader is not a neutral technician who merely dictates policies without conducting appropriate follow-ups. He or she is an educational expert who possesses professional knowledge and technical skills that enable him or her to analyze and solve problems with insight and imagination.

Unfortunately, many educators avoid research, condemning it as having dubious practical value. For these individuals, research is nothing more than theoretical formulations having little if any impact on schools. As James Olivero (1982) states, "unfortunately, practitioners frequently believe researchers are so protected from the hassles of everyday life that the ivory-tower types can't possibly understand the real world" (p. 343). The dichotomy between theory and practice has long been a chief complaint of many practitioners. The educational leader, however, is in a pivotal position in schools to bridge the gap between theory and practice by demonstrating the importance of research in the day-to-day operation of a school (Kagan, 1995). Research *is* a major professional responsibility of any educational leader.

Situation: Charles Daley, an elementary school principal in a midwestern urban setting, has been informed by two of his more experienced faculty that they would like to initiate a team teaching project. Inspired in large measure by an Association for Supervision and Curriculum Development conference from which they both recently returned, these two veteran teachers seem, to Mr. Daley, more enthusiastic than they've been in years. Concerned, attentive, and somewhat curious about their enthusiasm, Mr. Daley begins a computer search to collect information on team teaching. Using the Educational Resources Information Center CD-ROM database and a World Wide Web search on Yahoo, Mr. Daley begins to collect the latest research on team teaching. In a relatively short time, he has amassed an extensive number of articles published on the topic and has gathered information about schools that have experimented with team teaching for years. Mr. Daley forwards this information to his teachers and offers his continued support.

Analysis: Mr. Daley's interest in assisting his teachers by doing some preliminary research on team teaching demonstrates his sense of professionalism in two ways: (a) His willingness to encourage his faculty by collecting some basic research on a topic that interests them is admirable and is likely to promote a learning community, and (b) although Mr. Daley's efforts are very basic in terms of what can eventually be accomplished through action research, his initial efforts demonstrate not only his knowledge of data collecting but also his commitment to a spirit of inquiry.

Why Educational Leaders Might Avoid Research

Lack of Time. Educational leaders are confronted daily with a plethora of demanding tasks. The increasingly complex nature of the educational leader's job may indeed seem overwhelming (Whitaker, 1995). Principals and other educational leaders often complain of time management issues. Yet despite the apparent tensions and pressures that are characteristic of the principalship, for instance, lack of time to attend to necessary tasks and responsibilities may be remedied with effective time management strategies. Educational leaders would benefit from time management workshops to enable them to better cope with their ever increasing responsibilities. To simply say that one has no time to undertake research is not a viable or acceptable response. I have personally worked with many principals and other educational leaders who have utilized research to improve and renew their schools. If they were able to find time to undertake action research, then you certainly can, but only if you believe that such an undertaking is important.

Impractical. Many individuals assume that research is reserved for the research scientist or college professor but is not feasible for the practitioner. For these individuals, research is narrowly defined. Different types of research do exist. Although some types of research are best reserved for specially trained individuals, other forms, such as action research, are indeed viable. A growing literature base (e.g., Stringer, 1999) and the documented experiences of many practitioners (e.g., Palanki & Burch, 1995) attest to the practicality and usefulness of action research.

Ignorance. Many educational leaders simply lack the knowledge of how to best conduct and utilize research. They have not been formally trained in research strategies and methods that are appropriate and viable in schools. Consequently, many educational leaders often fear or eschew research. Action research is an attempt to provide technical knowledge and requisite skills so that you will feel more knowledgeable and comfortable in employing research strategies in your daily practice.

A Paradigm for Research

Although textbook authors of educational research have categorized types, methods, and forms of research differently (Best & Kahn, 1998), I have found the paradigm in Figure 1-1 to be a useful means to give my students an overall understanding of how action research is situated in a broader context as well as to highlight specific methods and research techniques that may be valuable to an action researcher.

Earlier in this chapter, I introduced the paradigm by defining research as disciplined inquiry that utilizes a systematic approach by applying the scientific method to study educational problems. There are two categories of research: basic and applied (Figure 1-2).They differ from one another in purpose but not necessarily in complexity or value.

Basic (also called *pure* or *fundamental*) research involves experiments that attempt to extend our knowledge in a given discipline or field of study. The goal of basic research is to develop **theory,** a statement of interrelated sets of assumptions and propositions. Basic research has no immediate practical value, but it is essential in furthering our understanding of important phenomena. Theories of learning, for example, are generated from basic research.

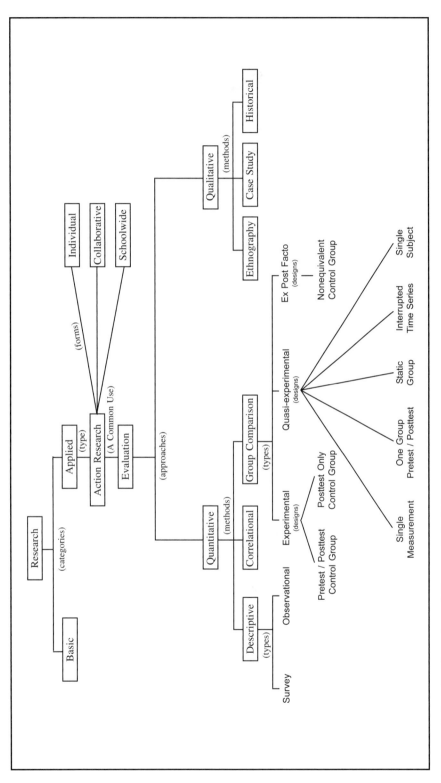

Figure 1-1. An Overview of Research in Education

Figure 1-2.

Applied research is conducted chiefly in order to improve practice by solving a specific problem. Attempts at applying learning theory to solve practical problems that teachers face in the classroom are examples of this category of research (e.g., Hunter, 1967).

Action research is one type of applied research (Figure 1-3). Administrators and supervisors (and other educational leaders) conduct action research in order to address a specific problem by using the principles and methodologies of research. Although action research utilizes less rigorous designs and methodologies than other forms of applied research, its benefits are enormous for the professional development of the educational leaders who use action research and for the school as a whole.

Figure 1-3.

Three forms of action research (Figure 1-4) allow educators to investigate areas of concern in their classrooms and schools: individual, collaborative, and schoolwide (Calhoun, 1993). Individual teachers and supervisors may conduct a research project that focuses on a specific class, program, or activity. The educator may define an area of investigation and then seek a solution or may simply collect data to determine a course of action. All action research projects begin with an individual educator who has the necessary knowledge, skills, and desire to carry out such an enterprise. Collaborative action research is taken on by a group or team of individuals that can focus on one classroom, several classrooms, or even a districtwide investigation (Oja & Smulyan, 1989). Schoolwide action research is undertaken by a community of practitioners including teachers, parents, students, and administrators to address schoolwide issues and solve common problems (Calhoun, 1994; Calhoun, Allen, Halliburton, & Jones, 1996; *Equity and Choice,* 1993; McNiff, 1995; Sagor, 1992; Stringer, 1999).

Figure 1-4.

The distinction between collaborative and schoolwide research may be subtle and even arbitrary. Certainly a school faculty committee that involves parents and students, for instance, is collaborative in nature. The difference between these two forms of action research is not important in this volume, which essentially deals with individual action research projects. Although collaborate and schoolwide action research are essential for school renewal (Glickman, 1998), this book primarily addresses the basics of how individual supervisors and other educational leaders may conduct action research. This approach is justified by the belief that before teams of committed professionals can deal with complex schoolwide problems, training in action research should be provided for dealing with classroom or gradewide projects. Action research projects are more likely to be encouraged and supported by educational leaders who have experienced firsthand the benefits of this type of research on a small scale. Furthermore, such training empowers administrators and teachers to conduct action research themselves without reliance on outside experts.

Like educational research in general, action research may utilize two approaches to inquiry: quantitative and qualitative. Although action research is generally thought of as entailing only qualitative approaches, sound action research may indeed benefit from a varied approach to disciplined inquiry that includes both qualitative and quantitative approaches.

Qualitative research relies on detailed verbal descriptions of the phenomena observed. Three methods of qualitative research that may be useful to the action researcher are ethnography, case study, and historical inquiry (Figure 1-5). Qualitative approaches do not utilize statistical or mathematical expressions. Action researchers often find that qualitative methods can be very easily adopted in school settings.

Figure 1-5.

Quantitative research relies on numerical data. Three methods of quantitative research that may be useful to the action researcher are descriptive, correlational, and group comparison research (Figure 1-6). Descriptive research can be broken down further into two types: survey and observational research (Figure 1-7). Correlational research has no subdivisions, whereas group comparison research can be divided into three types: experimental, quasi-experimental, and ex post facto research. Specific research designs are employed to conduct experimental, quasi-experimental, and ex post facto research.

Figure 1-6.

Figure 1-7.

As each approach, method, type, and design of research is explained in the text, Figures 1-1 through 1-7 should be referred to in order to help place the concept within context.

Evaluation Research: The Most Common Use of Action Research for Educational Leaders

> *Effective school principals must be evaluation-oriented leaders, and they need substantial competence in measurement and other aspects of evaluation.*
>
> —Stufflebeam, 1996

Evaluation research is the gathering of data in order to make a decision. Some authors include it as a separate category of research (McMillan & Schumacher, 2000). In this volume, however, evaluation research is considered as one possible use of action research. A goal of evaluation research is to assess the quality of a particular practice or program in a school. Evaluation research is very much involved in addressing a specific problem. In my experience, educational leaders as action researchers undertake evaluative studies quite often. Thus, evaluation research is considered the most common use of action research.

Educational leaders are likely to engage in evaluation research because they are involved in assessing a variety of educational concerns such as special programs, methods of teaching, and instructional materials.

Administrators and other educational leaders need to make many decisions on a daily basis. Unfortunately, many of these decisions are often made hurriedly and without the scrutiny of thoughtful, scientific investigation. What seems to be most expedient at the time is often the most important criterion for determining the fate of a new program. In my experiences in schools, I have found that when educational leaders are trained in sound research methodology, decisions are made more intelligently and equitably. To determine the fate of a new program, the educational leader would collect appropriate data from a number of sources before making the final decision to disband, modify, or even continue the program. The value of evaluation research is its ability to help leaders make informed educational decisions.

Parenthetically, evaluation research may also be used for the purpose of identifying problems. This strategy is usually undertaken during a needs assessment phase in which potential problems and issues are identified. Such an approach will be discussed in chapter 6 in the context of needs assessment. Furthermore, evaluation as action research may be used for benchmarking purposes by examining what other schools are doing in regard to a particular instructional strategy. In this way, the school might better assess itself in regard to its own instructional program. Although other uses of evaluation as action research are possible, this text will focus primarily on overall program evaluation because of its ubiquitous nature.

A Typical Day in the Life of a Vice Principal

Today was a typical day for Roberta Rodriguez, vice principal of Boynton High School, located in an affluent suburb of Chicago. In addition to preparing the day's scheduling and arranging for substitute teachers, she was involved in the mundane activities associated with the position of vice principal in a school of nearly 2,500 students. Today, Ms. Rodriguez did the following:

- Distributed newly obtained textbooks to the English Department
- Selected William Johnson to escort the school band to the district's open house celebration
- Decided to call an emergency grade conference to familiarize teachers about the newly adopted core content curriculum standards
- Recommended to the School-Community Council that Sylvia Barnett be selected as Parent of the Month

- Completed her evaluation report of the afterschool student at-risk program
- Began a needs assessment in order to implement an interdisciplinary team teaching program
- Placed a new student in Steve Goldman's already overcrowded homeroom
- Suggested that the art and science programs be revised
- Scheduled time for the Chess Club to meet during fourth period
- Recommended suspension for Maurice and Christopher for pulling the fire alarm at dismissal
- Interviewed a prospective teacher for a vacancy in the English Department
- Supervised first-period lunch duty in the cafeteria
- Determined that Joan Smith, an untenured teacher, should not be rehired for the next semester
- Observed Phyllis Williams, a veteran teacher, during fourth period
- Conducted a postconference with Ms. Williams during eighth period

As you can see, Ms. Rodriguez's day, like the days of most other educational leaders, was not only arduous and frenetic at times but was also filled with many situations in which decisions had to be made. Educational leaders are quite often challenged by decisions related to student discipline, administration of school policies, evaluation of teachers, graduation activities, emergency arrangements, efficacy of new curricula, implementation and evaluation of various school programs, and much more.

Taken together, decisions that educational leaders make help to establish, organize, and monitor various aspects of the school organization. Leaders' effectiveness is ultimately entwined with the overall efficacy of the school organization. It is imperative, then, that decisions be made thoughtfully yet decisively. The decisions Ms. Rodriguez made were based on many different kinds of evidence that she collected. Why, for example, did she suggest that the art and science programs be revised? How did she know that the programs were in serious trouble? Why did she decide to implement an interdisciplinary team teaching program? All of these decisions were based on information Ms. Rodriguez had gathered. This book is about the process of gathering and using information to help make better supervisory decisions, and that is what evaluation research is all about.

What to Evaluate?

Evaluation research can be divided into three types (the 3 Ps):

1. Program evaluation
2. Procedural evaluation
3. Product evaluation

Educational leaders are usually involved with making judgments about the effectiveness or desirability of various programs. They can and should assess such things as school goals and priorities, academic programs, extracurricular activities, school policies and rules, school climate, and special projects.

An educational leader might ask questions such as these: "Does the new program work?" "What impact does inclusion have on the attitudes of teachers?" "Does the whole-language program affect reading achievement levels among third graders?" Program evaluation that is regular, dynamic, and ongoing contributes greatly to the overall effectiveness of the school organization. This book, though not attending to all aspects of evaluation research, will describe program evaluation as one facet of action research that is often neglected.

Perhaps the most common form of decision making undertaken by educational leaders is procedural evaluation. This second type of evaluation research assesses personnel such as teachers and staff. Ensuring the competence of teachers is perhaps the foremost concern of educational leaders. Although personnel evaluation is important, I will not address this topic because much work has been published in this area (Peterson, 2000) and this form of research is not directly applicable to our discussion of action research.

Educational leaders also need to evaluate facilities and equipment, financial plans, school resources, and instructional materials on an ongoing basis. Product evaluation deserves special analysis (DeRoche, 1987) that is, however, beyond the scope of this volume.

Before proceeding with the remainder of the chapter, complete the following exercises to help reinforce some of the ideas expressed above.

Exercises

1. The process of gathering information to aid decision making is known as

   a. evaluation
   b. research
   c. sampling
   d. action projects
   e. networking

   Answer: b

2. The greatest obstacle faced by an educational leader in undertaking evaluative research is that he or she

   a. is deluged with other administrative and instructional tasks
   b. doesn't really care to go to the trouble of undertaking extensive research
   c. is not knowledgeable about research in schools
   d. is not given sufficient leeway from the building principal
   e. has no support from the district office or central board of education

   Answer: Choice "c" is correct because it is not that educational leaders are too busy, don't care, and/or don't have the authority or support to undertake research, but rather that their lack of professional development in this area precludes involvement in action research. Once equipped with the requisite knowledge, skills, and dispositions, leaders will apply the principles of research to improve their schools.

3. What images are conjured up in your mind when you think of *research*. Share responses with colleagues.

   _____

   _____

   _____

   Answers will vary

4. Research is a professional responsibility. Rate yourself on your knowledge and comfort levels in undertaking research. A score of 10 would indicate that you are "ready-to-go" and a score of 0 might mean that you have much to learn. Share responses with colleagues.

   _____

   _____

   _____

   Answers will vary

5. What kinds of programs might you evaluate in your school or district?

   _____

   _____

   Answers will vary

Evolution of Action Research

Kemmis (cited in Oja & Smulyan, 1989) outlines four phases in the history of educational research. The earliest phase of educational research is characterized by attempts to "make sense of practice by developing educational theory 'on a grand scale'" (p. vii). Developing theory to guide practice was a foremost concern to theorists such as John Dewey. Dissatisfied with the application of theory to practice, educators urged researchers to apply the techniques and principles of science to "examine and improve practice" directly. This second phase of research in education was direct and practical in the sense that once problems were identified, solutions through the application of the scientific method could be attained. A third approach appeared in opposition to this technical approach, which some thought simplified educational theory and practice by trying to find ready-made solutions to complex problems. During this phase, which Kemmis calls the pessimistic phase, tensions between practitioners and theoreticians were heightened. Research undertaken during this phase soon became seen as divorced from practice. Consequently, a fourth phase emerged, the self-reflective phase, which "recognizes practitioners' rights and skills as professionals and encourages their involvement in the examination of practice and the clarification of theory" (p. vii). Action research emerges from this self-reflective phase of educational research.

Although first popularized in the 1940s by Kurt Lewin (Adelman, 1993), action research was first systematically applied in education by Stephen Corey, a professor at Teachers College, Columbia University. Corey (1953) encouraged teachers and supervisors to use action research to improve their own practice. Corey, a man ahead of his time, advocated that fundamental change could not occur without the direct involvement of teachers and supervisors:

> The studies must be undertaken by those who may have to change the way they do things....Our schools cannot keep up with the life they are supposed to sustain and improve unless teachers, pupils, supervisors, administrators, and school patrons continuously examine what they are doing. Singly and in groups, they must use their imaginations creatively and constructively to identify the practices that must be changed to meet the needs and demands of modern life, courageously try out those practices that give better promise, and methodically and systematically gather evidence to test their worth....This is the process I call action research. (p. viii)

Action research gained further legitimacy when distinguished educators such as Hilda Taba, curriculum specialist and also a professor of education at Teachers College, Columbia University, advocated action research in the late 1950s. She believed that action research contributed much toward curriculum development. She saw two basic purposes for action research: (a) to produce evidence needed to solve practical problems, and (b) to help those who are doing the action research to acquire more adequate perspective regarding their problems, deepen their insights as to what is involved in their task, and extend their orientation toward children—toward methods of teaching them or toward what is significant in content of learning (Taba & Noel, 1957, p. 2).

Interest in action research waned in the 1960s because it was questioned as a viable research method by the scientific establishment. Foshay (1994) explained that the educational research establishment opposed action research, which was often reported merely in case study form, because "no attempt was made to see whether the examined population was representative of a larger population." Foshay continued, "the data often were flawed..., the movement was ridiculed in the publications of the American Educational Research Association (AERA), and it did not spread" (p. 320). Yet it emerged again in the late 1970s with the work of Lawrence Stenhouse and John Elliott in Europe (Kemmis, cited in Oja & Smulyan, 1989).

Historically, action research served as a problem-solving strategy for improving the school organization (Corey, 1953; Lewin, 1948), as a process of individual reflection on practice (Elliott, 1991), as a process to support staff development (Oja & Smulyan, 1989), as a collaborative process to support teachers' professional development (Sagor, 1992), and as a strategy to guide site-based school improvement (Glickman, 1998).

Calhoun, Allen, and Halliburton (1996) recently described the current fascination with and interest in action research. Whether undertaken by individuals or collaborative teams,

> part of the promise inherent in action research is to build the capability of individuals and organizations to move beyond current cognitions and practice. Recognized in the past as a powerful tool for simultaneously improving practice and the health of the organization, such is its appeal today. (p. 5)

Although few educators ever described the role of administrators or supervisors beyond overseeing or administering the action research process, thus enabling teachers to successfully complete a particular project, Taba and Corey were among the first educators to envision the supervisor as integral to the process. Taba believed that supervisors "needed to become learners along with the teachers....Instead of acting as experts, they had to become helpers...." Taba explained that supervisors needed expertise in action research not only to facilitate teachers' work but to "act as a research technician, devising, adapting, and borrowing research techniques as needed" (Taba & Noel, 1957, p. 50). Still, the suggestion that supervisors themselves might benefit from action research without engaging teachers was unrealized. One of the major intents of this book is to suggest that supervisors can and should become involved in action research for their own professional development.

Action Research Defined

Many practitioners will complain that much educational research has a minimal effect on practice. Teachers often identify themselves as "practitioners," and research, even in "action," sounds like some "university thing." Practitioners also assert that "research can be made to support anything" (Calhoun, Allen, Halliburton, & Jones, 1996). Breaking such stereotypical thinking based on erroneous assumptions and beliefs is difficult, though not impossible. The many attempts to involve teachers and principals in action research projects attest to its efficacy. My experience as both a teacher and an assistant principal also supports the notion that research is an invaluable tool for school improvement.

Action research is a kind of research that has reemerged as a popular way of involving practitioners, both teachers and supervisors, so that they better understand their work. Although originally developed primarily for the professional development of teachers, action research has recently gained favor among administrators, supervisors, other educational leaders, and school-based managed teams, including parents, community members, and students, as a way of improving schools. Corey (1953) explained that action research is undertaken "by practitioners in order that they may improve their practices" (p. 141). Corey was the first educator to include supervisors as they "attempt to solve their practical problems by using the methods of science" (p. 141).

Therefore, action research, a type of applied research, is conducted by practitioners to improve practices in educational settings. Action research, like other types of research, utilizes an array of methodologies and approaches. Although action research is generally identified with qualitative approaches, action research, as defined in this volume, incorporates both qualitative and quantitative approaches (Figure 1-8).

Figure 1-8.

Action research differs from traditional research in three ways:

1. Action research is often less sophisticated than traditional methods that incorporate, for example, complicated statistical techniques.
2. Action research is utilized primarily by practitioners to solve specific problems.
3. Findings from action research are often not generalizable to other groups and situations.

Benefits of Action Research

Although some educators think that research is impractical, irrelevant, and simply not feasible for practitioners, given the exigencies and pressures of working in a school, research can have immeasurable benefits if properly used, for it does the following:

- Creates a systemwide mindset for school improvement— a professional problem-solving ethos.
- Enhances decision making—greater feelings of competence in solving problems and making instructional decisions. In other words, action research provides for an intelligent way of making decisions.
- Promotes reflection and self-assessment.
- Instills a commitment to continuous improvement.
- Creates a more positive school climate in which teaching and learning are foremost concerns.
- Impacts directly on practice.
- Empowers those who participate in the process. Educational leaders who undertake action research may no longer, for instance, uncritically accept theories, innovations, and programs at face value.

Action research should not be viewed as just another technique or innovation in a long list of reform measures. If we've learned anything from educational history, it's to suspect such panaceas (Cuban, 1993). Though often heralded as a one-shot solution to school reform, action research is more realistically a viable tool used by practitioners to improve schools (Sagor, 1997).

Action Research Is Not Complicated

Equipped with technical knowledge and requisite skills, any educational leader can easily apply research methodology to almost any situation or problem area. Admittedly, there are areas or specific research strategies that are very sophisticated and require advanced knowledge. Aren't there aspects of the operation of your automobile that are beyond your comprehension? When was the last time you were able to dismantle a carburetor or change your transmission? Yet you still can drive a car! So too with action research. Understanding *how* a particular statistic, for instance, is able to consider disparate test scores from two groups and treat them comparably is immaterial as long as you know that it is the correct procedure to use. Anyone can utilize research without having to understand the minutiae or intricacies of advanced mathematical calculations.

As this book will demonstrate, any graduate student is capable of readily applying sound research strategies to solve real problems in schools. Don't avoid research simply because it seems complicated. It's really very simple, as you'll see.

Before proceeding with the remainder of the chapter, complete the following exercises to help reinforce some of the ideas expressed above.

Exercises

1. CLASS DISCUSSION

The rift between theoretician and practitioner is ever widening. One of the aims of *Action Research* is to indicate the necessity for the educational leader to assume leadership in bridging this gap. The educational leader is in a unique position to accomplish this by articulating the concerns of the school practitioner and applying theoretical research design to possibly alleviate existing problems.

Read the quotation below and consider the following questions:
  A. What is your reaction to the quote?
  B. What strategies might you, as an educational leader, employ to bridge the gap between theory and practice?
  C. What is the role of the educational leader in regard to interpreting and disseminating current research?

Quoted, with permission of the Association for Supervision and Curriculum Development, from Olivero, J. (1982). Principals and their inservice needs. *Educational Leadership, 39,* 343, 344.

RESEARCH TO PRACTICE: Unfortunately, practitioners frequently believe researchers are so protected from the hassles of everyday life that the ivory-tower types can't possibly understand the real world. On the contrary, theoreticians are confused by and irritated with practitioners who could benefit from learning better ways to function but don't.

What is needed is an intervention to bridge this gap. Lorre Manasee, staff member at NIE, offers a realistic solution to the problem. She has initiated a plan that calls for the dissemination of research through training. The idea is to incorporate the very best of what is known about the learning process into training programs for principals and other administrators. This notion is considerably different and potentially far more effective than the typical research paper that seems to be written by one researcher—certainly not for the benefit of the site leader.

WE NEED MORE PEOPLE WHO CAN INTERPRET RESEARCH RESULTS AND THEN SHOW OTHERS HOW THE RESULTS MAKE SENSE FOR STUDENTS [emphasis mine]. This calls for some rather unique people with unique skills, capable of making the link between research and practice and translating user needs into researchable problems. They could help researchers understand teachers' lives and problems. They would need to know something about both worlds and have resources and credibility in both.

Answers will vary

2. How might the benefits of action research, noted above, actually help to improve your school or district?

_____

_____

_____

_____

Answers will vary

Steps in Action Research

Action research is an ongoing process of examining educational problems in school settings. For those of you interested in applying action research, there are five guiding steps, as shown in Figure 1-9.

Steps in Action Research

REFLECT

SELECT A FOCUS

COLLECT DATA

ANALYZE AND INTERPRET DATA

TAKE ACTION

Figure 1-9.

1. Reflect

As a reflective practitioner, you continually seek ways of improving your school or district. You ask yourself, "What do I need to know to do a better job?" and "What concerns do faculty and staff raise?" During this initial phase, you examine the literature for ideas about school renewal or improvement. You explore "best practices" and find ways to implement innovative ideas that could work in your school or district.

2. Select a Focus

This includes three steps: (a) Know what you want to investigate, (b) Develop some questions about the area you've chosen, and (c) Establish a plan to answer these questions.

Come to an agreement on what aspect of the school program you would like to study. Ask "What am I concerned about?" and "Why am I concerned?" Identify what is known and what needs to be known about this program or practice. Ask "What do I know about this program?" and "What information should be known in order to improve the program?"

Identify specific aspects of the program that might need scrutiny such as: (a) student outcomes (e.g., achievement, attitudes), (b) curriculum (e.g., effectiveness of instructional materials, alignment with state content standards), (c) instruction (e.g., teaching strategies, use of technology), (d) school climate (e.g., teacher morale, relationships between teachers and supervisors), and (e) parental involvement (e.g., participation on committees, attendance at school events).

As you focus on a specific concern or problem, you need to begin to pose some questions that will serve to guide your research. If, for instance, low levels of parental involvement are a concern in your school, you might ask "How can I document these low levels of parent involvement?" "What impact do these low levels of participation have on students' completion of science projects?" "Will increased levels of involvement yield higher student achievement levels?" "How might parental involvement in school affairs be increased?"

Developing these guiding questions will eventually lead to specifying a **research question,** the question posed in a qualitative study, or a **hypothesis,** the question posed in a quantitative study. Selecting a focus also includes developing a research design, which is explained in detail in chapter 3.

3. Collect Data

Once you have narrowed your focus to a specific area of concern, have developed some research questions, and know how you plan to answer them, you are ready to gather information to answer your research questions. Let's say you're investigating the new science program adopted by the district. You've posed some research questions about achievement levels and students' attitudes toward science. You can now begin to collect data that will provide evidence for the effectiveness of this program in terms of achievement and attitudes.

You may administer teacher-made and standardized tests, conduct surveys and interviews, and examine portfolios. What other kinds of evidence could you collect to help you understand the impact of this new science program? How would you collect such evidence? Discuss these questions with a colleague.

Quite often action researchers collect data but do not organize them so that they can be shared with others. Raw data that just "sit around" in someone's file drawer are useless. Collected data must be transformed so that they can be used. Data that are counted, displayed, and organized by classroom, grade level, and school, for example, can then be used appropriately during the data analysis and interpretive phases. In order to present action research in the most concise and usable way possible, data organization is included in the data analysis phase that is described in detail in chapters 8 and 9.

4. Analyze and Interpret Data

Once you've collected relevant data, you need to begin the process of analysis and interpretation in order to arrive at some decision. Data analysis and interpretation of results will be major concerns of chapters 8 and 9.

5. Take Action

Finally, you've reached the stage at which a decision must be made. You've answered your research questions about the effectiveness of the new science program. At this point, three possibilities exist: (a) continue the science program as originally established, (b) disband the program, or (c) modify the program in some way(s).

Action research is cyclical (Figure 1-10). The process doesn't necessarily have to stop at any particular point. Information gained from previous research may open new avenues of research. That's why action research is ongoing. In the role of educational leader as action researcher, you're continually involved in assessing instruction and seeking ways to improve your school. Action research affords you the opportunity and tools necessary to accomplish these lofty goals.

Figure 1-10.

The Educational Leader
as a Reflective Practitioner

Reflection? Who has the time?" asks an assistant principal in an inner-city school in Los Angeles. "Certainly, we've learned about 'reflective practice' in graduate courses, but who has much time to really 'reflect' when you're on the job?" complains a principal in a suburban school in Westchester, New York.

Anyone who has worked as an educational leader in a fairly large school setting realizes that "educational leadership is riddled (or blessed) with situations that demand quick action and almost immediate response" (Beck, 1994, p. 128). In spite of the fact that leaders often have to make quick decisions, reflection is indeed possible.

Donald Schon (1983, 1984, 1987) advocates reflection in and on the practice of educational administration and supervision. Schon maintains that "the problems of real-world practice do not present themselves as problems at all but as messy, indeterminate situations" (1987, p. 4). Schon describes two types of reflective thinking: reflection-in-action and reflection-on-action. *Reflection-in-action* is the ability to "think on one's feet" when faced with the many surprises and challenges in our daily lives in schools. Educational leaders who are successful are able to "think on their feet" as they face the multitude of crises that are all too common in almost any school. Leaders must often decide quickly, for example, when confronted by an irate mother's demand that she be allowed to whip her child in front of the class. Even when challenged by less inflammatory situations, leaders must act decisively. Management by crisis is, unfortunately, all too common in today's schools. *Reflection-on-action* occurs when educational leaders look back on their work and consider what practices were successful and what areas need improvement. Reflection-on-action is critical to understanding and thinking about events and phenomena as they unfold in the school. Special time must be set aside to allow for reflection-on-action.

Overwhelmed and sometimes incapable of dealing with increased demands, educational leaders think that reflection-on-action is impossible when, in fact, it is not only possible but essential possible (Whitaker, 1995). How can an educational leader find the time to become a "reflective educator"? Here are some suggestions:

1. Set aside 15–30 minutes a day for reflective thinking. Build time into your schedule by informing your secretary that between 11:20 and 11:45 a.m. you are not to be disturbed, unless an emergency arises (and be sure to give your secretary some example of "legitimate" emergencies). During this time you should close and lock your door and deliberate on the overall structure of the day or on one specific issue.

2. Some leaders prefer to "reflect" before school begins or after school. Time for reflection should be determined by your schedule and preference. Choose a time during which you are alert and can seriously contemplate the many issues that need attention. Personally, I am a late-night person and find that 1 a.m. suits me just fine. I am most productive when the house is quiet and I am able to think undisturbed.

3. One principal I had the opportunity to work with held a "cabinet meeting" every day, from 7:30 until around 8:30 a.m., before students arrived. Such meetings allowed supervisory personnel to reflect and bring up important issues for general discussion. Anyone on the faculty or staff was allowed to attend these meetings to share their concerns or simply join in on reflecting.

One of the most important decisions an educational leader must make is whether to become a reflective practitioner. A reflective leader takes the time to think about what has transpired or what steps should be taken tomorrow. A reflective leader thinks before he acts. She is proactive, not reactive. A reflective leader takes responsibility for making tough decisions and is willing to admit error. Reflective leaders do not act impulsively or overreact to a situation. Instead, they carefully consider options and decide on a course of action.

Reflection is the heart of professional practice. Robert Starratt (1995) explains:

> Practitioners who analyze the uniqueness of a problem confronting them, frame the problem in ways that structure its intelligibility, think about the results of their actions, and puzzle out why things worked and why they did not tend to build up a reservoir of insights and intuitions that they can call upon as they go about their work. (p. 66)

Reflective Practice

Reflective process is a powerful approach to professional development.

—Osterman & Kottkamp, 2001

Reflective practice is a process by which educational leaders take the time to contemplate and assess the efficacy of programs, products, and personnel in order to make judgments about the appropriateness or effectiveness of these aspects so that improvements or refinements might be achieved. Research-oriented leaders have a vision that guides their work. As they plan and work to improve their schools, they collect and analyze data to better inform their decisions. Research-oriented leaders are engaged in ongoing self-study in which they assess the needs of their schools, identify problem areas, and develop strategies for becoming more effective.

Instilling habits of reflection, critical inquiry, and training in reflection is not usually part of a supervisor preparatory program. Supervisors should submit their own practice to reflective scrutiny by posing these questions, among others:

1. What concerns me?
2. Why am I concerned?
3. Can I confirm my perceptions?
4. What mistakes have I made?
5. If I were able to do it again, what would I do differently?
6. What are my current options?
7. What evidence can I collect to confirm my feelings?
8. Who might be willing to share their ideas with me?
9. What have been my successes?
10. How might I replicate these successes?
11. In what other ways might I improve my school?

Summary

Action research, as a disciplined inquiry, is an invaluable tool that allows educational leaders to reflect on their practices, programs, and procedures. Many practitioners avoid research for a variety of reasons. The foremost reason is that practitioners do not realize that implementing an action research project is not necessarily laborious, time-consuming, or difficult. Educational leaders who are truly concerned about improving their schools or programs will prioritize their responsibilities and expend appropriate energies toward undertaking some form of action research.

Although action research projects may be developed by teams of educational professionals, this book provides the impetus for individual leaders to acquire the requisite knowledge, skills, and disposition to make action research an effective and valuable experience. This chapter has provided an overview of various categories, types, and forms of research and has argued that evaluation research, discussed at length in chapter 6, is a primary use of action research that educational leaders are most likely to undertake on a regular basis.

In addition to providing you with a brief history, this chapter has explained the benefits and basic steps of action research. Finally, you may better understand that reflective practice is critically important in order to make intelligent judgments about the effectiveness of various programs, procedures, and practices. Research, as a tool of an educational leader, *is* reflection in action!

Before proceeding to the next chapter, complete the following exercises.

Exercises

1. Brainstorm some ideas for assessing a program in your school or district using the first step in action research, as described above.

   _____

   _____

   _____

   Answers will vary

2. How might you find more time for reflection-on-action? Be specific.

   _____

   _____

   _____

   Answers will vary

3. Submit your own practice to reflective thinking by answering the 11 questions noted in the section on Reflective Practice above. What other questions come to mind?

   _____

   _____

   _____

   Answers will vary

4. Which is *not* accurate regarding the five steps in action research?

   a. defining a problem can be teacher or supervisor initiated
   b. state the hypothesis
   c. in the research design you must state how the sample was formed and what statistical measures will be employed
   d. the final stage is to collect and analyze the data
   e. none of these

   Answer: d

References

Adelman, C. (1993). Kurt Lewin and the origins of action research. *Educational Action Research, 1*(1), 7–24.

Beck, L. G. (1994). *Reclaiming educational administration as a caring profession.* New York: Teachers College Press.

Best, J., & Kahn, J. (1998). *Research in education* (8th ed.). Needham Heights, MA: Allyn & Bacon.

Calhoun, E. F. (1993). Action research: Three approaches. *Educational Leadership, 51,* 62–65.

Calhoun, E. F. (1994). *How to use action research in the self-renewing school.* Alexandria, VA: Association for Supervision and Curriculum Development.

Calhoun, E., & Allen, L. (1996). The action research network: Action research on action research. In B. Joyce & E. Calhoun (Eds.), *Learning experiences in school renewal.* Eugene, OR: Clearinghouse on Educational Management.

Calhoun, E. F., Allen, L., & Halliburton, C. (1996, April). *A report on the implementation of and results from schoolwide action research.* Paper presented at the annual meeting of the American Educational Research Association, New York.

Calhoun, E. F., Allen, L., Halliburton, C., & Jones, S. (1996, April). S*choolwide action research: A study of facilitation.* Paper presented at the annual meeting of the American Educational Research Association, New York.

Charles, C. M. (1997). *Introduction to educational research.* New York: Addison-Wesley Longman.

*Corey, S. M. (1953). *Action research to improve school practices.* New York: Teachers College Press.

Cuban, L. (1993). *How teachers taught: Constancy and change in American classrooms, 1890–1980* (2nd ed.). New York: Longman.

DeRoche, E. F. (1987). *An administrator's guide for evaluating programs and personnel* (2nd ed.). Boston: Allyn & Bacon.

Eisner, E. (1991). *The enlightened eye.* New York: Macmillan.

*Elliott, J. (1991). *Action research for educational change.* Bristol, PA: Open University Press.

Equity and Choice. (1993). *10* (1).

Foshay, A. W. (1994). Action research: An early history in the United States. *Journal of Curriculum and Supervision, 9,* 317–325.

Glickman, C. D. (1998). *Renewing America's schools: A guide for school-based action.* San Francisco: Jossey-Bass.

Greenwood, J. M. (1891). Discussion of Gove's paper. *NEA Proceedings,* p. 227.

Hunter, M. (1967). *Reinforcement theory for teachers.* El Segundo, CA: TIP.

Kagan, D. M. (1995). *Laura and Jim and what they taught me about the gap between educational theory and practice.* New York: State University of New York Press.

Kemmis, S. (1980). *Action research in retrospect and prospect.* Paper presented to the annual meeting of the Australian Association for Research in Education, Sydney.

Lewin, K. (1948). *Resolving social conflicts.* New York: Harper and Brothers.

*McLean, J. E. (1995). *Improving education through action research: A guide for administrators and teachers.* Thousand Oaks, CA: Corwin Press.

McMillan, J. H., & Schumacher, S. (2000). *Research in education: A conceptual introduction* (5th ed.). Glenview, IL: Scott, Foresman.

*McNiff, J. (1995). *Action research: Principles and practice.* London: Routledge.

Oja, S., & Smulyan, L. (1989). *Collaborative action research: A developmental approach.* London: Falmer Press.

Olivero, J. (1982). Principals and their inservice needs. *Educational Leadership, 39* (5), 340–344.

Osterman, K. F., & Kottkamp, R. B. (2001). *Reflective practice for educators: Improving schooling through professional development.* Newbury Park, CA: Corwin Press.

Palanki, A., & Burch, P. (1995). *In our hands: A multi-site parent-teacher action research project.* (Report No. 30). Washington, DC: Center on Families, Communities, Schools, and Children's Learning.

Peterson, K. D. (2000). *Teacher evaluation: A comprehensive guide to new directions and practices* (2nd ed.). Thousand Oaks, CA: Corwin Press.

*Sagor, R. (1992). *How to conduct collaborative action research.* Alexandria, VA: Association for Supervision and Curriculum Development.

Sagor, R. (1997). Collaborative action research for educational change. In A. Hargreaves (Ed.), *Rethinking educational change with heart and mind* (pp. 169–191). Alexandria, VA: Association for Supervision and Curriculum Development.

Schon, D. A. (1983). *The reflective practitioner: How professionals think in action.* New York: Basic.

Schon, D. A. (1984). Leadership as reflection-in-action. In T. J. Sergiovanni & J. E. Corbally (Eds.), *Leadership and organizational culture: New perspectives on administrative theory and practice* (pp. 36–63). Urbana: University of Illinois Press.

Schon, D. A. (1987). *Educating the reflective practitioner: Toward a new design for thinking and learning in the professional.* San Francisco: Jossey-Bass.

Starratt, R. J. (1995). *Leaders with vision: The quest for school renewal.* Thousand Oaks, CA: Corwin Press.

*Stringer, E. T. (1999). *Action research: A handbook for practitioners.* Thousand Oaks, CA: Sage.

Stufflebeam, D. L. (1996, April). *Developing evaluation-oriented school principals.* Paper presented at the annual meeting of the American Educational Research Association, New York.

Taba, H., & Noel, E. (1957). *Action research: A case study.* Washington, DC: Association for Supervision and Curriculum Development.

Tuckman, B. (1999). *Conducting educational research* (5th ed.). New York: Harcourt.

Whitaker, K. S. (1995). Principal burnout: Implications for professional development. *Journal of Personnel Evaluation in Education, 9,* 287–296.

Wiersma, W. (1999). *Research methods in education: An introduction* (7th ed.). Boston: Allyn & Bacon.

Activity 3.   The Basics

1. Have I convinced you that action research is not all that complicated? Explain.

    _____

    _____

    _____

2. How does action research differ from traditional research? List three ways.

    _____

    _____

    _____

3. Why do some educational leaders avoid research? Are their excuses valid?

    _____

    _____

    _____

4. Which approach to research is best?

    _____

    _____

    _____

5. Describe an evaluative research project you or someone you know has undertaken.

    _____

    _____

    _____

6. Describe the five steps in action research to someone who knows nothing about them.

    _____

    _____

    _____

Teaching and Doing Action Research Through General Semantics

Focus Questions

1. How is it possible for an action researcher to remain objective?

2. Which approach to action research provides a more bias-free assessment of a situation—quantitative or qualitative?

3. Have you ever seen Akira Kurosawa's film *Rashomon,* and what can it tell us about research?

4. Why is it important for an action researcher to understand the relationship among language, thought, and human behavior?

5. Why is the concept of triangulation so important?

All seeing is essentially perspective and so is all knowing.

—Nietzsche

To attack such problems, one must "swarm all over them," the way an infantry team might attack a machine gun nest.

—Arthur Foshay, 1994

Introduction

Before getting into some of the nitty-gritty of action research, you need to be aware of an important principle or mindset that should guide any action researcher. Action research, at its best, examines phenomena from a variety of perspectives. Much of what is characterized as action research today, unfortunately, suffers from a lack of in-depth analysis from a variety of perspectives. I believe that maintaining a multidimensional perspective when conducting any form of research, especially action research, is imperative. This perspective is so important that I have devoted an entire chapter to explaining how I utilize the study of general semantics in both teaching and conducting action research.

I begin my course on educational research by relating a famous story told at Harvard Law School in which 175 eager, albeit anxious, first-year law students await the professor in their first course.

A middle-age, scholarly looking gentleman dressed in a dapper suit enters the huge auditorium through one of the doors adjacent to the stage. As the professor approaches the podium he peers out at his students and selects his victim.

"You," pointing to a male student in the rear of the auditorium, "state the facts in the case before you." Nervously and hurriedly, the 175 students read the case. The student selected by the professor offers no response. Once again the professor repeats his request. The student again freezes. Again the request is made. "State the facts in the case before you." The student gives an inadequate answer.

The professor nonchalantly reaches into his pocket and takes out a dime and says, "Take this dime, call your mother [it's an old story!], and tell her to pick you up because you'll never become a lawyer." Shocked, yet thankful they weren't called upon, the 174 other students anxiously await the student's reaction. No response.

"You heard what I said. Take this dime and tell your mother to pick you up." The student rises and walks slowly towards the stage. Hushed silence pervades the auditorium. Suddenly the student stops, looks up, and shouts, "Sir, you are a bastard." Without batting an eyelash, the professor looks up and says, "Go back to your seat. You're beginning to think like a lawyer."

"This story," I inform my class, "epitomizes the purpose of law school, which is to instill habits of skepticism, verbal aggressiveness, and the readiness to challenge the authority of a lawyer." I continue by conveying my expectations and hopes for them this semester. "My purpose in teaching this course is very different from that professor at Harvard. I do, however, want to help you begin to *think* and *act* like action researchers." To accomplish this objective I not only provide hands-on activities that challenge my students to apply many principles of action research, I also incorporate the study of general semantics in order to help them avoid narrow frames of reference while conducting research.

Before discussing some implications of the study of general semantics for the teaching and practice of action research, I begin with an overview and short history of general semantics. Then I examine how I was introduced to the field of general semantics and explore some of its implications for action research.

What Is General Semantics?

Action research is above all a matter of language.

—Gauthier, 1992

General semantics is concerned with ways of increasing the truth content of our language, which inevitably influences our perceptions of the world. To achieve this, general semanticists examine the relationship between language, thought, and human behavior. More specifically, the field of general semantics is based on a fundamental principle that language is arbitrary. According to general semantics, there is no inherent relationship between a word and what it stands for. Because many of us speak only one language, we unconsciously assume that there is some inherent relationship between words (verbal maps) and the things they represent. Calling an object a *chair* is arbitrary, for example. The word *chair* in English in no way more accurately describes what it is than calling it a *kisei* ("key say") in Hebrew. Anyone who speaks several languages knows that there are as many words for things as there are languages; and there is no "right" one.

The arbitrariness of language, representing only one of many principles of general semantics, was first systematized by Alfred Korzybski (1879–1950) in a book that, according to some, is "one of the ten most influential books of the twentieth century" (cited in Read, 1970). Korzybski's (1933/1995) analysis in *Science and Sanity* laid the groundwork for what later became known as the field of study called general semantics (Bois, 1967). Korzybski, a Polish scientist and engineer, became convinced that discourse framed in right-wrong, yes-no, true-false, or what he called an "Aristotelian" way of thinking (a term he coined from the system of deductive logical reasoning originating with Aristotle) was potentially limiting (de Bono, 1972). According to Korzybski, phenomena do not lend themselves to such dichotomous thinking. For Korzybski, reality is too complex and diverse to rely on one perspective in pursuing knowledge, truth, and inquiry. Thus, Korzybski's non-Aristotelian formulations held that we could never fully define reality, that all theories were tentative to some extent, and that language is arbitrary. "Korzybski cryptically denied the identity of theory and reality by saying, 'Whatever you *say* a thing is, it is not'" (Pula, 1970, p. 153).

Emanating from this non-Aristotelian premise is another one of Korzybski's contributions, known as **multiordinality,** or multiple meanings. Given the unreliability and inadequacy of language to precisely describe phenomena, Korzybski maintained that a word can often have very different meanings depending on, for instance, the context in which it is spoken and the manner in which it is expressed. Multiple meanings are common and have significant implications for how we communicate. According to the general semanticist, words are ambiguous and can be used in many different ways. For example, I might ask you, the reader, the following three questions: Who crosses the bridge on your nose? How can you sharpen your shoulder blades? Does the calf on your leg eat the corn on your toe? (Berman, 1974). Although there is obviously a high degree of social acceptance and agreement of meaning among people, misunderstandings are too common because we unconsciously expect people to have the same understanding as we do. Meanings are not in words, they are inside people, according to general semanticists. Confusion of this basic premise often leads to errors in thinking, communication, and behavior.

The study of general semantics attempts to help people use language more scientifically and accurately. General semantics is concerned with increasing the correspondence between the words we use to describe reality and the structure of reality itself. Conceived as such, the study of the field of general semantics has important implications for the teaching and practice of action research.

I was initially introduced to the fascinating study of the relationship between language, thought, and human behavior when a colleague, quoting Voltaire, said to me: "There are too many of us present." To which I replied an incredulous, "What's that?!" He reiterated, "There are too many of us here." "But there are only two of us in this room," I responded. "I'm sure there are at least six of us," he said. "There is what you are, what you think you are, and what I think you are. And there is what I am, what I think I am, and what you think I am." What did this mean? Momentarily stunned, I regained my composure and realized an inherent truth that I perhaps knew subconsciously but never articulated. I had taken for granted the multifaceted dimensions of reality. My assumptions erroneously shaped my perceptions and behavior. I also realized that the picture I have of myself is due to my unconscious assumptions. What I think I am is not me—it's an abstraction, a map of my real self: What did this mean for me as an action researcher?

Initial curiosity quickly turned into intrigue, fascination, and compulsion. I read Korzybski's (1933/1995) *Science and Sanity,* Chase's (1938) *The Tyranny of Words,* Hayakawa's (1939) *Language in Thought and Action,* and listened intently to Berman's (1974) audiocassette program "How to Think, Communicate, and Behave Intelligently: An Introduction to General Semantics." I learned the importance of increasing the correspondence between the structure of my verbal map of "what's out there" and the structure of reality itself. Aside from many personal lessons I learned, I became more interested in the implications that general semantics had for my students engaged in action research. How might I help them become better researchers?

Course Description

I begin my graduate-level research course by asking students to stand and walk over to the window. As they peer through the window I ask them to describe what they see. As they convey their perceptions, I record responses on the board. "Is there anything else you see?" "Is what you are seeing representative of what is out there?" "Is what you are describing an accurate assessment of what you have seen?" Students assume that their responses are accurate, if not definitive, descriptions of "what's out there."

I ask them now to examine a chair at the front of the room. I inform them that on the underside of the chair the word *Taiwan* is imprinted. "Write down what you know about this object." Nearly every student writes that the object is a chair made in Taiwan. After a brief, albeit intense, discussion it is apparent that the students have not thoroughly examined their assumptions and perceptions. "Why did you assume that the object was made in Taiwan? Is this object a chair made in Taiwan, or is it an object we call a chair that has the word *Taiwan* printed on it?"

Our assumptions are lenses that affect what we see and how we interpret meaning. As researchers we should try to neutralize our assumptions, at least temporarily, in order to maintain objectivity. Doing research demands understanding that the chair may or may not have been made in Taiwan. Additional information is needed before a conclusive statement can be made about the origin of the object. Seeing things using multiple lenses or frames is a better way of ensuring a more accurate understanding of "what's out there."

Quoting Nietzsche, I explain that "all seeing is essentially perspective, and so is all knowing." I read *It Looks Like This* (Webber, 1976) to them and have them peruse *The True Story of the 3 Little Pigs* (Scieszka, 1996). We discuss the implications of these stories for their work as educational researchers. Researchers attempt to explain phenomena systematically through the application of the scientific method. To know something about anything necessitates a global or multidimensional perspective. One should acknowledge and consider a variety of perspectives or points of view before making a decision or reaching a conclusion.

Using the metaphor of detective can inform our work as action researchers. If a detective arrived on the scene of an automobile accident and proceeded to interview the drivers without attending to bystanders and even the elderly gentleman peering through the window of his apartment located above the scene of the accident, he or she would certainly not adequately ascertain the facts. Moreover, if one of the drivers was an elderly woman and the other a 40-year-old man dressed in a neat blue suit, the detective might infer that a detailed investigation was unwarranted. In this case, the detective's assumptions would be prejudicial and misleading and would lead to inaccurate conclusions.

Similarly, I explain to my class, we as action researchers are detectives of sorts. We collect an array of data to inform the conclusions that we can justifiably make. This is called **data collection.** A data collection technique is called an **instrument.** To utilize a few sources may lead to incomplete analyses, if not misevaluations. Although general semanticists originally questioned the truth claims of quantitative research (Payne, 1977), qualitative research too is particularly susceptible to misevaluations.

Questions about the "truth value" (Lincoln & Guba, 1985, p. 290) of qualitative research have emerged. Questions about the applicability, consistency, and neutrality of qualitative research persist. We need to ask questions such as "how truthful are the particular findings of qualitative investigations?" "How applicable are these findings to other settings?" "Can other researchers replicate these findings?" "How can we assure that the findings are not based on the researcher's unique biases and erroneous assumptions?"

The credibility of qualitative paradigms is enhanced by employing, for instance, a technique known as **triangulation,** a term first coined by Webb, Campbell, Schwartz, and Sechrest (1999). "Triangulation is the act of bringing more than one source of data to bear on a single point" (Marshall & Rossman, 1999, p. 146). As Marshall and Rossman explain, "designing a study in which multiple cases are used, multiple informants or more than one data gathering technique can greatly strengthen the study's usefulness for other settings." I tell my students that incorporating multiple sources of data is critical to ensuring a more accurate view of reality. To reinforce this multidimensional framework that underlies triangulation, whether in regard to quantitative or qualitative analyses, I draw Figure 2-1 on the board and explain that multiple use of data collection methods will provide us with a more complete understanding of a given problem or research question.

To demonstrate the strength of triangulation, students, in groups of four, develop a problem and select a different data collection technique for each person in the group (e.g., interview, questionnaire, historical inquiry, unobtrusive measures). They confer on defining the problem and later work independently for 2 weeks gathering data using only one technique. They reconvene to share observations, findings, and tentative conclusions. Students are then en-

Figure 2-1.

couraged to address questions such as "Did my observations, findings, and conclusions coincide with those found by other members in my group?" "In what way was my data collection limiting?" "How can I more fully understand the problem?" "How does the combination of techniques offer greater insights into the problem?" Students realize that triangulation rests on the assumption that the weakness in a single method will often be compensated by the strengths of another method. Triangulation therefore exploits the assets and neutralizes the liabilities of different data collection methods (Jick, 1979).

Not surprisingly, therefore, I encourage students undertaking their individual projects to use a mixed-methodology design incorporating both qualitative and quantitative analyses (Creswell, 1994). Using one modality is limiting and will not reveal all that can be known about the impact of a particular treatment. Students begin to explore a specific issue or problem of concern to them in the classroom. They are encouraged to view the problem or topic from a multidimensional view. Students realize the complexity of the "world of reality" and that, although everything cannot be known about anything (a central premise of general semantics called the *allness principle*), assuming a multiple framed perspective gives a student a more realistic insight into a given educational problem.

Assignments, then, encourage students to use an array of data collection techniques that are likely to preclude myopia and provincialism, which often lead to unidimensional thinking about a given research topic. To this end, students complete two additional assignments prior to undertaking their own research project. First, I ask them to select a field site of some sort such as a health care facility, a restaurant, or a college cafeteria. They must describe the environment and interactions therein during a specified time frame, using as many data collection techniques as is readily feasible. Students must report their findings and describe how each technique offers a unique dimension to the "reality" of their particular situation.

A second assignment is designed to help them view situations from different perspectives. Students are asked to describe how different people in given settings might view a particular situation. A student, for instance, would describe how a waitress, customer, and cash register attendant might view services offered in the restaurant.

We also watch Akira Kurosawa's film *Rashomon,* which recounts the same event through the eyes of several witnesses. Each witness tells a different story about how a murder took place. Students are asked to write four different versions of what happened and are encouraged, through class discussions, to realize and appreciate the social construction of reality and how what is perceived as "truth" depends on one's perspective.

Before proceeding with the remainder of the chapter, complete the following exercises to help reinforce some of the ideas expressed above.

Exercises

1. How does the study of general semantics inform our work as action researchers?

   _____

   _____

   _____

   > Although answers will likely vary, a correct response should include the notion that action researchers should use a variety of data collection and research methods so that decisions will not be based on just one approach.

2. Here's a fun exercise: Korzybski discussed the term *multiordinality* and described that our use of language is often ambiguous and arbitrary. Here are some excerpts from an unknown author: "English is a crazy language, isn't it? There's no egg in eggplant or ham in hamburger; neither apple nor pine in pineapple. English muffins weren't invented in England or French fries in France. Sweetmeats are candies, while sweetbreads, which aren't sweet, are meat. We take English for granted. But if we explore its paradoxes, we find that quicksand can work slowly, boxing rings are square and a guinea pig is neither from Guinea nor is it a pig....How can a slim chance and a fat chance be the same, while a wise man and a wise guy are opposites?... Your house can burn up as it burns down....When stars are out, they are visible, but when the lights are out, they are invisible. And why, when I wind up my watch, I start it, but when I wind up this essay, I end it?"

Can you think of other examples of the "unique lunacy of a language"? What does all this have to do with action research, anyway?

_____

_____

_____

Answers will vary

3. Define a problem you'd like to investigate and select four different data collection techniques you would use to better understand the problem you identified. Share your views with colleagues.

_____

_____

_____

Answers will vary

4. Visit the video store and rent Kurosawa's film *Rashomon,* which recounts the same event through the eyes of several witnesses. Each witness tells a different story about how a murder took place. Review the four different versions represented in the film and discuss the lessons relevant to action research.

_____

_____

_____

Answers will vary

Another Lesson From General Semantics

A specific important lesson from general semantics that I review with my students as action researchers is to always test their hidden premises as they, for instance, observe principal-teacher interaction at a faculty conference. We all have beliefs and assumptions that shape our perspective. Often we react too impulsively. We make false assumptions and inferences based on inadequate data. "Avoid making snap judgments," I tell them. As you observe a class, ask yourself, "What am I assuming?" Typically an overly zealous student might arrive at some premature conclusions after perusing preliminary data. Withholding judgments until a thorough consideration of multiple data sources is recommended (Morain, 1977).

Misevaluations are common when analyzing data derived from interviews, for example. One student, seeking to ascertain a principal's attitude toward school reform, assumed that the principal suggested that bureaucracy as the organizational structure of schooling should be dismantled. The principal used the word *bureaucracy* when referring to his inability to obtain necessary resources for a particular school program. *Bureaucracy* for the interviewer connoted red tape, waste, and inefficiency. He assumed that the principal concurred that the dysfunctional aspects of bureaucracy precluded successful school reform and that few if any substantive changes could occur until alternative forms of school organization were considered. I urged this student to pursue this line of questioning with the principal and not to assume that he disavowed bureaucracy completely. As the interview continued, the principal acknowledged the importance of bureaucracy in terms of providing stability and structure. He maintained that change within a bureaucracy was feasible. He was not, in fact, advocating a dissolution of the school bureaucracy.

The study of general semantics helps us to use and understand language more scientifically. The unconscious assumptions we have about our language can result in many misevaluations, as in the case previously cited. Disagreements over meanings of words are not uncommon. Meaning is not in the words we use but in the person's mind. Rather than asking the interviewee what he meant by *bureaucracy,* my student assumed that what he meant was based on his own assumptions of the meaning and implications of the word. General semantics offers much insight into interpreting meanings of words derived from interviews, case studies, surveys, and other qualitative sources. Action research is more meaningful and accurate when we become aware of some of the unconscious assumptions that we make in thinking, communicating, and behaving.

Similarly, misevaluations can also occur between the doctoral or master's degree advisor and student. Students are often anxious as they initiate their study. Numerous ideas flood their thoughts as they eventually narrow their focus to one fuzzy idea. Their thoughts may focus on the assumption that the professor will consider their idea foolish and unworthy of scholarly investigation. At the same time, the faculty advisor might have his or her own version of what topic deserves study and how the investigation should proceed. Unless meanings are articulated, confusion and misevaluations are inevitable. In my course, in which students must select an action research topic, I encourage them to share their ideas first with their peers and then with me. Shared meanings often lead to effective communication and successful research projects.

Summary and Conclusion

One of the tasks of an action researcher is to understand that reality, language, and behavior are complex. Any attempt to understand and describe phenomena is necessarily incomplete, given the multifaceted nature of reality. General semantics suggests that every point of view has built-in assumptions. Although we attempt to gain wide perspective, we also understand the inherent bias of any investigation. Nevertheless, our goal as action researchers is to achieve perspective through the use of a multitude of data sources. As Kurman (1977) notes, "a shift of perspective is not a violation of the true order of things, but a viable alternative" (p. 267).

For instance, let's say you're interested in assessing the impact of the new stress reduction program implemented 2 years ago. You're interested in knowing the impact of these stress-reduction techniques on students' attitudes and achievement levels in mathematics. Before concluding that the program is a failure or success, you need to collect data or information to inform your decision. That's what research is all about, collecting data. However, if you were to only interview 30 students in one class or merely examine test scores on a given grade, you would not get a true or valid picture of the program's impact. Examining scores of teacher-made tests and standardized tests; interviewing teachers, parents, and students; and reviewing anonymous surveys distributed to all participants would give you a much better picture of the current state of the program than merely looking at one narrow aspect. Once those data are collected and analyzed, you're in a much better position to make a decision about the effectiveness of this program.

Examining a multitude of data before making a decision is what this chapter has tried to convey. This message may seem obvious and somewhat simplistic, but in practice action research has been plagued by a very limited use of alternate methods for collecting data. Employing qualitative and quantitative measures, and employing various data sources and data collection methods, thereby achieving triangulation, the educational leader as action researcher is most certainly in a better position to arrive at an intelligent, thoughtful decision (O'Connor, 1990).

References

Berger, P. L., & Luckmann, T. (1966). *The social construction of reality: A treatise on the sociology of knowledge.* New York: Doubleday.

Berman, S. I. (1974). *How to think, communicate, and behave intelligently: An introduction to general semantics.* [Audiocassette]. San Francisco: International Society for General Semantics.

Berman, S. I. (1982). *Words, meanings, and people.* San Francisco: International Society for General Semantics.

Bois, J. A. (1967). *Art of awareness.* Dubuque, IA: Brown.

Bolman, L. G., & Deal, T. E. (1997). *Reframing organizations* (2nd ed.). San Francisco: Jossey-Bass.

Chase, S. (1938). *The tyranny of words.* New York: Harcourt, Brace.

Creswell, J. W. (1994). *Research design: Qualitative and quantitative approaches.* Thousand Oaks, CA: Sage.

de Bono, E. (1972). *Po: Yes and no.* New York: Penguin Books.

Foshay, A. W (1994). Action research: An early history in the United States. *Journal of Curriculum and Supervision, 9,* 317–325.

Gauthier, C. (1992). Between crystal and smoke: Or, how to miss the point in the debate about action research. In W. Pinar & W. Reynolds (Eds.), *Understanding curriculum as phenomenological and deconstructed test* (pp. 184–194). New York: Teachers College Press.

Hayakawa, S. I. (1939). *Language in thought and action.* New York: Harcourt, Brace.

Jick, T. D. (1979). Mixing qualitative and quantitative methods: Triangulation in action. *Administrative Science Quarterly, 24,* 602–611.

Korzybski, A. (1995). *Science and sanity* (5th ed.). Lakeville, CT: International Non-Aristotelian Library. (Original work published 1933)

Kurman, P. (1977). Research: An aerial view. *Et Cetera, 34,* 265–276.

Lincoln, Y., & Guba, E. (1985). *Naturalistic inquiry.* Beverly Hills, CA: Sage.

Marshall, C., & Rossman, G. B. (1999). *Designing qualitative research* (3rd ed.). Newbury Park, CA: Sage.

Morain, M. S. (1977). *Teaching general semantics: A collection of lesson plans for college and adult classes.* San Francisco: International Society for General Semantics.

O'Connor, B. N. (1990). About action research versus formal research. *Business Education Forum, 44* (4), 8–9.

Payne, D. (1977). The biases of inexact hypothesis testing. *Et Cetera, 34,* 330–338.

Pula, T. J. (1970). General semantics as an educative tool in the electrical curriculum. In L. Thayer (Ed.), *Communication: General semantics perspectives* (pp. 151–162). New York: Spartan Books.

Read, C. (1970). Alfred Korzybski: His contributions and their historical development. In L. Thayer (Ed.), *Communication: General semantics perspectives* (pp. 339–347). New York: Spartan Books.

Scieszka, J. (1996). *The true story of the 3 little pigs.* New York: Viking Press.

Webb, E. J., Campbell, D. T., Schwartz, R. D., & Sechrest, L. (1999). *Unobtrusive measures.* Chicago: Rand McNally.

Webber, I. E. (1976). *It looks like this: A point-of-view book.* San Francisco: International Society for General Semantics.

Activity 4. Importance of Triangulation

1. What does general semantics tell us about action research?

_____

_____

_____

_____

2. What must you begin to do before undertaking an action research project?

_____

_____

_____

_____

3. Brainstorm a possible topic and ideas for action research. Record in detail your ideas, then share your ideas with a colleague.

_____

_____

_____

_____

4. How did you alter your ideas after exchanging your topic and plan?

_____

_____

_____

_____

5. What is triangulation and why is it so important when undertaking research?

_____

_____

_____

_____

Cut here

Getting Started
on an
Action Research Project

Focus Questions

1. What do you think you need to know to get started on an action research project?

2. What are the advantages of employing quantitative *and* qualitative approaches?

3. List three things you think are most important to get you going on a project.

4. What else would you need to get started on an action research project?

For those seeking whole-school improvement in terms of increasing student learning and creating a healthier professional workplace, action research captures the notion of disciplined inquiry (thus "research") in the context of focused efforts to improve the quality of the organization and its performance (thus "action").

—Calhoun, Allen, & Halliburton, 1996

Our discussion of triangulation in the previous chapter emphasized the importance of two approaches of research: quantitative and qualitative. These approaches have different purposes, each having its own strengths and weaknesses. Current thinking in the field of educational research suggests that neither approach is superior to the other, but earlier views held that the quantitative approach, with its emphasis on traditions of positivism, was far more "scientific" than a qualitative approach. The predominance of this social science perspective has only recently undergone criticism in light of the emergence of qualitative, including ethnographic and biographical, analyses. Still, the quantitative research approach is appropriate in some situations, whereas a qualitative research approach is more suitable in other situations. Sometimes both approaches can be applied in a given research project. Utilization of a particular approach depends on what is being researched, the aim of the project, and the researcher's preference rather than the inherent superiority of one approach over another.

Quantitative and qualitative approaches have arisen from different research needs. The quantitative research approach seeks to establish facts through the utilization of the scientific method. In quantitative research, the researcher is considered to be "an outsider to the research" (Carr & Kemmis, 1986, p. 16), or an objective observer. Results from quantitative analyses are presented numerically, often using some statistical procedures. The research goal of this approach is discovery of some truth through generalizability, the degree to which findings in one context may be applied to other settings.

In contrast, qualitative research emphasizes the researcher's subjective viewpoint as integral to disciplined inquiry. Qualitative inquiry provides in-depth analysis of a given problem that might not otherwise be gleaned from statistical results derived from quantitative studies. Results of qualitative studies are verbally expressed in great detail. A qualitative approach enables in-depth analysis of social, interpersonal, and cultural contexts of education more fully than a quantitative study does. For many educators, qualitative research provides richer and wider-ranging descriptions than quantitative methods (see the Picasso story in chapter 13).

Thus, rather than conceptualizing quantitative and qualitative approaches as diametrically opposed to each other, both approaches should be seen as part of one naturalistic (qualitative) positivistic (quantitative) continuum (Figure 3-1).

An action researcher may, then, choose a variety of approaches from anywhere on the continuum. As you are introduced to various strategies below, keep in mind that both quantitative and qualitative approaches are equally viable and that use of both, if possible, is optimal. Your projects will be much richer and more meaningful. See chapter 4 for a discussion of a quantitative approach and chapter 5 for a discussion of a qualitative approach to action research.

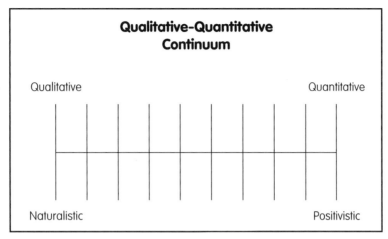

Figure 3-1.

Getting Started:
The Overall Research Plan

Thus far, we have learned that although action research is not complicated, educational leaders can apply rather sophisticated methods in order to solve practical problems they confront daily. Action research, as disciplined inquiry, can involve simple surveys to inform supervisory or teaching decisions or involve statistical analyses to determine the efficacy of given practices or programs. Educational leaders are professionals well equipped to utilize research methodologies and strategies for school improvement.

Mindful of the importance of triangulation, as described in the previous chapter, you're ready to get started. A teacher who prepares to teach a lesson must begin by planning. A teacher plans a sequence of learning experiences and activities centered around a goal and a number of objectives. In the same vein, an action researcher begins by developing a plan. This chapter will guide you through the steps in developing such a plan.

A **research design** is an overall plan for conducting action research. An action researcher begins by clarifying the purposes for undertaking a study and then plans the logistics or administrative items that are necessary to conduct a successful project. Research approaches and methods are then considered. Planning and carefully considering an appropriate design are also essential elements in any action research project.

In order to get started by choosing a sound research design, several steps should be followed:

1. Clarify the purposes of your research.
2. Attend to administrative and logistical aspects of your study.
3. Decide on a quantitative and/or qualitative approach.
4. Select a method and type of research.
5. Choose a design that is appropriate for the area of investigation.

Clarifying Purposes

The first step to consider is the purpose for undertaking action research. Four sets of questions should initially be addressed:

1. What is the purpose of my study or action research project?
2. What do I want to accomplish, or what are my objectives?
3. Why is such a study important? Why do I want to spend time doing this?
4. How will information gleaned from my study help to improve the overall instructional program?

Here are some additional questions to ponder:

- Why do I want to conduct an action research study?
- What are the primary concerns about my current instructional program?
- What areas (instructional, curricular, administrative) need improvement?
- How do I know that our instructional programs are working at top efficiency and effectiveness?
- What is the impact of the new reading series on pupil achievement?
- Are the new computers and multimedia technologies being used effectively?
- Are parents adequately involved in instructional and curricular planning activities?
- What are student attitudes toward the new extracurricular afterschool program?

- Are teachers adequately prepared to implement the new math series?

- Does the school climate foster a sense of collegiality?

- How might the recently mandated science program be effectively implemented?

- What other programs require implementation, and how will I assess their effectiveness?

- Are instructional materials current and being optimally utilized?

- How do teachers feel about the new clinical supervisory methods incorporated by the principal?

- Are the needs of students, parents, and teachers met?

- Are school goals and objectives continually evaluated?

- How productive are the semiannual parent-teacher conferences?

- Is portfolio assessment meeting its intended objectives in grades K–3?

- What alternatives are there to traditional grading practices in grades 7–9?

- Are discipline codes collaboratively developed and rigorously enforced?

These are only some of the questions you might consider before undertaking any study or research project. Before you begin, you must clarify your purposes for conducting the study by focusing on what needs are to be addressed in your school, what you hope to accomplish, and why this project is so important.

Before proceeding with the remainder of the chapter, complete the following exercise to help reinforce some of the ideas expressed above.

Exercise

What specific area(s) would you like to study as part of an action research project? Develop some ideas and share them with a colleague.

Clarify your purposes for conducting action research by brainstorming and recording answers to the questions enumerated in the previous section.

Articulate the overarching purpose of your study.

Why and how will the action research project improve your school?

What goals and objectives do you want to accomplish?

Answers will vary

Considering Logistics

You have now identified the overarching purpose of your study, including why and how the study will further improve your school and what goals and objectives you want to accomplish. You also know that data should be gathered from a variety of sources. You will try to utilize both qualitative and quantitative measures, including experimental and nonexperimental types of research and including a variety of data gathering instruments (see chapter 7). Before we consider the heart or essence of research design (deciding which specific form of research to use), we need to consider some logistical matters first: Who will be involved in this study? Who will collect data? How long will it take? What will it cost in terms of time and resources? Additional concerns are knowing how data are to be collected, analyzed, and reported, by whom, and what will be done with the results.

In summary, then, the first step in choosing a sound research design is to develop an overall plan for your study so that you are clear about your purposes, understand the value of this undertaking, and have attended to some logistics. The following questions will serve as a guide in developing any research plan:

- What research study will I undertake?
- Why am I conducting this study?
- How will this study help my school to improve?
- What are my goals and objectives?
- Who will be involved in this study?
- For what other logistical concerns should I prepare?
- How will data be collected?
- How will data be analyzed?
- How will data be reported?
- What will I do with the results?

Answers to these questions will enable you to start framing and preparing a plan. You need not answer all of the questions above definitively. Just begin thinking about them as you continue to plan the project. Complete the activity sheet at the end of the chapter to get you going.

You are now ready to select an appropriate research design matched to your particular needs and concerns.

The Plan

Now that you have clarified the purposes for conducting an action research project and attended to various logistical concerns, a plan that specifies a research design must be articulated. Selection of a research design is really quite simple. The design used depends on the question(s) you ask. Then select the appropriate research methods that can answer the questions you posed.

Preliminary steps in choosing a research design are as follows:

1. Specifying research questions and/or hypotheses

2. Selecting an appropriate **sample,** or group of subjects

3. Assigning individuals to a **treatment,** the procedure implemented to determine its effect

Ask yourself the following questions:

- What questions will guide your research?
- Who will participate in your study?
- How will they be selected?
- Which group will be exposed to the treatment?

Answering these questions is a prerequisite for selecting a suitable research design.

Complete the following exercise to help reinforce some of the ideas expressed above.

Exercise

Given the topic you chose in the previous exercise, what logistical areas will need immediate attention?

After answering the questions above in regard to the plan, describe your sample, how participants of your study will be utilized or assigned to a treatment, and what research questions you will attempt to answer as a result of undertaking your research action project.

_____

_____

_____

Answers will vary

Suggestions for Getting Started

Here are several key suggestions to help you get started on an action research project. Review and follow the five steps discussed earlier in this chapter:

1. Clarify the purposes of your research.
2. Attend to administrative and logistical aspects of your study.
3. Decide on a quantitative and/or qualitative approach.
4. Select a method and type of research.
5. Choose a design that is appropriate for the area of investigation.

Think through the process before you begin. When asked to explain his high percentage of successful free throws from the line, basketball legend Michael Jordan said that before approaching the line he imagines himself holding the ball, aiming, and shooting. "I see the ball dropping into the hoop." We can learn from Jordan's approach by envisioning what our project will "look like down the road." Develop a vision of your project, then follow the next suggestion.

Articulate your vision of action research to a colleague. Talking about your plans to someone else will help to clarify your project. New ideas will naturally arise, or revising existing ones might be suggested.

Collaborate with a colleague on a project. Often it is easier to begin a project by teaming up with someone. The other person, if chosen correctly, will serve to spur you on toward success. Collaboration is also exciting and fun.

Avoid those inevitable roadblocks (stumbling blocks). Setbacks will naturally occur. More often than not these obstacles are beyond your control. As long as you keep your goal in mind, you will be able to circumvent nuisances that might serve to thwart your project.

At this point, you might want to read chapter 13 for some concrete examples.

References

Calhoun, E. P., Allen, L., & Halliburton, C. (1996, April). *A report on the implementation of and results from schoolwide action research.* Paper presented at the annual meeting of the American Educational Research Association, New York.

Carr, W., & Kemmis, S. (1986). *Becoming critical: Education, knowledge, and action research.* London: Palmer Press.

Activity 5.   Planning a Research Project

1. Why do I want to undertake this action research project? What do I want to investigate? What do I hope to learn?

   _____

   _____

2. What preliminary information should I gather to help me get started?

   _____

   _____

3. What question or questions should I ponder?

   _____

   _____

4. What are my short-term and long-term goals?

   _____

   _____

5. Who will be involved in this research project?

   _____

   _____

6. To what administrative or logistical concerns should I attend?

   _____

   _____

7. How will data be collected, analyzed, and reported?

   _____

   _____

8. What will I do with the results?

   _____

   _____

9. Will I incorporate quantitative and/or qualitative approaches?

   _____

   _____

Quantitative Approaches to Action Research

Focus Questions

1. What are different types of quantitative approaches?
2. What are the advantages of using a quantitative approach to action research?
3. What is the difference between a survey and a questionnaire?
4. How might you incorporate a quantitative approach in your project?
5. Can you think of an action research project that would not call for a quantitative approach?

Action researchers may not use all or even many of the approaches described in this chapter. Still, an action researcher should have at his or her disposal a variety of research methods. The quantitative approaches to action research are clearly explained, and only information that action researchers would actually use is provided. Readers are encouraged to peruse all the methods and approaches discussed in this chapter. Familiarity with them will provide ideas for how an action research study may be undertaken. Selection of one or more of the methods should occur afterwards.

As I have mentioned, three quantitative methods are commonly used in educational research: descriptive, correlational, and group comparison research (see Figure 1-6).

Descriptive Research

Descriptive research is one of three methods of research that assumes a quantitative approach in studying a given educational issue or problem. Descriptive research may use statistics or numbers (usually percentages) to describe data.

Although descriptive research is treated as a quantitative method, its two types of research, surveys and observations (described below), can in fact be reported qualitatively if nonnumerical findings are reported. Some authorities in the field of educational research consider descriptive research as nonexperimental and as either quantitative or qualitative. Yet in action research, surveys and observations are usually reported quantitatively.

Let's say you distributed a questionnaire to teachers in your district and collected data about their attitudes toward bilingual education. To report your findings, you decide to note what percentage of teachers in various categories is favorably or unfavorably disposed to bilingual education. You report, for example, that 56% of elementary school teachers are in favor of bilingual education, compared to 34% and 23% of middle school and high school teachers, respectively. This is an example of descriptive research because you describe the findings of your study numerically.

Descriptive research may utilize simple mathematical notations, such as percentages, or more complicated statistical formulations (see chapter 8). Two types of descriptive research can be employed by action researchers: surveys and observations.

Surveys

A **survey** is any instrument used to assess attitudes or views of respondents. Discussion of surveys in this section will highlight the most common type of survey used in action research: questionnaires. A **questionnaire** is a type of survey that is distributed to a sample to ascertain attitudes about a particular issue or concern. Although questionnaires can be assessed qualitatively, a discussion of questionnaires has been included in this section because results are most often reported numerically.

Two other types of surveys, interviews and focus groups, whose results are reported verbally, are discussed in chapter 7.

Questionnaires are very useful tools to collect data about almost any given topic. Because they are relatively easy to construct and analyze, questionnaires are very popular in action research projects. Questionnaires, especially those conducted anonymously, provide keen insights that might otherwise be overlooked or unrealized.

Questionnaires can be used to describe what teachers in your school think about the new literature-based reading program recently adopted. Questionnaires are one of the most common types of data collection instruments (or data sources) used in action research projects.

Questionnaires, as a descriptive research methodology and as a data collection instrument, will be explained further in chapter 7.

Under what circumstances do you think you might utilize a questionnaire?

Observations

Surveys and observations can really be considered *both* quantitative and qualitative in approach. The determining factor that categorizes one or the other is the way the data are reported. I have included surveys and observations as quantitative approaches because in action research projects they are often reported numerically.

Observation, in this context, refers to studies that measure behavior of an individual or group of individuals by directly watching them and reporting what you see in some numerical way.

Two common forms of observations are *nonsystematic* and *systematic.* When a supervisor, for instance, nonsystematically observes a classroom she may simply walk into a classroom unannounced, watch classroom interaction, and begin taking notes on the interactions she observes. Nonsystematic observations are usually anecdotal and subjective. Systematic observation refers to a formal process of collecting data that is more scientific than nonsystematic observations in that data are collected with the aid of predetermined observation forms, audiovisual equipment, or some other observation instrument. Systematic observations are generally more accurate and desirable when conducting action research.

An example of observational research conducted systematically in action research projects is as follows. An assistant principal and a principal observe three students in a classroom. These students have been identified as seriously disruptive. Both supervisors may simultaneously observe these students and record the number of instances of misbehavior within a predetermined period of time. The observers must, of course, agree on what is considered "serious misbehavior." Prior to the observation they agree that serious misbehavior will be defined as any behavior that includes striking someone else in the class with one's body or any other object, as well as verbal and nonverbal disruptions that include cursing, incessant calling out without permission, or getting out of one's seat repeatedly.

During an observational research session both supervisors will record occurrences of misbehavior (i.e., target behavior) at various intervals or designated times using the Interval Recording Observation Form (Figure 4-1).

Interval Recording Observation Form

Student's Name: _____

Environment: _____

Target Behavior: _____

Start Time: _____

Observer: _____

Date: _____

10-minute observation period: 30-second intervals

9:00		9:01		9:02		9:03		9:04		9:05		9:06		9:07		9:08		9:09	
1	2	3	4	5	6	7	8	9	10	11	12	13	14	15	16	17	18	19	20

Key: + is marked for each occurrence of target behavior; – is marked if target behavior did not occur.

Figure 4-1.

Validity—the extent to which the instrument measures what it is intended to measure—is maintained by predefining "serious misbehavior." **Reliability**—the degree to which the instrument yields consistent results—is determined through the percentages of agreements between observers.

Any numerical recording of data collected through direct observation is considered observation. Several noteworthy works describe in detail various ways or methods of collecting data through observational research. Consult, for example, Acheson and Gall, 1997; Glickman, Gordon, and Ross-Gordon, 1998; Moore, 1995; and Willerman, McNeely, and Koffman, 1991. The latter work provides detailed explanations of how to use seating charts, verbal flow charts, nonverbal communication patterns, and anecdotal recordings using audio- and videotapes. I usually require my students to read portions of that excellent book.

Correlation Research

Correlational research is used to explore the degree of relationship between two variables. A **variable** is a factor that has distinguishably different properties (e.g., gender, whose properties are *male* and *female*). An action researcher will rarely correlate more than two variables, but it is possible to do so. For example, as an educational leader you might be interested in correlating students' scores on math and science tests. You might hypothesize that the higher a student scores on math tests, the higher he or she is likely to score on science tests. A correlational analysis will indicate the degree to which these two variables (math tests and science tests) relate to one another. The strength of the **correlation** (or relationship) between two variables may warrant a specific instructional measure to be taken on a grade level or by an individual teacher.

Correlational research cannot indicate causality between variables. Therefore, any predictions based on correlational research are tentative. Although it is not frequently employed by action researchers, correlational research might be useful, for example, to study the following questions:

1. What is the relationship between leadership styles of principals and faculty morale?

2. What is the relationship between levels of stress among high school freshmen (or any group, for that matter) and achievement levels in a given subject?

3. What is the relationship between the availability of technologically oriented instructional materials in science and science achievement?

As will be explained in chapter 8, correlational analyses are relatively easy to compute with appropriate computer programs.

Group Comparison Research

Group comparison research, the third quantitative research method, compares two or more groups according to some variables (usually two). There are three types of group comparison studies: experimental, quasi-experimental, and ex post facto. The type of research you choose depends to a large extent on the situation you are involved with and the degree of independence that you, as researcher, have to assign your subjects to an **experimental group,** which receives the experimental treatment, or a **control group,** which remains untreated or receives a placebo treatment.

Experimental research assigns individuals to an experimental or control group through a process of **randomization,** in which all participants have an equal chance of being selected.

Quasi-experimental research assigns groups, rather than individuals, to experimental and control groups, and no process of randomization occurs.

Ex post facto research uses groups that are already formed, such as two classrooms, assigning each to the experimental or control condition. Again, no randomization occurs.

Regardless of which type of group comparison research you employ, the same basic structure applies: two groups are formed, a treatment is administered, posttests are given after a reasonable period of time, statistical comparisons are made, and conclusions are drawn.

Let's say you randomly assigned students to two groups. The experimental group will receive computer instruction to reinforce writing skills, while the control group will learn the same writing curriculum without computers. After a 4-month period, you compare the writing abilities of each group. Such comparisons enable you to assess the impact or effect of the **independent variable** (the variable that is manipulated—in this case, computer assisted writing instruction) on the **dependent variable** (the outcome, or affected variable—in this case, writing achievement). In chapter 8, I will discuss precisely how results from group comparison studies are analyzed.

Experimental research may be the least suitable type of group comparison research for most educational researchers because of the requirement of randomization. Yet some educational leaders might indeed want to undertake experimental research. Sometimes leaders do have the opportunity to randomize, as I did, when I was an assistant principal in New York City (Glanz, 1994). I studied the effect of stress reduction strategies on fifth-grade students by randomly assigning students to two groups: the experimental group received the treatment—stress reduction instruction—while the control group did not receive the treatment. The independent variable was stress reduction training, and the dependent variable was the levels of stress exhibited by students at various times during the school year. The fact that randomization was incorporated indicates the experimental nature of the study.

How does randomization work? Although randomizing individuals or classes is not often very feasible in educational settings or frequently employed in action research, opportunities may emerge in which randomization is possible and desirable. There are many ways of assigning the **subjects,** or participants, randomly to groups. Although a detailed discussion of randomization and its variant forms (e.g., stratified random sampling, cluster sampling, etc.) is unnecessary, educators should know the following rules when wishing to randomize:

1. Select the **population**—the total group from which you want to pull your sample—and make certain that all members of that population have an equal chance of being selected. For example, when I surveyed assistant principals in New York City (Glanz, 1994), I obtained a list of 3,000 assistant principals.

2. Next I assigned each subject (assistant principal) a number from 0000 to 2999.

3. I then consulted a table of random numbers (which can be found in almost any book on statistics) and arbitrarily selected a number.

4. I looked at the last four digits of the numbers.

5. If that number was also assigned to a subject, that subject was selected for the sample; if not, I went to the next number. For example, notice this list of random numbers:

21880	78677
16899	90867
22500	12490
09823	73033
23460	89780
30494	23111
92412	80003
99780	00986

If you start with the top number and look at the last four digits (1880). That represents the assistant principal who was assigned number 1880; in other words, the 1,880th assistant principal on the list was chosen for my study. I then look at the last four digits of the next number (6899) and realize that it is a larger number than the list of names of assistant principals (maximum of 3,000), so I skip that number and continue with the next number. The last four digits of the next number is 2500, so I select the 2,500th assistant principal on my list, who becomes the second subject in my study.

6. I continue this procedure until I have the desired sample (usually 10% of the population, which in this case was 300 assistant principals).

Other sampling techniques are defined in the glossary, and further discussion of group comparison studies can be found later in this chapter.

Before proceeding with the remainder of the chapter, complete the following exercises to help reinforce some of the ideas expressed above.

Exercises

1. You are a superintendent who wants to sample teacher attitudes toward supervision, and there are 5,000 teachers in the population. Describe how you might select a random sample using the table of random numbers.

   _____

   _____

   _____

   > Answer:
   > POPULATION = 5,000 teachers
   > SIZE = 10% of 5,000 = 500 teachers
   > SELECT = assign each a number from 0001 to 5000
   > Arbritrarily start in the Table of Random Numbers and look at first or last four digits and go down the list until you select 500 teachers. Note: Today, samples can be easily generated through computer printouts without the use of the Table of Random Numbers.

2. Can you think of a situation in which you might set up
   a. an experimental study
   b. a correlational study
   c. a descriptive study

   Describe each study in detail.

   _____

   _____

   _____

   _____

   _____

   _____

   Answers will vary

Choosing a Research Design

Thus far, you have selected a topic or an area of investigation, clarified your purposes in undertaking this research venture, and begun to plan to conduct an action research study. At your disposal are quantitative and qualitative approaches to research. Within each approach, different methods may be chosen. Selection of a particular method depends on a variety of factors such as the nature of the study, the kinds of questions asked, and the resources available. In this section of the chapter, in order to assist you in getting started, I will discuss another aspect of research design that is of utmost importance.

Why is a design necessary? As an educational leader, you'll likely have to implement various programs, establish certain procedures, and/or institute specific practices. Evaluating the efficacy of these instructional concerns will be a challenging yet urgent task. Program evaluation, for example, is an essential responsibility of any professional supervisor. Evaluating a program with intelligence, thoroughness, and technical sophistication is essential. Any such evaluation requires attention to design as the foundation for setting up an action research project. Paying no attention to design would be like building a home without a blueprint.

Before you can choose a sound research design, you'll need to know what designs are readily available and when and how they should be used. Then you can select the appropriate design to suit your objectives.

This section will discuss eight frequently used research designs that can be used, to varying degrees, in action research. All of these designs are suitable for quantitative approaches, except for the single measurement design, so they are included in this chapter. In the next chapter, a design for evaluation research will be introduced.

An Inadequate Research Design

There is really only one inadequate or unacceptable research design, and that is called the *unassessed treatment design* (Popham, 1972). Unfortunately, this approach is often used by practitioners in school settings. A program may be implemented or a practice established without thorough and thoughtful consideration of its efficacy. The program or practice is continued or discarded without undertaking any sort of evaluative measure. Does this sound familiar?

An unassessed treatment design is characterized by an educator's inaction. The educational leader, for example, makes no effort whatsoever to assess whether the treatment is effective. Popham (1972) characterizes this design as T = nothing; that is, no assessment is conducted to determine the impact of the given treatment. I knew a supervisor who once introduced a new procedure requiring teachers to more closely monitor student progress. At the end of the semester, he "felt" that the program was a good idea. He decided to expand the program to the entire grade. When I asked him why he decided to take this action, he replied, "It sounds good, doesn't it?"

Popham (1972) describes the unassessed treatment design as follows:

> In this approach, the instructional treatment developer simply implements a new instructional treatment or alters the existing instructional treatment without making any kind of systematic effort to measure whether the treatment is effective. Usually, of course, judgments have been made regarding whether the treatments are likely to prove worthwhile, but these evaluations are often made without any evidence whatsoever. A school administrator, for example, may introduce a new procedure requiring pupils to spend more time in the school library. At the end of the semester, he may "feel" it was a good idea and should be continued. Or a teacher may decide to alter the nature of his homework assignments so that students do half their assigned work during class sessions. Intuitively, he may decide that this new treatment worked out well, but he makes no attempt to measure the results produced by the innovation. (p. 140)

Popham concludes by cautioning against such an approach. "It is preferable for educators to remain open-minded, postponing all decisions about treatment until such time as appropriate measurements can be collected" (p. 142).

Mini-exercise: Can you think of a situation in which such an approach was taken? Explain.

Adequate Research Designs
(or Simplified Designs for School Research)

A treatment, also known as an **intervention,** is specific instructional practice, program, or procedure that is implemented by a researcher in order to investigate its effect on the behavior or achievement of an individual or a group. A treatment might include, for example, a reading series recently adopted by a school, the use of computers to assist problem solving, or a behavioral contract system implemented to positively influence behavior of three seventh graders. As a researcher, you want to understand the impact these treatments have on various outcomes (e.g., achievement or attitudes). The following research designs adequately allow you to gather evidence to demonstrate the efficacy of the treatment. Below, seven categories of research design are discussed that might prove useful for action research projects (Table 4-1).

Table 4-1. Summary of Research Designs

Unassessed Treatment	T →
Single Measurement	T → M
One-Group Pretest and Posttest	M → T → M
Static-Group Comparison	T → M
	→ M
Nonequivalent Control Group	M → T1 → M
	M → T2 → M
Pretest and Posttest Control Group	R M → T1 → M
	R M → T2 → M
Posttest-Only Control Group	R T1 → M
	R T2 → M
Interrupted Time Series	M1 → M2 → M3 T M4 → M5 → M6
Single Subject	A-B
	A-B-A
	A-B-A-B
	Multiple Baselines

Single Measurement Design

The **single measurement design** is commonly employed in qualitative research but is included in this chapter for the sake of convenience. It may be depicted as follows: T → M. The T stands for treatment and the M indicates the measurement—that is, the impact that the treatment has on the sample.

Although single measurement designs do not necessarily consider factors that may have influenced a particular outcome, these designs are frequently employed in action research projects because they are relatively easy to use. When single measurement designs are employed, the educator introduces a treatment and attempts to measure its impact. Often the measurements take the form of a traditional test.

Let's say you were writing a case study (see chapter 5) to indicate the positive influence that behavior contracting had on the behavior of John, a fifth grader. This would involve detailed descriptions of John's behavior over time as a result of several observations. The researcher would provide anecdotal evidence demonstrating how, for instance, John's behavior has changed since the introduction of behavior contracting. Observations are recorded anecdotally; that is, explicit descriptions of observable acts are recorded without interpretation. Note the following statements that are made anecdotally:

> Jerry got out of his seat at 9:15 a.m. and walked over to Susan and took her pen without permission.
>
> Juanita dropped her pen on the floor.
>
> There are 40 students in this class.

Note the difference between anecdotal annotations and inferences:

> He is a trouble maker.
>
> The information on this test may be too difficult for Susan.
>
> She is hyperactive.
>
> Fred behaves very nicely.
>
> She appears neurotic at times.

As you learn about case study research you will see that the anecdotal records and interpretations of them are considered "measurements," albeit qualitative. Single measurement designs may be used in quantitative research, too.

One-Group Pretest and Posttest Design

A second design commonly used by practitioners is known as the **one-group pretest and posttest design** and is depicted as follows: $M \rightarrow T \rightarrow M$. In this design, one group is selected and is pretested (M) on some variable. A treatment (T) is then introduced, and its impact is assessed by a posttest (M) of some sort.

This research design is not as powerful as the following designs, yet it is commonly used by action researchers because very often only one group is available for study. Growth from pretest to posttest can be assessed. The serious weakness of the one-group pretest and posttest design is that you can never be certain that an increase in achievement, for example, is a consequence of the treatment itself. No control is provided for intervening variables that might have influenced posttreatment findings. Suppose you find an increase from pretest to posttest; how confident can you be that the gain was attributable solely to your treatment and not due to some other factor (an unknown variable)? Learners could have gained due to maturation or experiences not associated with the intervention or treatment. Too many other plausible explanations exist.

Some people maintain that pretest-posttest comparisons may be effectively used to ascertain achievement gains. Yet most researchers caution against such a procedure because it may be possible for one group with very low initial scores to make large gains, compared to another group that starts off with a high average and then makes smaller gains. Groups who score higher on pretests will not always make the same degree of significant improvement as groups who start with lower averages. This is called the *test ceiling factor.*

Nevertheless, despite this serious flaw, use of this design is feasible if two conditions are met: (a) you don't rely only on this design but rather you triangulate to every extent possible; and (b) you analyze data using the sign test, which will be explained in detail in chapter 8.

Static-Group Comparison Design

The **static-group comparison design** is used in quasi-experimental research involving two groups in which only one group, the experimental group, receives a treatment. Although a posttest is administered to each group (experimental and control), no pretest is usually administered. Individuals are not randomly assigned to groups. This design is schematically depicted as follows: T → M and → M.

Let's say you want to conduct a study with one class. This design is often used by action researchers who have only one class in which a study can be conducted. You divide the class into two groups. No pretest is used to accomplish this division. Rather, you, the leader-teacher, merely estimate two equivalent or comparable groups. Then one treatment (e.g., use of stickers as a positive reinforcement for math achievement) is administered to the group designated as experimental. The control group is intentionally not offered this form of positive reinforcement for its math work. At the end of a period of time (perhaps after a unit of instruction), you administer an achievement test (see chapter 7). You would then use a statistical test (the Mann-Whitney U-test; see chapter 8) to determine whether there is a significant difference between the two groups.

Nonequivalent Control Group Design

The next four designs are among the most powerful designs that can be used by action researchers (Popham, 1972). They include classic group comparison studies that involve two contrasting groups: the experimental group receives one treatment, while the control group receives another.

The **nonequivalent control group** design is useful for educational leaders as action researchers. This design, frequently used in school research, involves administering one treatment (T1) to an experimental group and another treatment (T2) to a comparison (control) group. This design is schematically depicted as follows: M → T1 → M and M → T2 → M.

Nonequivalent control group designs usually involve intact experimental and control groups. For instance, if you taught high school English, you might select two classes (such as your fourth and sixth periods) to be involved in a study. You selected these two classes because both groups are somewhat equivalent in achievement levels or comparable in relation to the variable under study. (The word *nonequivalent* in the title of this design refers to the different, or nonequivalent, treatments that *both* groups receive). Because nonequivalent control group designs involve intact classes, this design is associated with ex post facto research.

Nonequivalent control group designs can be used with two separate classes with or without the same teacher. You may even divide one class into two equivalent groups using the **matched pairs** technique, in which each member of one group has a direct counterpart in the other group. Let's say you have a fifth-grade class comprising 28 students, and you want to divide them into two equivalent or comparable groups to assess the impact of a particular instructional strategy. To divide the class using matched pairs, you would follow these steps:

1. Administer a test to the entire class. If the content area of your study involves mathematics, for example, you would administer a mathematics test.

2. Rank the students who completed the test according to the grade achieved on the test. In other words, rank each member of the class from highest score to lowest score. For example, your results, in part, may appear as follows:

Mohammed B.	97
Fred D.	96
Juan S.	96
Fran Y.	93
Anita G.	91
Kim W.	88
Wendy L.	83

3. You then take the first pair (Mohammed B. and Fred D.) and randomly assign them to the experimental and con-

trol groups as follows, for example, Fred D. to the experimental group and Mohammed B. to the control group.

4. Continue the same procedure for the next pair (Juan and Fran) and do so with all 28 students.

Using matched pairs ensures that you now have two comparable groups, at least in terms of mathematics achievement. You are then ready to conduct your study using, for instance, a nonequivalent control group design.

Nonequivalent control group designs can only work when you begin the study with comparable groups (although, as we'll discuss in chapter 8, if comparability cannot be achieved for some reason, then a statistical procedure known as an ANCOVA can be used). Generally, the nonequivalent control group design is used when randomization is impossible but groups are essentially comparable.

The next two designs are similar to the previous design except for the fact that randomization is possible. Randomization ensures equivalence between groups; that is, whenever you randomize you can be certain that both groups are comparable. However, randomization is not easily used within classes because moving pupils from one classroom to another for research purposes may not be feasible or practical.

When could randomization be used? You may be able to randomly distribute students into classes before the start of the school year during reorganization, as I have done in some circumstances.

Pretest and Posttest Control Group Design

The **pretest and posttest control group design** is a powerful design that incorporates randomization or sampling. This design may be depicted as follows: EXPTL R M → T1 → M and CONTRL R M → T2 → M. The R indicates that the two groups have been formed by randomization procedures. As before, the M refers to the measurements taken prior to and after the introduction of the treatments (T1 and T2).

Since randomization ensures equivalence between groups, the pretest and posttest control group design allows you to draw conclusions about the effectiveness of the treatment. Statistically higher posttest scores of the experimental group compared to the control group would indicate that, for example, the special use of a new mathematics series with the experimental group contributed to the higher achievement scores.

A pretest is not necessary to establish a baseline so that a comparison can be made when the posttest is given. As will be explained in chapter 8, pretest to posttest gains are not measured to ascertain the impact of a given treatment. Statistical work on posttest scores is all that has to be done once group equivalence is assured.

As stated earlier, randomization ensures comparability or equivalence between groups. Therefore, if randomization is employed, why give a pretest?
One might respond that a pretest can confirm equivalence, but such an asser-
tion is really unnecessary because it is readily acknowledged that randomization assures equivalence. Sometimes, however, a pretest may yield some
important information about content validity. Sometimes a pretest can be a
reactive measure that produces a change in the subject's behavior. For instance,
a pretest that is given orally may be reactive in the sense that respondents or
subjects obtain clues about possible answers from the voice inflections of the
tester. If pretests appear to be reactive, then an alternate design, such as the
posttest-only control group design, should be employed.

Posttest-Only Control Group Design

The **posttest-only control group design** may be depicted as follows: R T1 →
M and R T2 → M. This design should be used when the pretest may be a
reactive measure; that is, participants completing a test or a survey may receive
clues from the pretest that influence a positive score on the posttest. If a pretest
is potentially reactive, don't use it. Because randomization is employed, there
is no need to worry about equivalence between groups. This design allows you
"to make defensible judgments about the value of a given treatment" (Popham,
1972, p. 149).

Interrupted Time Series Design
(Single Subject Design)

The **interrupted time series design** is somewhat different from the previous
designs. Also commonly known as the **single subject design,** it is schematically depicted as follows: Ml → M2 → M3 T M4 → M5 → M6. In this design, one group is repeatedly pretested, exposed to a treatment, and then
repeatedly posttested. In other words, a series of measurements is taken both
before and after the introduction of the treatment. Measurements (M) may be
taken from existing archival data such as attendance records, standardized test
scores, disciplinary records, and school profiles.

Interrupted time series designs usually involve *group* analyses with respect
to a given variable, such as academic progress over time. When progress over
time is assessed for *individuals,* it is usually called a single subject design. This
allows a researcher to investigate one or just a few individuals with respect to a
given variable. Subjects are exposed to a treatment and then multiple measurements are taken over a period of time. The objective of this sort of research is to
determine whether the treatment had any effect on the behavior of the subject(s).

Single subject design is a powerful method of studying the effectiveness of
an intervention or treatment on a single subject. Measurements are repeatedly

made until stability is established—this is called a **baseline**—after which treatment is introduced and an appropriate number of measurements are made. The treatment phase is followed by a second baseline, which is followed by a second treatment phase.

Single subject design is popular for action researchers because it is very useful to monitor and assess a particular treatment on individual students. This design is advantageous because results are easy to interpret, usually by visual inspection of the charted data points. Statistical analysis is also unnecessary.

A-B; **A-B-A**; or **A-B-A-B research designs** are types of single subject designs. Before we discuss these, three basic terms must be explained.

Baseline condition (Condition A). This refers to information collected on a specific target behavior before an intervention strategy is employed (Figure 4-2). The purpose of establishing baseline data is to provide a description of the target behavior as it occurs naturally, without treatment. The baseline serves as the basis of comparison for assessing the impact of a treatment. Taking a number of baseline measurements to establish a pattern of behavior is known as *baseline stability.* For instance, observing Sarah for a period of 3 days in a row for 45 minutes each time and noting the number of times she gets out of her seat without permission would establish baseline stability.

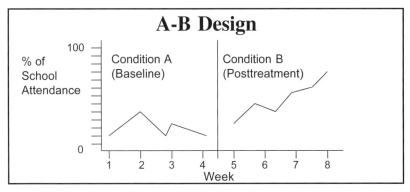

Figure 4-2.

Treatment (or intervention) condition (Condition B). During this phase, the treatment is introduced while data collection continues.

Target behavior. Directly observing any subject in a school setting involves identifying a target behavior. The target behavior must be defined in such a way as to allow the observer to objectively and independently note and measure each occurrence of the behavior. Target behavior must be observable and measurable. Independent observers must be able to see the behavior occurring and be able to quantify the behaviors by noting, for instance, the frequency and duration of each act of the behavior. For example, observing Michael raising his hand in class for any reason is a target behavior, because the observer can see the behavior occurring and is able to note the number of times Michael raises his hand in a 45-minute period. An example of a nonobservable target behavior might be to see if Joshua is cooperative during group work. The difficulty here, of course, is with the word *cooperative*. What does it actually mean? What does it mean to you? Can two independent observers agree that a particular student is being cooperative?

Here's a mini-exercise: Place a check next to the target behavior that can be observed and measured by two independent observers without defining the behavior prior to observation:

1. Johnny is acting out in class.
2. Natasha says "thank you" during the lesson.
3. Felicia is disruptive during art class.
4. Billy completes his class assignments.
5. Sally is behaving well.
6. Kisha raises her hand to ask or answer a question.

Frequency Recording Observation Form

Student's Name: _____

Environment: _____

Target Behavior: _____

Start Time: _____

Observer: _____

Date: _____

5 minute observation period: 30-second intervals

NAME		1		2		3		4		5
Maria										
Ronald										
Steve										

Key: + is marked for each occurrence of target behavior; − is marked if target behavior did not occur.

Figure 4-3.

Numbers 2 and 6 are target behaviors that can easily be observed. The other choices require observers to define what is "acting out," "disruptive," "completing assignments," and "behaving well." Undertaking a single subject design requires observers to clarify behaviors in advance.

The most common way to record data is to use frequency charts (checklists). These allow an observer to note the frequency of each target behavior. Interval recording is sometimes used to divide the observation period into equal intervals of smaller time periods (Figure 4-3). Observers can then note whether the target behavior occurred (+) or did not occur (–) during each interval. The frequencies are not recorded; the target behavior is merely noted in a specified period of time.

Regarding accuracy, here are some factors to consider that may potentially affect your data collection during baseline and treatment periods:

1. *Reactivity.* The student observed realizes that you are counting or noting the number of times, for example, that she is talking to a neighbor. Reactivity can be minimized by not staring at the student as observations are being made.

2. *Observer drift.* This occurs when an observer daydreams or when an observer is unclear if a target behavior is occurring. An **operational definition**—an observable, measurable, and quantifiable definition—is the best method by which to minimize observer drift. For instance, how might you operationalize "getting out of his seat"? Answer: When his buttocks are approximately 12 inches from his chair.

3. *Recording procedures.* Make certain that charts for recording data are available at the time of the observation.

4. *Location of observer.* The best place to observe is usually from the back of the room, as long as you have an unobstructed view of the class.

5. *Observer expectations.* Biased observations or conclusions are minimized when target behaviors are clearly defined in advance.

6. *Lack of practice.* The observer should practice recording behaviors prior to actual study.

7. *Reliability.* Interrater reliability is achieved when there is a high percent of agreement between two or more observers.

Let's say two individuals are watching the number of times Jose leaves his seat without permission and the following data are collected by each observer: observer A frequency = 5; observer B frequency = 10. Reliability could then be calculated as follows: $5 \div 10 = 0.5 \times 100 = 50\%$. You should strive for at least a 70% reliability factor.

A-B

The first type of single subject design is known as A-B. Note Condition A (the baseline condition) and Condition B (the intervention condition). Don't forget, with single subject designs you are studying individuals, not groups of individuals.

The line in the center of Fig. 4-2 indicates that the treatment has been introduced. You'll notice that the baseline was kept over a 4-week period to establish stability before the introduction of the treatment. Measurements continue after the treatment is introduced to note any changes in attendance. From perusing the figure you may reasonably conclude that the treatment did indeed have a positive effect on school attendance.

Can you draw a chart showing no change after the treatment is introduced? Can you think of a situation in which you as an educational leader might employ a single subject design? *Hint:* Think of a situation in which you want to monitor student behavior of some sort. Choose a target behavior—what exactly you are going to observe. Be very specific about the target behavior (e.g., the number of times Howie gets out of his seat or the number of times Juan praises a fellow student in his cooperative group). Once a target behavior has been specified, start collecting baseline data during a specified period of time. Then introduce the treatment and keep collecting data. Record your data in chart or graph form.

One of the potential problems with an A-B design is how to determine that the change after the treatment was definitely due to the treatment and not, perhaps, to some intervening variable or outside influence. That's why some researchers prefer a second type of single subject design known as A-B-A.

A-B-A

A-B-A design is similar to the A-B design, except that you withdraw the intervention and then maintain baseline data. For example, as an educational leader you might want to introduce a program to increase attendance among students who are identified as at-risk of dropping out of high school. At a national convention you learn about a marvelous intervention strategy. You decide to implement this program (after, of course, becoming more familiarized with the program). How do you proceed? First, keep baseline data (Condition A) on each student's attendance records for a period of 4 weeks to establish baseline stability. Then, introduce the treatment for a similar period of 4 weeks. You'll note, for example, that attendance rates dramatically increase. Before you conclude that the program is successful, you would withdraw the treatment and monitor student attendance rates by keeping additional baseline rates for another 4 weeks. You might find that attendance drops but that its rates are better than they were prior to the introduction of the treatment.

An A-B-A design allows you to more confidently attribute the change in behavior to the treatment, as opposed to some extraneous factor or chance factor. Can you draw a chart or graph that illustrates the experiment described above?

A-B-A-B

The third type of single subject design is known as A-B-A-B. This is similar to the previous design, but it reintroduces the treatment. This design adds further credibility to your treatment. Can you explain why? Can you draw a graph illustrating this design? Can you think of a reason that an A-B-A-B design should not be used? *Hint:* Consider the ethics of removing a successful treatment.

A variation of the designs above is known as the alternating treatment design (A-B-C-A-D-A) and is characterized by the introduction of three separate treatments (B, C, and D):

1. It starts off the same way as A-B, with B representing the use of positive reinforcement through verbal praise.

2. The first of two other treatments is introduced. The first treatment (B) is removed, and a new treatment designated as C is introduced (e.g., positive reinforcement using only tokens, no praise), followed by A, which is a phase in which you record baseline data.

3. Treatment C is withdrawn, and a new treatment (D) is introduced (e.g., positive reinforcement offered by sending daily letters home), followed by a phase in which you continue to record baseline data, A.

This design can be used when you want to assess the impact of various treatments before you select one as your primary choice.

Another major category of single subject designs is known as *multiple baseline design.* This is a modification of the single subject design. With the use of multiple baseline designs you can collect data on more than one subject, behavior, and/or situation. Multiple baselines are recorded because different subjects, behaviors, and situations are observed.

A *multiple baseline across subjects design* involves utilizing one of the three single subject designs (A-B, A-B-A, or A-B-A-B) on two or more different subjects. For example, you may want to observe three of your students in terms of their frequency of violent behavior (i.e., your target behavior might be the number of times Steve, Maria, and Ronald hit someone in the classroom). Baseline data for Steve might be graphed as shown in Figure 4-4. Completing similar graphs for Maria and Ronald will allow for comparisons to be made regarding the frequencies of hitting, pretreatment, and posttreatment for all three students.

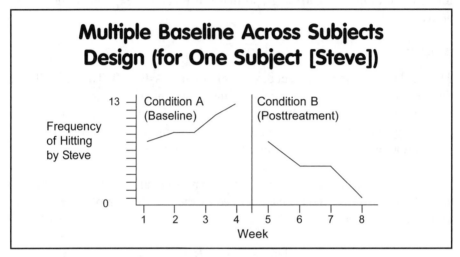

Figure 4-4.

A *multiple baseline across behaviors design* involves utilizing one of the three single subject designs (A-B, A-B-A, or A-B-A-B) on one subject while observing two or more different behaviors. For example, you may chart the frequencies of hitting, yelling, and kicking for a given student or among three students. Comparisons, as before, can be easily made.

A *multiple baseline across situations design* involves utilizing one of the three single subject designs (A-B, A-B-A, or A-B-A-B) in two or more different settings for one or more subjects. For example, you may chart the behavior of a given student or among three students in different settings (math class, cafeteria during lunch, and in the gymnasium). Comparisons, as before, can be easily made.

The reader is urged to consult Zirpoli and Melloy (1996) for an excellent overview of single subject designs and other relevant information.

Mini-exercise: Pair with a colleague, describing each of these aforementioned designs, making certain to provide an example for each.

Before proceeding to the next chapter, complete the following exercises (culled, in part, from Popham, 1972) to help reinforce some of the ideas expressed above.

Exercises

1. INTERRUPTED TIME SERIES DESIGN
    Write in the space provided the letter or letters of the graph lines that support the conclusion that improvement was due to the treatment.

    _____ In this hypothetical research situation, we have measured pupil performance on equivalent problem-solving tests every 2 months during the year, and we have introduced a 3-week teaching unit (i.e., the treatment) on problem-solving problems during the middle of the year.

    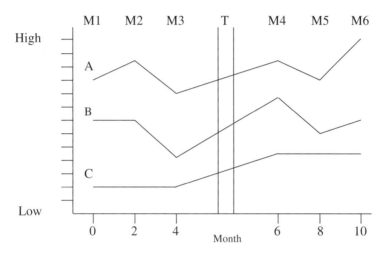

    Answer: C. Only to group C can we attribute the increase to the treatment. Groups A and B reveal fluctuating pre- and posttreatment performance records, thus indicating that the same stimuli causing the pretreatment fluctuations could also have caused the posttreatment fluctuations.

2. IDENTIFYING TYPE OF DESIGN

    Write the name of the design employed in this example in the space provided.

    A school superintendent introduces a new music appreciation program throughout her school district that depends heavily upon tape recordings of classical masterworks. Although rather costly, the new program is considered a success by the superintendent and her staff at the end of the year.

    DESIGN EMPLOYED:

    _____

    _____

    Answer: Unassessed treatment (because no attempt is made to investigate the program)

3. IDENTIFYING TYPE OF DESIGN

    Write the name of the design employed in this example.

    A 10th-grade biology teacher institutes a new approach to the teaching of one-celled animal life based on a series of 7-minute single-concept films. Prior to starting the new unit, she develops a test covering the material and administers it to her class before and after the unit, noting with satisfaction a dramatic improvement by her pupils on the test.

    DESIGN EMPLOYED:

    _____

    _____

    Answer: one-group pretest and posttest

4. IDENTIFYING TYPE OF DESIGN

    Write the name of the design employed in this example.

    A researcher uses a table of random numbers to subdivide 15 junior high school classes into three groups of five classes each (30 pupils per class), as follows: Treatment A, Treatment B, and Control. The treatments are administered during the first 4 months of the school year, and at mid-semester a posttest is given to all of the 450 pupils involved.

    DESIGN EMPLOYED:

    _____

    _____

    Answer: posttest only

5. IDENTIFYING TYPE OF DESIGN

    Write the name of the design employed in this example.

    A school principal has received a federal grant to institute a new mathematics enrichment program. Using school records, he computes the average mathematics achievement score on a nationally standardized examination for his 5th-, 9th-, and 12th-grade pupils during each of the preceding 3 years. He plans to have the same tests administered for the 2 years following the institution of the new program. He wishes to compare the relative positions of the three classes during the 5-year period.

    DESIGN EMPLOYED:

    _____

    _____

    Answer: interrupted time series

6. SELECTING THE APPROPRIATE DESIGN

Select the design best suited to the following research problem and write its name in the space provided.

> A school researcher hopes to test the merits of a new series of third-grade reading booklets. The booklets, commercially produced, are sold with a test that covers the skills ostensibly developed by learners during the 4-week period when the booklets are to be used. The researcher suspects that the pretest may structure the thinking of the pupils if it is administered to them prior to their exposure to the booklets. Twenty third-grade teachers have indicated a willingness to have their classes involved in the research as members of either the experimental or control groups.

BEST DESIGN:

_____

_____

Answer: posttest only (because of possibility for randomization and the potentially reactive nature of pretest)

7. SELECTING THE APPROPRIATE DESIGN

Select the design best suited to the following research problem and write its name.

> A high school government teacher wishes to conduct a study in his class of the difference that weekly issues of current events newspapers will make in his pupils' scores on a current events test. He realizes that pupils will learn about current events outside school, so he is particularly interested in their pretest to posttest growth. He has a series of literature selections that he can give to students in the class who are not assigned to read the current events newspapers.

BEST DESIGN:

_____

_____

Answer: pretest and posttest control group design or nonequivalent

8. SELECTING THE APPROPRIATE DESIGN

Select the design best suited to the following research problem and write its name.

> A school counselor wishes to test the influence on students' attitudes toward narcotics of a particular commercial film dealing obliquely with the use of narcotics. He devises a self-report questionnaire but is afraid if pupils complete the questionnaire prior to viewing the film, they will become sensitized to the narcotics issue. Random assignment of pupils is possible.

BEST DESIGN:

_____

_____

Answer: posttest only (because of the reactive nature of questionnaire)

9. SELECTING THE APPROPRIATE DESIGN

Select the design best suited to the following research problem and write its name in the space provided.

Faced with the necessity for evaluating a new set of general science kits, members of a small high school science department decide that they cannot randomly assign pupils among their first-semester general science classes because there would be conflicts. They have, however, administered science aptitude tests and have found that their four classes are remarkably similar. They hope to use the science kits with two complete classes, since two teachers have indicated unwillingness to use the kits with only a portion of their class.

BEST DESIGN:

_____

_____

Answer: nonequivalent control group design (with previously administered aptitude test at pretest)

10. SELECTING THE APPROPRIATE DESIGN

Select the design best suited to the following research problem and write its name.

Ms. Barbara Lewis, a school principal, wishes to assess the interest-building contribution of a school club program instituted 4 years ago. She decides to use daily attendance rates as an index of pupils' interest in school. She discovers that such data has been accumulated (in the school's archives) for every year since the club was inaugurated, as well as for the 10 years before it was initiated.

BEST DESIGN:

_____

_____

Answer: interrupted time series

11. Which statement is not true?

a. Nonequivalent designs are used when randomization is not possible and groups are comparable.

b. Posttest control group designs are used when randomization is possible.

c. Interrupted time series designs are used when randomization is impossible or in a case in which two parallel treatments are not readily available.

d. The purpose of matched pairs is to develop an accurate testing instrument.

Answer: d

12. Divide into groups of three and consider that you are all principals who are evaluating some sort of program in your school. How could you use the following quantitative and qualitative approaches?

   a. observations
   b. surveys
   c. group comparison research
   d. ethnography   Answers will vary

13. Identify the correct design:

   a. As a high school principal, I introduced a schoolwide restructuring program known as Housing. The high school was in desperate need to restructure because of high dropout rates and low SAT scores. The ninth grade has completed its first year in the Housing program. The program appears successful, so I plan on including grade 10 next year.

   _____

   b. A supervisor of curriculum wanted to assess a new fourth-grade reading series used in two elementary schools in the district. Each school has three fourth-grade classes with comparable standardized reading test scores. She introduces the new reading series to one school in September, while the other school is monitored as they use the traditional reading series. Scores on the standardized reading test are compared at the end of May.

   _____

   c. An assistant principal wants to see the impact of a new in-school suspension program on the attendance record of selected students at-risk. She reviews attendance records for 3 years prior to the implementation of the in-school suspension program. She will compare these records to the attendance records for 3 years after the program starts.

   _____

   Answers: a) unassessed; b) nonequivalent control group design; c) time series

14. Write three realistic cases describing the use of any three adequate research designs. Cases should be drawn from either personal experience or an experience any supervisor or lead-teacher might encounter. Be specific, realistic, and practical.

   _____

   _____

   _____

                                                      Answers will vary

15. MATCH

X		Y
___	A. unassessed treatment design	a. R T1 → M R T2 → M
___	B. single measurement design	
___	C. one-group pretest and posttest design	b. M → T → M M → T1 → M
___	D. nonequivalent control group design	c. T →
___	E. pretest and posttest control group design	d. M1 → M2 → M3 T M4 → M5 → M6
___	F. posttest-only control group design	e. T → M
___	G. interrupted time series design	f. RM → T1 → M RM → T2 → M
		g. M → T → M

Answers: A(c), B(e), C(g), D(b), E(f), F(a), G(d)

References

Acheson, K. A., & Gall, M. D. (1997). *Techniques in the clinical supervision of teachers.* New York: Longman.

Glanz, J. (1994). Redefining the roles and responsibilities of assistant principals. *Clearing House, 67* (5), 283–288.

Glickman, C. D., Gordon, S. P., & Ross-Gordon, J. M. (1998). *Supervision of instruction: A developmental approach* (4th ed.). Boston: Allyn & Bacon.

Moore, K. D. (1995). *Classroom teaching skills.* New York: McGraw-Hill.

Popham, W. J. (1972). Simplified designs for school research. In R. L. Baker & R. E. Schutz (Eds.), *Instructional product research* (pp. 137–160). New York: American Book.

Willerman, M., McNeely, S. L., & Koffman, E. C. (1991). *Teachers helping teachers: Peer observation and assistance.* New York: Praeger.

Zirpoli, T. J., & Melloy, K. J. (1996). *Behavior management: Application for teachers and parents* (2nd ed.). New York: Macmillan.

Activity 6.   Quantitative Methods and Designs

1. In Activity 5, nine questions were posed to help you start a research project. Given that you find a quantitative approach useful and feasible, complete the information below. Check the methods and designs that you may use in the action research project you are developing. Realize that your selections now may be changed later.

METHODS

Descriptive research

_____ surveys   _____ observational

Correlational research

Group Comparison research

_____ experimental   _____ quasi-experimental   _____ ex post facto

DESIGNS

_____ single measurement   _____ one-group pretest and posttest

_____ static-group comparison   _____ nonequivalent control group

_____ pretest and posttest control   _____ posttest-only control group
        group

_____ interrupted time series   _____ single subject

Qualitative Approaches to Action Research

Focus Questions

1. What are different types of qualitative approaches?
2. What are the advantages of using a qualitative approach to action research?
3. What is the difference between a case study and an ethnographic study?
4. How might you incorporate a qualitative approach in your project?
5. Can you think of an action research project that would not call for a qualitative approach?

Qualitative research approaches "are used to examine questions that can best be answered by *verbally* describing how participants in a study perceive and interpret various aspects of their environment" (Crowl, Kaminsky, & Podell, 1997, p. 499). A study involving how a principal, for instance, fostered shared decision making in her school could be reported qualitatively. By interviewing key participants in the school, observing decision-making committees in action, and describing in detail how participants relate with one another, and analyzing written documents and other sources about site-based management, the researcher may reach certain conclusions about the effectiveness of shared decision making in this particular school.

Qualitative approaches, as you recall, are just as viable as quantitative ones. Yet quantitative research attempts to describe outcomes, the "what" (product) of a study; qualitative studies examine the "how" (process) and the "why" questions. The power of qualitative research is in its ability to enrich our understanding of a given phenomenon.

Although results cannot usually be generalized to other schools, qualitative research offers a unique opportunity to conduct an in-depth analysis of the intricate processes at work when attempting to implement, for example, a collaborative model in a school, as described in the opening paragraph of this section. The value of qualitative approaches is that they provide rich detail and insight often missing from quantitative studies.

Other differences exist between qualitative and quantitative studies. Qualitative research captures behavior occurring in naturalistic settings and does not involve purposeful manipulation of subjects for experimental purposes, as do many quantitative studies. Qualitative research is not just another methodology (a set of data collection and analysis tools) but can be conceived as a paradigm or a way of thinking about how knowledge is created and best understood. A fundamental belief that qualitative researchers espouse is that events cannot be understood unless one understands how they are perceived and interpreted by the people who participated in them. Moreover, a quantitative approach assumes that social facts have an objective reality that can be studied scientifically; qualitative modes assume that reality is socially constructed and is best represented by the subjective perceptions or observations of individuals. Qualitative research can occur naturally by simply walking into a classroom, for instance, and recording behavior objectively or anecdotally without any prescribed or predetermined criteria. Qualitative research is therefore more flexible and inductive than quantitative research, which by definition requires a more structured, prescribed, and deductive format.

The quantitative researcher tries to maintain a degree of objectivity and detachment from whatever is examined. In contrast, a qualitative researcher may be more actively involved by participating at the same time, for example, that observation is undertaken. Whereas quantitative researchers attempt to identify a problem in advance of a study, qualitative researchers feel comfortable waiting for problems or issues to emerge. In essence, quantitative research attempts to establish facts, whereas qualitative research tries to develop an understanding of a problem.

Situation: Georgina Urbay, a lead-teacher in a suburban elementary school on the West Coast, just completed her master's degree at a local university. Her master's thesis was on a topic relevant to her work situation, as described below.

Ms. Urbay investigated gender influences on the quality of attention students receive in their class. Having reviewed the literature in this field, Ms. Urbay wondered whether gender biases existed in the classes she was responsible for supervising. When she had observed some of the newer teachers in the past, her observations had focused on the quantity of thought-provoking questions asked during a lesson or identifying, numerically, which students were on- or off-task. In these visits, Ms. Urbay and the teachers had predetermined the nature of each observation. This time Ms. Urbay just wanted to get a general feeling about the classroom without previously established criteria for observation, so she read about qualitative observation tools like the *wide lens strategy* (Acheson & Gall, 1997). With this procedure, the observer makes brief notes of events as they occur in the classroom. A favorite technique used by anthropologists, the wide lens strategy enables intensive, direct observations of behavior. No prearranged categories or questions are developed. The recorder may perceptively determine how wide a lens to make. The wider the lens, the more behaviors are observed. As narrower lenses are used, specific behaviors of individuals may be focused upon.

Anecdotal records usually consist of short descriptive sentences summarizing a particular event or situation. These recordings are usually made objectively and nonevaluatively. Rather than recording that "Susan was daydreaming," Ms. Urbay might write, "Susan was gazing out the rear window of the classroom." Ms. Urbay decides to reserve the right to make interpretive observations as well, but she includes her interpretive comments in brackets. Although audio recordings would help to capture the lesson, Ms. Urbay decides that such a recording would make the teacher feel uncomfortable. Because Ms. Urbay knows short-hand, writing data is not a problem for her.

Ms. Urbay decides that rather than sit in the back of the room as a detached observer, she will get a "better feel" for the classroom environment by participating to any extent possible in the lesson at the same time she is recording observations. Ms. Urbay entered Eric Jones's classroom. Mr. Jones was a second-year teacher who was still receiving mentoring from Ms. Urbay. Ms. Urbay informed Mr. Jones that she would be observing and participating in his lesson. She informed Mr. Jones that this was not a formal observation but merely an opportunity to get a better sense of the classroom climate. She spoke with Mr. Jones about her research into gender-related issues in the classroom and indicated that she was curious how gender might influence teacher behavior. It is important to add that Ms. Urbay is not responsible for personnel evaluation, so this would have no reason to make Mr. Jones nervous. In addition, Ms. Urbay has established good rapport with Mr. Jones, just as she has with the other teachers she mentors.

Ms. Urbay took the following notes during one segment of the lesson:

> 5th grade class; 13 boys and 12 girls; self-contained classroom; Eric Jones, teacher; 9:45 a.m.; I enter as Mr. Jones tells class to take out their readers. As Mr. Jones gives instructions for silent reading, three students (2 male and 1 female) are out of their seats hanging their clothing in the rear classroom closet. The girl is talking. Mr. Jones tells her to be quiet and sit down. During silent reading students are reading quietly. After about 3 minutes a monitor enters classroom and teacher is recording daily attendance. Noise level in class rises. Monitor leaves room. Teacher walks back and forth as students get quiet. At 9:49 a.m., Mr. Jones asks a boy to tell the class what the story was about. Student responds. Class attentive. Mr. Jones asks a girl, "Why do you think Billy in the story was so upset?" Student responds. Teacher calls on a boy who also responds, albeit differently. Mr. Jones probes and asks boy to explain. Mr. Jones asks another thought-provoking question to a girl. Girl responds. Teacher asks another question to a boy and probes. [10 minutes elapse and I note that it appears that Mr. Jones calls on boys and girls evenly, but he consistently probes male responses, and rarely probes a female response. Curious, ask Mr. Jones about this!] Time elapses. Teacher divides class into study groups. I join one of the groups with 2 boys and 1 girl. Teacher circulates. Students answer reading questions and discuss story. I ask them if they liked the story and to explain why or why not. Teacher requests attention from class. Mr. Jones continues asking many thought-provoking questions and follows the same pattern of probing more for boys than for girls. Interestingly, when the boy sitting to my right in the group was asked a question, he was probed, but the girl to my left was not. I could not discern any concern among the students.

This situation is one in which the lead-teacher, Ms. Urbay, decided that a qualitative approach would be best suited for her observation of Mr. Jones's lesson. Her primary purpose was to obtain a better understanding of the lesson given by Mr. Jones. Although her observations focused on teacher questions and student responses, she had the flexibility to note any usual or unusual behavior in the classroom. Her format was flexible and unstructured. Her recordings occurred in the natural classroom environment without any manipulation of subjects or classes. What other features of the scenario above demonstrate its qualitative nature? Can you create a scenario, different from the example above, that illustrates a qualitative approach? Note that qualitative approaches are not always applied to an observation of a teacher's lesson. In the scenario you provide, describe qualitative research in a setting outside the classroom.

Although qualitative and quantitative procedures differ in purpose, orientation, and in how research is conducted (Table 5-1), other differences center on how data are collected and analyzed and how conclusions are reached. Unlike with quantitative research, few authorities in the field agree on precise methods for data collection, analysis, interpretation, and even the reporting of findings derived from qualitative procedures (Creswell, 1994). Notwithstanding these differences, patterns or similarities emerge among those individuals who conduct qualitative inquiry. Although data collection and analysis are described in later chapters, a brief overview of data collection and methods of analysis for qualitative studies is in order.

Table 5-1.

Characteristics of Quantitative and Qualitative Research	
Quantitative	*Qualitative*
numbers or statistics	*verbal descriptions*
generalization possible	*specific to situation*
describes the "what"	*describes the "how"*
positivistic	*naturalistic*
testable hypotheses	*tentative hypotheses*
structured	*flexible*
reality is objective	*reality is constructed*
detached	*involved*
deductive	*inductive*
predetermined	*emergent*
establishes facts	*develops understanding*

Data collection in qualitative approaches depends on the purpose for the study and the type of information sought. If the researcher is interested, for instance, in understanding meanings given to certain events such as reactions to faculty meetings, then a combination of direct observation, participant observation, and interviewing may be used. On the other hand, if visual evidence of a particular situation is required (e.g., a student's behavior during a lesson), then a video recording may be more appropriate than distributing surveys. Although primary and secondary data collection techniques (such as observations, interviews, documents, and audiovisual materials) will be discussed in chapter 7, the following data collection approaches are commonly used in qualitative research (Creswell, 1994):

- Gathering observational notes as a participant-observer
- Gathering observational notes by an observer

- Conducting unstructured, open-ended interviews
- Keeping a journal during a research project
- Collecting personal documents (e.g., letters and official records)
- Analyzing public documents (e.g., memoranda and minutes)
- Videotaping a social situation of an individual or a group
- Examining photographs or videotapes
- Watching and recording nonverbal behaviors

Can you think how you could use any of the data collection techniques above?

Data analysis in qualitative research, discussed in chapter 9, is also varied. According to Patton (1990), "sitting down to make sense out of pages of interviews and whole files of field notes can be overwhelming" (p. 297). Data analysis can certainly be overwhelming, but certain basic principles can be applied (these and other data analyses will be explained in chapter 9). These are as follows:

- *Simultaneity.* Data analysis and even interpretation can be conducted at the same time that data are collected. Sorting similar pieces of information into categories and attaching meaning to them is commonly used in qualitative projects.

- *Reduction.* Seemingly disparate pieces of data can be reduced into categories, patterns, or themes. Reduction is often accomplished by a procedure known as *coding*, which involves attaching meaning to a particular scene, document, or event. For example, in viewing different types of leaders in films, one may categorize the different leaders by their style by first coding each leader with a given leadership style. Reduction also involves content analysis, which will be discussed in chapter 9. A distinction between data analysis and data reduction should be made. *Data analysis* in qualitative research refers to the process of categorizing, describing, and synthesizing data. *Data reduction* is used to better describe and interpret data under analysis.

- *Display.* Data can be displayed in numerous ways (visually and otherwise) to aid analysis and interpretation.

- *Computer.* Data can be easily analyzed using qualitative text software packages.

Suppose you had carefully conducted some interviews with teachers and collected some open-ended anonymous questionnaires that dealt with teachers' perceptions of effective, or "good," principals. After spending several weeks collecting data, you now wonder how you can make sense of it all. "Qualitative data analysis is primarily an inductive process of organizing the data into categories and identifying patterns (relationships) among the categories. Unlike quantitative procedures, most categories and patterns emerge from the data, rather than being imposed on the data prior to data collection" (McMillan & Schumacher, 2000, p. 501).

Creswell (1994) describes qualitative data analysis as an inductive process in this way:

> Treat the responses and documents like a giant inductive set: At the simplest level you are searching for categories and their attributes—figuring out what things go together (convergence). For responses to open-ended survey or interview questions, read through the set quickly for a general impression. Then take each item, and list or group all responses together. Look at this list and decide if there are responses similar in content that appear frequently.
>
> For example, one team interviewed a sample of eighteen students...using four questions....As the team looked at these eighteen responses on the first pass, they noticed immediately that projects of various sorts were mentioned frequently. On the next pass, they looked more closely at the comments students made during their discussion of projects. They noticed that students gave descriptions of projects across subject areas in science, social studies, math, and reading. (p. 75)

Further discussion of this inductive process will be undertaken in chapter 9.

Although we have been discussing the use of the qualitative research approach, quantitative research has for many years been the research of choice in the social sciences. The model of social research—the scientific method—and the logic that underpins it—positivism—have dominated educational and administrative theory. The predominance of this social science perspective has only recently undergone criticism in light of the emergence of qualitative, including ethnographic and biographical, analyses. The traditions of positivism and the scientific method in educational research, though still popular, have given way somewhat to alternative approaches for conducting research (Denzin & Lincoln, 2000).

Three types of qualitative methods may be applied by the action researcher: historical inquiry, ethnography, and case study. While other qualitative methods exist, I have personally used and found these forms useful. Qualitative methods do not, of course, utilize statistical or mathematical expressions. Qualitative approaches rely on detailed verbal descriptions of observed phenomena. Action researchers often find qualitative methods most suitable and more easily adopted in school settings.

No randomization is employed in nonexperimental qualitative studies. The researcher may select a particular individual to observe using "thick descriptions" (intensive, daily, observation over an extended period of time). For example, a day in the life of a city superintendent may be investigated by following the superintendent around. Observations are recorded anecdotally (verbatim). Since this form of research is qualitative and nonexperimental, findings are based primarily on the investigator's perceptions and interpretations. See the glossary entries of *validity* and *reliability* for a description of how these may be enhanced in qualitative approaches.

Historical Inquiry

Historical inquiry attempts to explain the past and its interconnectedness to present conditions. History can be understood as an attempt to study the events and ideas of the past that have shaped human experience over time in order to inform current practice as well as to make more intelligent decisions for the future.

Although historical inquiry would not usually be an action researcher's first line of research, historical study does have particular relevance, especially when undertaking a needs assessment prior to initiating a new program (see discussion of this in the next chapter). For example, a new principal would want to examine past records of levels of student achievement, records of dropout rates, or teacher attendance patterns. Data sources might include cumulative record cards, files, newspapers, original documents, and other archival information often found in school profiles.

Oral histories may be particularly useful for qualitative researchers. Oral histories involve open-ended interviews with a series of individuals involved in a particular issue. Can you think of an issue or situation in which an educational leader might want or need to undertake oral histories?

Ethnographic Research

Ethnography, perhaps the most common qualitative approach, is a branch of anthropology. It is a method of research in which individuals are observed in natural settings and are described in detail. In ethnographic research there is no attempt to generalize findings. An example of an ethnographic study would be to ask: What is a typical week in the life of five city school superintendents?

One would follow or shadow these superintendents and take a lot of notes (called *thick descriptions* or *field notes*) describing anecdotally the activities of these individuals. After a week, you would have accumulated a plethora of notes. You would read and reread your notes and perform a content analysis to determine if any themes emerge from your data.

Note that it is possible to take detailed written descriptions of what was observed and, at the same time, make specific reflective or interpretative comments. As long as these subjective comments are kept separate from the descriptive data, use of the researcher's speculative comments is common in ethnographic research. In the brief excerpt that follows of field notes taken on October 27, 1998, at an afterschool faculty conference at Lakewood Middle School, note that the researcher's subjective comments are identified and kept separate from the descriptive, more objective portion:

> I walked into the Lakewood Middle School main auditorium at 3:10 p.m. as the principal, Ernest Malcomb, was calling the meeting to order. Twenty-six people were sitting in seats scattered about the large auditorium. The principal requested that those individuals in the rear of the auditorium sit near the front. Three individuals moved from the rear to the middle of the auditorium. Seven individuals remained in the rear. The principal began to read the faculty notes. After two minutes had elapsed, he requested that Ms. Chapman report on the curriculum committee's findings and recommendations.

> *Comments:* The teachers in the rear of the auditorium seem defiant in their refusal to move their seats closer to the principal. As Mr. Malcomb read the faculty notes, many teachers appeared bored.

Field notes, then, are the researcher's written chronological account of what transpired during an observation session. Field notes consist of two parts: (a) an objective section that contains a detailed description of what has taken place, and (b) a subjective part that contains the observer's reflections or speculations about what was observed.

Ethnographic research, then, clearly separates description from interpretation and judgment.

Some authorities in the field consider ethnography a form of descriptive research. Although ethnography does describe a particular situation, it usually does so without numbers, frequencies, or statistics. I have classified ethnography under qualitative research to indicate its nonmathematical orientation.

As an action researcher employing ethnographic research, you would identify a topic, pose a research question or two, and collect data by documenting and explaining in great depth what you are observing. Data sources for an ethnographic researcher might include the following:

1. Study of the social behavior of individuals (examples might include shadowing an associate superintendent during the course of her day; observing the occurrences of misbehavior among three special education students; observing teachers during a grade conference)

2. Communication patterns among individuals or groups (examples might include observing interactions between faculty and a principal at an afterschool conference; observing students as they play in the school yard)

3. Environmental conditions (examples might include studying the impact of block scheduling on student movement in the hallways; observing the impact of early dismissal procedures on the number of incidents of reported accidents)

Many detailed ethnographic studies have been published in education (e.g., Goodlad, 1984). Educational leaders, in their role as action researchers described in this volume, are unlikely to undertake an extensive ethnographic study. Readers who are interested in more in-depth analyses of ethnography, for purposes of doctoral work or otherwise, should consult other volumes such as Glesne and Peshkin (1999), Gay (1996), and Wiersma (1999).

Several principles related to ethnography as well as all qualitative research approaches should be reviewed. Ethnographic research does the following:

- Occurs in a natural setting
- Attempts to explore the why, what, and especially how of an issue
- Concentrates on field work that may include observations and interviews
- Focuses on a research problem and selection of a research site
- Explores sites that are related to the problem but not randomly selected
- Stresses extensive use of field notes
- Generates questions, collects data, and interprets data as a combined process
- Generates theory from data (grounded theory)
- Involves analyzing data as they are collected

Discussion of the data collection methods useful in ethnographic research is presented in chapter 7, whereas data analysis for other qualitative approaches in general is discussed in chapter 9.

Case Study Research

Case studies are actually ways of reporting ethnographic research, but they are so common that I have included them as a separate category.

A **case study** involves an in-depth investigation of an individual, a group of individuals, a site, or a scene. Findings are stated verbally, not numerically. Case studies are reported by describing in detail observations made of individuals, groups, or school settings. Special education teachers, for instance, who use IEPs (Individual Educational Programs) are actually involved in some aspects of case study research. Case studies are written so that a better understanding of a situation is likely and so that educators may discuss possible implications for an individual, a group, or a school.

Case study research can also be conducted by examining a specific phenomenon such as a program, an event, a process, an institution, or a social group (Merriam, 1997). An example of how a case study approach was used in an action research project can be found, for example, in Glanz (1995), in which a martial arts program for students at risk was implemented.

Case studies differ subtly from ethnographic research in that they are written descriptively and objectively, whereas ethnographic accounts may contain interpretive material. Case studies are also more narrowly focused on a particular person, place, or scene. Case studies may tend to create an idealized situation merely by using descriptive accounts. Case studies are often guided by a series of questions that the researcher tries to answer. The case study provides an in-depth, descriptive account.

Incorporating a qualitative research methodology through the use of portraits (Donmoyer, 1993; Lawrence-Lightfoot, 1985) has recently gained favor. Donmoyer and Kos (1993) have recently demonstrated the efficacy of this case study approach in examining the at-risk population. I would like to present, as an example, a brief yet descriptive case study excerpt of one particular student who was in many ways representative of the students involved in the martial arts program mentioned above (Glanz, 1995). Data were gathered through the use of observations based on field notes, interviews, questionnaires, and videotape recordings. Information was gleaned from school personnel, especially the classroom teacher, the parent, the sensei (martial arts teacher), and the student himself. Multiple observers, multiple data collection methods, and extensive thick descriptions were employed to attain as accurate a portrait as possible.

Ernest is a 10-year-old African-American fourth-grade student attending P.S. 563 in Elizabeth, New Jersey. Ernest was held over once in grade 3 and is two years below grade level in reading and math. Ernest has had excellent attendance in school but has been a severe discipline problem since the first grade. He has been suspended four times within the last 2 years for the following incidents: striking another child across the face with his fist, causing severe swelling and bleeding; throwing a chair at another student and hitting the substitute teacher by accident; pulling the fire alarm during the school day; and threatening another child in his class with a knife.

Ernest has had an unstable family life in that he has not seen his father for nearly 5 years. His father is incarcerated for robbery and attempted murder and is serving a 15-year sentence. His mother, who has reported to the school only once in the past 3 years, is a crack addict. Ernest lives with an "aunt" across the street from school. He is an only child.

Ernest has recently been involved in a neighborhood gang of approximately 15 other youth, mostly of junior high school age. Ernest is very intelligent and mature for his age. Although he is quite verbal, he does not participate in school. Teachers have reported the following comments appearing on report cards and cumulative record cards:

- Ernest is an active youngster who needs constant supervision. (Grade 2)

- Ernest is intelligent and can do work if he wants to. (Grade 1)

- Ernest is very aggressive and hostile to his classmates. (Grade 2)

- Ernest needs help in reading and math. He does not participate and is very playful in class. (Grade 3)

- Ernest threatens others and shows no interest in school. (Grade 4)

- Ernest has the potential but clearly needs a more restrictive classroom environment.

- Ernest has been referred to the guidance counselor, assistant principal, and principal without any significant, longstanding change in behavior and attitude. Psychological tests indicate that he is of above average intelligence. Standardized tests as well as teacher-made tests indicate that Ernest is low-achieving.

When the guidance counselor tried to explore Ernest's thoughts and feelings the conversation typically went like this:

GC: How are you doing, Ernest?

E: (*no response*)

GC: Well?

E: Fine.

GC: Well, you know, Ernest, I have been receiving very disturbing reports about your behavior.

E: (*silence*)

GC: Do you like school?

E: Yeah.

GC: Well, if you like school, that's great, but—

E: Do I have to be here? I wanna go.

GC: We know you are a very bright boy and want the best for you. Your teacher and Mr. Smith really care about you.

E: (*shrugs shoulders*) I wanna go.

GC: Go where?

E: Out of here.

Ernest storms out and runs through building for 10 minutes before he is apprehended by security and brought to the assistant principle's office, where the same conversation repeats itself to no avail. Ernest is escorted back to class in time for lunch. He returns to class after lunch 30 minutes late. His excuse is that he was playing basketball in the yard.

The case study continues to document attempts to assist Ernest. After participating in a martial arts class specifically designed to encourage greater self-discipline for students like Ernest, the following data were collected as part of the case study: "Ernest showed much enthusiasm about the karate class in his discussions with the assistant principal" (AP).

E: Yeah, I'm really interested. When can I begin?

AP: You know, martial arts are very demanding and require disci-
      pline and lots of hard work.

E: I can do it.

AP: Why are you so interested in the martial arts?

E: I don't know, I just am.

AP: You like the violence and fighting?

E: Yeah, I guess. You know karate?

AP: Yep.

E: (*nodding head in approval*)

AP: You know, the sensei, the teacher, is very strict and will not
      tolerate fooling around.

E: (*no comment*)

AP: You also should know that you can continue in the class as
      long as you continue to receive good reports from your teach-
      ers and me. And that you'll have to do homework and all
      that...sensei will explain all that. Okay?

E: Okay.

Two weeks into the program, the following was noted:

> Mr. Shurack, a state-certified teacher and first-degree black-belt
> instructor, was interviewed about Ernest's progress in the karate
> class. The sensei reported that Ernest had much difficulty adjust-
> ing to the rigors and demands of the class. Ernest grew impatient
> and had difficulty maintaining concentration. There seemed to be
> a dramatic change in his attitude and attention as a result of the
> number of visits to Ernest's classroom during the school day by
> the assistant principal and Sensei, in which conversations were
> conducted about his progress. "It is due, I think," stated Sensei
> Shurack, "to the fact that Ernest received positive reinforcement
> and encouragement from his classroom teacher, the AP, the prin-
> cipal, and me that he was able to stick it out in class. The books
> and magazines (e.g., *Karate Illustrated* and *Kung-fu,* which were
> ordered through our school library) seemed to sustain Ernest's
> interest in those early weeks.

As you can see from this excerpt, case studies provide descriptive and detailed information that is often missing from quantitative approaches.

Try writing a case study of your own school as an organization. The sample questions in Table 5-2 should serve as a guide. In the end, your case study will represent an attempt to describe your school as thoroughly as possible so that an outsider would be able to get a good sense of what your school is like.

Table 5-2.

Some Guiding Questions in Writing a Case Study of Your School

1. *Describe the area in which your school is located. How is it reached by transportation? What is the social class that predominates in the area? Is the school in a residential or business area? Do many students come from the local community? Where else do students come from? Are students bused to the school? What is the ethnic makeup of the student body?*

2. *Is the school plant in good condition? How old is the building? How is it decorated, outside and inside? How do student treat the physical plant? Are the corridors well-lighted? What are the colors of the walls? Are they clean? Are bulletin boards displayed in the hallways? What do they contain? How many floors are there in the building? What special facilities or equipment exist?*

3. *What is the makeup (number, ethnicity, gender, etc.) of the faculty, staff and administration? What are the responsibilities of administrators? teachers? What hierarchical relationships exist, if any? What is the relationship between teachers and administrators?*

4. *What services exist in the school? Are there nurses, doctors, and custodians in the school? Where is the cafeteria? What is the quality of the food services? Who is in charge? Are teachers and administrators on duty? Is there a library? What library resources exist? Are multimedia technologies present? Does each class have computers? What are the different kinds of software and hardware?*

5. *Does the school have a written statement of philosophy? Is there a student and/or teacher handbook? Are parents welcome and involved in the school? How do faculty and administration involve parents?*

6. *How much emphasis is placed on constructivist instructional strategies? What motivational strategies are employed? Describe the state of student discipline. What classroom management techniques and strategies are employed?*

7. *How are decisions made in the school? Who is involved in instructional decision making? Who is involved in administrative decision making? Does a learning community exist in the school? What is the relationship of the district office to the school?*

These are only sample questions. Many more questions about grouping practices, other instructional procedures, and logistical operations may be posed. Case studies provide an in-depth understanding of a particular situation. Remember, the action researcher is likely to use a case study to describe a particular situation that can be then discussed or analyzed by others. Once a school, for instance, is described in detail using a case study, discussion of educational and/or instructional implications may occur.

Can you think of a situation in which a case study might aid decision making? How might action researchers use the case study method?

Note that use of case studies by educational leaders, as action researchers, might be very specific and limited. For readers interested in a more detailed explanation of case studies, especially as they are used for doctoral theses, see Merriam, 1997.

References

Acheson, K. A., & Gall, M. D. (1997). *Techniques in the clinical supervision of teachers.* New York: Longman.

Calhoun, E. P., Allen, L., & Halliburton, C. (1996 April). *A report on the implementation of and results from schoolwide action research.* Paper presented at the annual meeting of the American Educational Research Association, New York.

Creswell, J. (1994). *Research design: Qualitative and quantitative approaches.* Thousand Oaks, CA: Sage.

Crowl, T. K., Kaminsky, S., & Podell, D. M. (1997). *Educational psychology.* Madison, WI: Brown & Benchmark.

Denzin, N. K., & Lincoln, Y. S. (Eds.). (2000). *Handbook of qualitative research* (2nd ed.). Thousand Oaks, CA: Corwin Press.

Donmoyer, R. (1993). The purpose of portraits: Rethinking the form and function of research on students at risk. In R. Donmoyer & R. Kos (Eds.), *Students at risk: Portraits, policies, programs, and practices* (pp. 37–48). New York: State University of New York Press.

Donmoyer, R., & Kos, R. (1993). *Students at risk: Portraits, policies, programs, and practices.* New York: State University of New York Press.

Gay, L. R. (1996). *Educational research: Competencies for analysis and application* (5th ed.). Englewood Cliffs, NJ: Prentice-Hall.

Glanz, J. (1995). A school/curricular intervention martial arts program for students at risk. *Journal of At-Risk Issues, 2* (1), 18–25.

Glesne, C., & Peshkin, A. (1999). *Becoming qualitative researchers* (2nd ed.). New York: Longman.

Glickman, C. D., Gordon, S. P., & Ross-Gordon, J. M. (1998). *Supervision of instruction: A developmental approach* (4th ed.). Boston: Allyn & Bacon.

Goodlad, J. I. (1984). *A place called school.* New York: McGraw-Hill.

Lawrence-Lightfoot, S. (1985). *The good high school.* New York: Basic Books.

McMillan, J. H., & Schumacher, S. (2000). *Research in education: A conceptual introduction* (5th ed.). New York: Longman.

Merriam, S. B. (1997). *Qualitative research and case study applications in education.* San Francisco: Jossey-Bass.

Patton, M. Q. (1990). *Qualitative research methods* (2nd ed.). Beverly Hills, CA: Sage.

Wiersma, W. (1999). *Research methods in education: An introduction* (7th ed.). Boston: Allyn & Bacon.

Willerman, M., McNeely, S. L., & Koffman, E. C. (1991). *Teachers helping teachers: Peer observation and assistance.* New York: Praeger.

Activity 7. Qualitative Methods and Designs

1. In Activity 5, nine questions were posed to help you start a research project. Given that you find a qualitative approach useful and feasible, complete the information below. Check the methods and designs that you may use in the action research project you are developing. Realize that your selections now may be changed later.

_____   Historical Inquiry (Needs Assessment)

_____   Ethnography

_____   Case Study

Purpose: _____

_____

_____

Data Collection Methods: _____

_____

_____

Data Analysis and Interpretation: _____

_____

_____

Tentative Findings: _____

_____

_____

Easy Steps to Program Development and Evaluation Research

Focus Questions

1. What is the first step you would take to initiate a new program in your school or district?

2. What does the term *supervision* mean to you?

3. If asked to explain the value of parental involvement, how would you do so?

4. What are some major questions to consider in developing an evaluation plan?

5. Have you ever undertaken a formal evaluation of a program? If so, what caveats would you recommend to a novice leader?

The challenge for today's educational leaders is to set an example that clearly demonstrates that schools can be the one institution where human relationships are enhanced...as it deals with internal and external evaluation processes and accountability requirements.

—DeRoche, 1987

What should be clear is that...evaluation is a complicated endeavor, and that there is no single approach that will solve all problems.

—Herman, Lyons Morris, & Fitz-Gibbon, 1988

Evaluation conducted at the school level can improve the quality of information used to make management, program, and instructional decisions.

—Herman & Winters, 1992

Successful program development cannot occur without evaluation. Program evaluation is the process of systematically determining the quality of a school program and how the program can be improved.

—Sanders, 1992

Program evaluation projects provide educators with the information and insights they need to refine and improve the services and programs they provide to their students. And that is a worthy goal.

—Brainard, 1996

As an educational leader, you'll most likely want to implement some sort of instructional program and then establish procedures for evaluation. Program development and evaluation are so common among those individuals in leadership positions that I have devoted this entire chapter to its discussion. I recall my first position as an assistant principal in an elementary school in New York City when I was confronted with some serious misbehavior in the upper grades by a few students at risk. I decided to initiate a unique program to deal with this troublesome situation: The martial arts program I discussed briefly in the last chapter. In establishing this program, I also realized that its effectiveness had to be assessed. For a complete description of this program, how and why I implemented it, and how I undertook program evaluation, see Glanz (1995).

For an introduction to evaluation research, see chapter 1.

Eight Steps of Program Development

The following eight steps will guide you in establishing almost any program in a school. My students, who have applied this design, have found these steps useful.

What is the first step you would take to initiate a new program in your school or district? As a leader you realize that the success of any new program depends on understanding the unique culture and history of the school. Attempts at implementing reforms over the past 20 years have taught us that "reform through fiat" simply doesn't work. Meaningful and lasting change occurs best when implemented gradually at a grassroots level. Reform efforts that consider the unique culture and history of a particular school or district have a much better chance of succeeding (Cuban, 1993). Therefore, the first step in initiating any new program is not to "storm the fortress" and demand that teachers comply with newly mandated curricula or programs. The first step that any thoughtful, professional educational leader takes is to undertake a needs assessment.

In order to enliven this discussion about program implementation, I will relate these steps to a program that I tried to implement many years ago while undertaking a supervisory internship with the curriculum coordinator of a district who wanted to implement a gifted program in a particular school. This was my first experience at implementing a program that helped many youngsters to achieve their potential.

Needs Assessment

Leaders sometimes attempt to change or implement programs without considering many important factors. The first task of a competent educational leader who wants to start any sort of program is to analyze the situation by describing and identifying problems or areas of concern. In other words, a leader should undertake a needs assessment. There are four steps in undertaking needs assessment.

Reflect by Posing Questions

- Does the school need a gifted program?
- What evidence indicates that the school might need such a program?
- Has a gifted program ever been implemented before?
- If so, what happened to the program and why was it discontinued?

- What will my new program contribute to addressing the needs of gifted students?
- Who is considered a gifted student?
- How do I (we) plan to implement such a program?

Posing key questions is the first step in implementing any program. These questions should be addressed by the individual leader in collaboration with the supervisory staff and interested faculty.

Observe

Prior to making any decision about implementing the program, "walk around" the school and get to know the faculty, staff, students, and parents. Observe students and teachers at work. Get a sense of the culture of the school. We call this MBWA: Management By Wandering Around. This doesn't mean aimless wandering, but rather purposeful observation. Too many principals, from my experience, manage their schools from the main office, rarely observing and talking with their faculty and staff on a daily basis. Successful implementation of your program involves "getting out there" and finding answers to some key questions:

- What are faculty interested in?
- Who are the influential members of the faculty?
- What instructional strategies are commonly employed by teachers?
- Do students seem enthusiastic about learning?
- Are parents involved in the instructional or curricular program?
- Is there some grassroots support for the need of change?
- Who might you confide in and ask to participate in the initial stages of program implementation?
- What resistances to change exist?

Observing includes examining records, school files, and profiles. Examining records such as cumulative student folders, school profile sheets that provide summaries of standardized test scores, and teacher files may give you some valuable clues as to the direction you may take to implement this program. Such an analysis will help to ascertain existing strengths and weaknesses that should be addressed during the initial stages of program implementation.

Meet With Key Personnel

Meeting with key school personnel, informally through MBWA and formally through invitation, will not only demonstrate your concern about faculty input into program development but will provide valuable insights that observation alone cannot offer. Meet with the following personnel, among others: teachers, union representatives, parents (especially the PTA president and board), superintendent, coordinators, guidance counselors, secretarial staff, lunchroom personnel, deans, and other supervisors.

Speak with everyone, for four reasons: (a) to allow them to voice their concerns and opinions about the new program, (b) to apprise them of possible future developments, (c) to share information with them, and (d) to invite their input in terms of suggestions, comments, and participation.

Although such attempts at shared leadership may be unusual and difficult to attain, my experiences have convinced me that effective and lasting change occurs best through collaboration among faculty, staff, administrators, community, and students.

Public education has continued to receive voluminous criticism for being bureaucratic and unresponsive to the needs of teachers, parents, and children. One of the prominent proposals for disenfranchising bureaucracy is the dissolution of autocratic administrative practices in which overbearing supervisors rule by fiat. Most favored is the side of greater and more meaningful decision making at the grassroots level. This translates into giving teachers more formal responsibility for setting school policies, thus enhancing democratic governance in schools. Susan Moore Johnson (1990) observed that "although schools have long been under the control of administrators, local districts are increasingly granting teachers more formal responsibility for setting school policies" (p. 337). The argument for greater involvement goes something like this: When teachers participate in decisions about their schools, there will be a significant improvement in their attitudes that will strengthen their commitment toward their work and will translate into better academic improvement. The new vision, then, calls for empowered teachers, democratic governance, and heightened professionalism (Glanz, 1992).

Establish a Needs Assessment Committee

A final step in needs assessment might be to form a committee composed of interested teachers, supervisors, parents, and students to assist in the implementation of the program. This committee can plan implementation of the project and engender support from other faculty and interested parties.

I was once asked to conduct a series of cooperative learning workshops for a school district in New Jersey. The principal, realizing the importance of faculty involvement in staff development, formed a needs assessment committee to ascertain interest in these workshops before I was hired. The committee designed a questionnaire to determine levels of experience with cooperative learning. The committee forwarded their findings to me before the workshops so that I might gain a sense of the nature and level of sophistication I would need in these workshops. My workshops were successful, in large measure, because of the preplanning strategies implemented by the needs assessment committee at this school.

Goals

The second step you should take once you've decided that the program is needed is to develop short- and long-term goals. Framing a vision of what this new program has to offer is critical in program development. Goal development should be done collaboratively by involving as many stakeholders as possible. Setting up a committee for this purpose is recommended. This committee can be composed of the same members as the needs assessment committee, although involving others is advisable. This committee would be charged with brainstorming goals or program objectives, prioritizing goals, and disseminating goals to faculty, staff, and community.

Whenever you form a committee to evaluate something, keep in mind these three questions:

1. Why have we formed a committee? (Purpose)
2. What are our short-term plans? (Objectives)
3. What are our long-term plans? (Goals)

Short-term goals should be accomplished within a 1- to 6-month framework. Examples of short-term goals are establishing criteria for admission into the gifted program or forming a planning committee of two teachers, one staff developer, one parent, one assistant principal, and a student.

Examples of long-term goals are increasing parental involvement by 10%, decreasing teacher burnout, implementing a portfolio program next year for the upper elementary grades, and raising standardized reading test scores by 15%.

Administrative Aspects

Administrative or logistical concerns should be worked on throughout the implementation phase. As an educational leader, you should attend to the following concerns: staffing considerations, scheduling, advertising, room allocations, ordering materials and supplies, securing funding sources publicity, and delegating responsibilities.

Supervision

In establishing any new program, attending to supervisory issues is imperative.

Supervision is a process that involves strategies to enhance instructional improvement. An educational leader is concerned with facilitating an environment that is conducive to learning. A competent leader should attend to PCOWBIRDS!

P = Plans. Planning is integral to instructional success, and an educational leader should help a teacher to develop appropriate and meaningful instructional activities and learning experiences. Checking plans, offering suggestions, co-planning, reviewing procedures, and framing thought-provoking questions are essential. Supervision involves assisting teachers to better plan their lessons and units of instruction.

C = Conferences. Conferencing with teachers, formally and informally, in order to share ideas and develop alternate instructional strategies is an essential supervisory responsibility.

O = Observations. An educational leader should offer expertise by both formally and informally observing classroom interaction. A skilled leader who utilizes various observation systems (e.g., Acheson & Gall, 1997; Glickman, Gordon, & Ross-Gordon, 1998) can facilitate instructional improvement by documenting classroom interaction so that a teacher might reflect upon and react to what has been observed. Observations play a key role in supervision. As Yogi Berra once quipped, "You can observe a lot by watching."

W = Workshops. Educational leaders should conduct or organize various workshops for teachers on relevant instructional topics such as cooperative learning, alternative teaching strategies, and multiple intelligences.

B = Bulletins. Bulletins, journals, reports, and newsletters can be disseminated to interested faculty. One of my teachers became interested in cooperative learning after attending a reading conference. I sustained her interest by placing several articles about cooperative learning in her mailbox.

I = Intervisitations. Teachers rarely have the opportunity to visit and observe colleagues. A leader can facilitate intervisitations by rearranging the schedule so that teachers might observe one another and then share common instructional strategies or discuss common problems. Intervisitations, to be effective, must be voluntary and nonjudgmental.

R = Resources. Leaders should make available for teachers a variety of instructional materials and technologies to enhance instructional improvement.

D = Demonstration lessons. An educational leader is presumably a teacher of teachers. A leader is not necessarily the foremost teacher in a school, but he or she should feel comfortable in providing "demo" lessons for teachers, when appropriate. Providing such lessons enhances supervisory credibility among teachers and provides instructional support. For instance, I once noticed during a formal observation that the teacher was not using wait time effectively. He posed good questions but waited only about 2 seconds before calling on some-one. As his supervisor, I suggested that he watch me teach a lesson and notice how long I wait after posing a question before calling on a pupil. These observations were the basis for a follow-up conference at which we discussed the research on "wait time" and the advantages of waiting before calling on a pupil. As the saying goes, "A picture is worth a thousand words." Having this particular teacher watch me demonstrate effective use of "wait time" was more valuable than had I merely told him what to do. Competent supervisors not only "suggest" how to do something, they also must "demonstrate" how it should be done.

   S = Staff development. Educational leaders can aid instructional improvement by providing staff development that is "purposeful and articulated," "participatory and collaborative," "knowledge-based," "ongoing," "developmental...and "analytic and reflective" (Griffin, 1997).

Curriculum

Curriculum includes all the planned experiences, programs, and subjects that are designed to enhance student learning. As an educational leader, you are always actively engaged in curricular and instructional matters. Too much time is often spent on what I call *administrivia.* Administrative exigencies must, of course, be attended to, but instructional improvement will not be enhanced without direct and specific attention to curricular concerns, such as the following (Glatthorn, 1994):

1. Reviewing current curriculum guidelines and other instructional materials

2. Reviewing materials for instruction (e.g., texts, workbooks, computers), making certain that curriculum materials are matched to appropriate instructional levels of students

3. Arranging assembly programs, fairs, exhibits, contests, and other incentives such as banners, T-shirts, buttons

4. Facilitating interdisciplinary curriculum

5. Encouraging curriculum development and renewal

Parents and Pupils

Implementing any program involves parental input in terms of advisement and participation. While being interviewed once for an assistant principalship, I was asked if I believed in parental involvement. Not wanting to offer the usual or typical canned response, I rose from my seat and demonstrated for the committee my commitment to parental involvement in the following way (Mamchak & Mamchak, 1983):

"Let me show you what I mean when I say that parental involvement is essential." I held up a blank piece of paper (Figure 6-1). I continued, "Within a school there are basically three groups of individuals. There are faculty (including administration and teachers), there are students, and there are parents." As I mentioned each group, I drew a small oval until I developed the configuration seen in Figure 6-2. "Quite often," I lamented, "when faculty work on their side, and the parents work on their side, all without partnership and commitment, the students are left in the middle." As I mentioned "the faculty," I placed a dot in the center of the left-hand oval; as I mentioned "the parents," I placed a dot in the center of the right-hand oval; and as I mentioned "the students," I merely pointed to the center oval. I ended up with the configuration in Figure 6-3.

Figure 6-1.

Figure 6-2.

Figure 6-3.

"When this happens," I continued, "when there is no communication and teamwork between these two sides, the whole system can get looking pretty unhappy." As I said "when there is no communication" I drew the curved line above the three ovals. Then, as I said "the whole system can get," I drew the curved line under the three ovals. The configuration now resembled the sad face shown in Figure 6-4.

Figure 6-4.

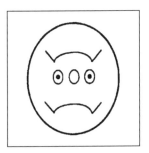

Figure 6-5.

"But, let's add teamwork. Let's get everyone working together to help our children. When parents and faculty work together constructively, the whole school is unified." As I mentioned "working together," I drew a large, encompassing oval around the sad face so that it looked like Figure 6-5.

"Then," I concluded, "thanks to teamwork and spirit of cooperativeness, students will succeed and we will have a happy and functioning school; one we may all be justly proud of." As I said the last words, I turned the drawing around 180 degrees. Before the eyes of the committee, it turned into the happy face as seen in Figure 6-6.

Although this was a somewhat contrived and simple demonstration of my philosophical commitment to parental involvement, several committee members did smile and I'm certain I effectively communicated my point. Involve parents in any reasonable way possible. Here are some suggestions:

Figure 6-6.

1. Invite their participation on needs assessment and goal committees through formal and informal invitations.

2. Sponsor an open house at which you will provide refreshments and outline the nature of participation you desire.

3. Develop a parent hotline so that parents may keep abreast of "what's happenin'" in the school.

4. Invite parents to a parent-student picture night.

Students are all too often not considered in program development. Soliciting their participation on committees offers a unique opportunity to benefit from their keen insights and perspectives.

Resource People

Program implementation involves the active participation of several other personnel, depending, of course, on the nature of the program. The following individuals may be valuable resources: guidance counselors, teachers with special expertise, social workers and psychologists, specialty coordinators from the district office or neighboring townships, lunchroom and office staff, health department officials, and consultants.

Evaluation

Evaluation is a decision-making process. In an era of accountability in which productivity is demanded, evaluation assumes greater priority and attention. We as educational leaders can increase productivity by (a) setting goals, (b) determining where we are, and (c) identifying strategies for getting where we want to be.

In a nutshell, when we evaluate we want to answer two fundamental questions: (a) How are we doing? and (b) How can we improve?

Evaluation is a comprehensive, ongoing process. Many consider evaluation synonymous with some sort of posttest and that's it. This volume has demonstrated the importance of taking a comprehensive approach to school improvement by incorporating quantitative and qualitative approaches.

Also, many individuals are not aware of the formative *and* summative nature of evaluation. Evaluation is ongoing to the extent to which you provide for formative evaluation. Assessing progress along the way makes sense. Why wait 6 months or a year before realizing that changes are warranted? Formative evaluation allows for program adjustments and modifications. Research has indicated that programs that incorporate formative evaluative measures are more likely to succeed.

Summative evaluation that is triangular in nature (see chapter 2), leads to one of three conclusions:

1. Modification of the program or procedure

2. Elimination of the program or procedure

3. Continuation of the program or procedure

Any programs, practices, and procedures should be evaluated—such as school goals and objectives, parent-teacher conferences, assessment procedures (including report cards), faculty meetings, assembly programs, music programs, administrative procedures, dropout rates, attendance policies, schoolwide discipline plans, curriculum materials, pupil achievement, accounting procedures, and school climate.

To evaluate, keep this mnemonic in mind: *ROTC.*

R = Records and rating scales—examine records, develop rating or attitudinal surveys and checklists

O = Observations, both formal and informal

T = Tests, standardized or nonstandardized or both

C = Conferences with everyone

In developing a general evaluation plan, keep in mind these points:

1. What is the purpose of evaluation?

2. What needs to be evaluated?

3. What are your goals?

4. How will data be collected?

5. How will data be organized and analyzed?

6. How will the data be reported?

Problems are inevitable in program evaluation. Keep in mind these five steps for solving problems:

1. Analyze the situation
2. Examine research (data collected or evidence)
3. Examine results
4. Develop alternative solutions
5. Act (modify, discard, or continue)

A Mnemonic for Establishing a Program

I highlighted and detailed eight steps to consider in implementing any educational program. Can you recall the eight steps? Here are two acrostics my students came up with. Which do you prefer? Can you develop your own? If so, please email your ideas to: jglanz@wagner.edu.

I
Negative
Grades
Always
Scar
Children's
Parents
Really
Emotionally

II
Never
Give
A
Strange
Child
Permission to
Run the
Exam

Five Steps of Program Evaluation

The following steps of **program evaluation** were employed when I evaluated a program that I had established in a school while serving as assistant principal. The discussion that follows is based on information gleaned from Sanders, 2000. (See also Wholey, Hatry, & Newcomer, 1994.)

The program I evaluated was first established at a public elementary school to address some of the needs of at-risk students. What made this program noteworthy was that martial arts training was incorporated as part of an overall curricular approach aimed at assisting selected fourth and fifth graders who were either currently involved in gangs or likely to join them. Program evaluation involved the following five steps.

Focusing the Evaluation

This itself consists of three steps: (a) clarifying evaluation purposes, (b) clarifying what is to be evaluated, and (c) identifying questions to be answered.

The purpose of our evaluation of the martial arts program was twofold: (a) to monitor pupil progress academically and socially, with the intent to conduct formative (in-progress) evaluations of the students' academic and social progress, and (b) to monitor pupil motivation, with the intent to provide insights about the effort and persistence among student participants.

Our primary purpose for evaluating the program was to determine whether a program of this nature, which had never been attempted in our school before, should be continued and expanded to include other students at risk. Formative evaluative steps would enable us to monitor the program on an ongoing basis. Midcourse corrections could be made if necessary to improve the quality of the program. A summative evaluation was planned at the end of the school year by accumulating overall data relating to our two purposes outlined above as well as bringing in an outside consultant to provide his reactions to the program. The consultant was a principal of a school in another district who was also a black belt instructor in the martial arts.

After clarifying evaluation purposes, another set of decisions was needed to get a clear sense of what was to be specifically evaluated. Criteria were specified separately for each of the evaluation purposes noted above. Five aspects were identified for pupil academic and social progress:

1. Incidence of aggressive behavior (physical fights with other students and/or physical acts toward faculty and staff)

2. Degree to which basic school and class rules were adhered to

3. Rates for tardiness and attendance

4. Number of homework assignments completed

5. Number of in-class assignments completed

Two specific aspects were identified for pupil motivation: the degree to which students demonstrated effort and persistence in class, and the degree to which students demonstrated effort and persistence in martial arts class. Once we had a sense of what was to be evaluated, the following questions were posed:

1. What were the expected academic outcomes for students who participated in the martial arts program?

2. What were the expected social outcomes for students who participated in the martial arts program?

3. Were students motivated to participate in in-class and school-related functions as well as in the martial arts class itself?

4. How well were the students performing on the expected outcomes noted above?

5. To what extent was the program meeting expectations of principal, assistant principal, martial arts instructor, teachers, parents, and student participants?

Collecting Data

In order to answer each of the evaluation questions, sources of information and methods for each evaluation question had to be identified. Scheduling the collection of data and assigning responsibility for collecting data was also completed.

Sources of data collection were culled from existing resources such as school files and records, direct observation of the program, and people connected to the program. Evaluation methods that were deemed appropriate and feasible were matched to each evaluation question as follows:

1. What were the expected academic outcomes for students who participated in the martial arts program?

    Data collection methods: teacher and pupil interviews, teacher-made tests, and checklists for completed assignments.

2. What were the expected social outcomes for students who participated in the martial arts program?

   Data collection methods: teacher, supervisor, and pupil interviews; number of reported suspensions; number of times students were reported to assistant principal's office for misbehavior; attendance reports; and observations.

3. Were students motivated to participate in in-class and school-related functions as well as in the martial arts class itself?

   Data collection methods: teacher, supervisor, and pupil interviews; attendance reports; observations; student journals and portfolios; and visual anthropology or film ethnography (Marshall & Rossman, 1999).

4. How well were the students performing on the expected outcomes noted above?

   Data collection methods: methods noted above through formative and summative evaluations.

5. To what extent was the program meeting expectations of principal, assistant principal, martial arts instructor, teachers, parents, and student participants?

   Data collection methods: interviews and questionnaires.

Organizing and Analyzing the Data

Evaluation methods provided much qualitative information. Much data was especially gathered through the use of multiple observers, multiple data collection methods, and extensive descriptions. Field notes, thick descriptions, transcripts of interviews, written responses to questionnaires, student journal entries, and copies of written documents, files, and reports were organized and analyzed according to each evaluation question. My concern was to summarize the data collected as accurately and clearly as possible. At every opportunity, I attempted to verify and validate the findings by getting reactions from people involved in the project.

Reporting the Data

Results of this program evaluation revealed that the students at risk who participated in this integrated school-curricular martial arts program improved in the following ways:

1. *Academically.* Although teachers initially reported little if any change in the number of completed homework and in-class assignments, by the end of the 6th month of the program teachers did in fact state that these assignments were increasingly being completed. Teachers who were interviewed stated that they were pleased by this academic progress. Teachers attributed this success not necessarily to the martial arts program per se but to the close contact with and supervision of these students by supervisors and the martial arts instructor. In fact, the martial arts program did provide an incentive for these students to improve academically.

2. *Socially.* Teachers and supervisors reported fewer incidents of aggressive behavior exhibited by these students. A reduction in the number of discipline referrals was clearly evident. Classroom teachers also reported greater adherence to rules and procedures, as did teachers on lunch duty. Improved attendance and tardiness rates were noted.

3. *Motivation.* Classroom teachers and the martial arts instructor related that these students demonstrated greater effort, interest, and enthusiasm.

4. *Expectations.* Results from interviews, questionnaires, and informal observations and talks with parents, teachers, supervisors, and students themselves revealed positive feelings about the curricular martial arts program. Teachers and parents, in particular, asserted that they expected students to continue to improve.

Throughout the course of the evaluation, adult participants were informed about the evaluation process and the progress being made toward its completion. Time was spent obtaining comments from teachers, supervisors, and an outside consultant regarding any possible errors or omissions of evidence and other plausible interpretations that were missing. It was decided that the publication of an article describing our program could enhance efforts to expand the martial arts program to possibly include a larger sample and even expand the program to other schools. Reports of this evaluation, then, were to be disseminated throughout the district.

Administering the Evaluation

Administering this evaluation plan was a complex and arduous undertaking. Many logistics had to be considered, including scheduling data collection, allocating time for data analysis, and budget. Although budget constraints were minimal, scheduling problems emerged fairly regularly. At times, certain teachers, due to their own pressures and concerns, did not readily provide needed data. Programs had to be occasionally adjusted and arrangements coordinated with participants. Establishing and maintaining open communications among all participants were a priority. Anonymity of participants was assured.

Complete the following exercises to help reinforce some of the ideas expressed above.

Exercises

1. What steps would you take to assess the needs of your school or district? Whom would you contact and meet with? What sorts of data would you collect? Who might be involved in the process?

    _____

    _____

    _____
                                                      Answers will vary

2. Imagine that you are a principal who is interested in doing a needs assessment of your school. You want to survey how staff, parents, and students feel about the effectiveness of the school's goals in three areas: curriculum, organization, and school climate. Your questionnaire should include items about academic goals, monitoring of student progress, teacher effectiveness, administrative leadership, rewards and incentives for students, order and discipline, parent and community involvement, positive school climate, and opportunity for student responsibility. Describe how you would use these results to improve your school. Be specific, realistic, and practical.

    _____

    _____

    _____
                                                      Answers will vary

3. Using the steps described above, implement and evaluate any program of your choice. Be as specific as possible in your descriptions.

    _____

    _____

    _____
                                                      Answers will vary

4. A quasi-experimental design involving one group that is repeatedly pretested, exposed to an experimental treatment, and repeatedly posttested is known as a

    a. pretest and posttest design
    b. posttest-only design
    c. time series design
    d. revolving series design
    e. none of these

    Answer: c. Explanations to this question and the next five can be found in chapter 4.

5. A true experimental design that involves at least two randomly selected groups in which both groups are pretested, one group receives a new treatment, and both groups are posttested is called a

    a. time series design
    b. posttest-only control group design
    c. pretest and posttest control group design
    d. nonequivalent control group design
    e. none of these

    Answer: c

6. Which is the weakest design?

    a. nonequivalent control group design
    b. posttest-only control group design
    c. interrupted time series design
    d. single measurement design
    e. pretest and posttest control group design

    Answer: d

7. You take 50 fourth-grade students, assign 25 randomly to one class and 25 randomly to the other class. Both groups are measure beforehand. Two different treatments are presented, then a follow-up measurement is given. Which type of design is this?

    a. pretest and posttest control group design
    b. posttest-only design
    c. case study
    d. nonequivalent control group design
    e. one-group pretest and posttest design

    Answer: a

8. Mrs. James teaches computers at P.S. 999. She has a new textbook that she wishes to use with her classes. She decides to test the effectiveness of the new textbook. She chooses two classes that rank similar in ability on a pretest in computer literacy. She gives her programmed text to group A, but with group B she continues her normal instruction. At the end of the semester, she gives a test on computer knowledge and discovers that the class using the new text outperformed the other group (B). She concludes that the new text should be incorporated in all the classes. What research design did Mrs. James use?

    a. nonequivalent control group design
    b. interrupted time series design
    c. pretest and posttest control group design
    d. posttest-only control group design

    Answer: a

9. Mr. Solomon is a supervisor in an elementary school. Mr. Jones, a 6th-grade teacher, complains that one student, Billy, is disruptive and recalcitrant. Mr. Solomon tells the teacher to record Billy's behavior in anecdotal form for 2 weeks before a conference with the guidance counselor. During the first week, Mr. Jones discovers that Billy acts out 26 times. During the second week, he acts out 22 times. During the third week, Mr. Jones meets with the guidance counselor to work out Billy's problems. The counselor sets up a special reward system for Billy. During the fourth week, Billy acts out 18 times. During the fifth week, the disturbances decrease to only 5 times. Mr. Jones and the counselor conclude that the technique is successful. What research design was employed?

    a. pretest and posttest control group design
    b. control group only design
    c. interrupted time series design
    d. single measurement design
    e. nonequivalent control group design

    Answer: c

10. If you are an educational leader who wishes to establish a new science program in your school, what is the first step that should generally be taken?

    a. consult with parents
    b. hand out new textbooks and get feedback from teachers
    c. establish summative evaluative criteria
    d. disseminate goals and objectives to all staff
    e. needs assessment

    Answer: c

11. *Complete the 5 steps in program evaluation by being as specific as possible:*

Focusing the Evaluation: *What are my purposes? What is to be evaluated? What questions will be developed?*

Collecting Data: *What data collection methods will be employed? (Match them to each evaluation question previously posed.)*

Organizing and Analyzing the Data: *How will I organize and analyze my data?*

Reporting the Data: *How will results of this program evaluation be reported?*

Administering the Evaluation: *What administrative and logistical items must be addressed?*

References

Acheson, K. A., & Gall, M. D. (1997). *Techniques in the clinical supervision of teachers.* New York: Longman.

Brainard, E. A. (1996). *A hands-on guide to school program evaluation.* Bloomington, IN: Phi Delta Kappa.

Cuban, L. (1993). *How teachers taught: Constancy and change in American classrooms, 1890–1980* (2nd ed.). New York: Longman.

DeRoche, E. F. (1987). *An administrator's guide for evaluating programs and personnel* (2nd ed.). Boston: Allyn & Bacon.

Glanz, J. (1992). School-based management and the advent of teacher empowerment: One administrator's view of reform. *Record in Educational Administration and Supervision, 12,* 40–45.

Glanz, J. (1995). A school/curricular intervention martial arts program for students at risk. *Journal of At-Risk Issues, 2* (1), 18–25.

Glatthorn, A. A. (1994). *Developing a quality curriculum.* Alexandria, VA: ASCD.

Glickman, C. D., Gordon, S. P., & Ross-Gordon, J. M. (1998). *Supervision of instruction: A developmental approach* (4th ed.). Boston: Allyn & Bacon.

Griffin, G. A. (1997). Is staff development supervision? No. In J. Glanz & R. F. Neville (Eds.), *Educational supervision: Perspectives, issues, and controversies* (pp. 162–169). Norwood, MA: Christopher-Gordon.

Herman, J. L., Lyons Morris, L., & Fitz-Gibbon, C. T. (1988). *Evaluators handbook* (2nd ed.). Newbury Park, CA: Sage.

*Herman, J. L., & Winters, L. (1992). *Tracking your school's success: A guide to sensible evaluation.* Newbury Park, CA: Corwin Press.

Johnson, S. M. (1990). *Teachers at work: Achieving success in our schools.* New York: Basic Books.

Mamchak, S., & Mamchak, S. (1983). *School administrator's public speaking portfolio.* Englewood Cliffs, NJ: Center for Applied Research in Education/ Prentice-Hall.

Marshall, C., & Rossman, G. B. (1999). *Designing qualitative research* (3rd ed.). Newbury Park, CA: Sage.

*Sanders, J. R. (2000). *Evaluating school programs: An educator's guide* (2nd ed.). Newbury Park, CA: Corwin Press.

Wholey, J. S., Hatry, H. P., & Newcomer, K. E. (1994). *Handbook of practical program evaluation.* San Francisco: Jossey-Bass.

Activity 8: Starting a Program and Planning Its Evaluation

This activity allows you to plan a program and incorporate the steps in evaluation. The worksheet is meant to allow you to brainstorm different ideas. Changes in your plan can always be made at a later date. This worksheet also serves as a review of the ideas discussed in this chapter.

1. What program do I wish to initiate? Why do I want to develop this program? What do I hope to accomplish? (Use additional paper to record your responses if necessary.)

   _____

2. What preliminary information should I gather to help me get started? _____

   _____

3. What question or questions should I ponder? _____

   _____

4. Who will be involved in this project? _____

   _____

5. How will data be collected, analyzed, and reported? _____

   _____

6. What will I do with the result? _____

   _____

7. What will I do when problems develop? _____

   _____

8. Complete the 8 steps in program development by being as specific as possible:

   Needs Assessment: What do I intend to do to adequately assess whether or not a need exists far my program?

   Goals: What are my short- and long-term goals? How do I plan on disseminating these goals?

   Administrative Aspects: What administrative or logistical concerns need to be addressed?

   Supervision: How will I facilitate instructional improvement?

   Curriculum: What curricular matters must be addressed? How will curricular changes be addressed?

   Parents and Pupils: How will I involve both of these groups?

   Resource People: How can specialists assist in program development?

   Evaluation: What is my evaluation plan?

(Continued on back)

9. Complete the 5 steps in program evaluation by being as specific as possible:

Focusing the Evaluation: What are my purposes? What is to be evaluated? What questions will be developed?

Collecting Data: What data collection methods will be employed? (Match them to each evaluation question previously posed.)

Organizing and Analyzing the Data: How will I organize and analyze my data?

Reporting the Data: How will result of this program evaluation be reported?

Administering the Evaluation: What administrative and logistical items must be addressed?

Data Collection Techniques That Work

As professionals, the process of reflecting, hypothesizing, and testing our theories about how students learn best is perhaps one of our most important undertakings.

—Linda Ramon, superintendent,
quoted in *Journal of Action Research*

Popular Data Collection
Techniques Used in Action Research

Having emphasized a triangular approach to action research that favors both quantitative and qualitative approaches, this chapter will continue along this same vein by discussing various ways of collecting data. Data collection is the process of collecting information to answer one's research questions and/or confirm or reject a hypothesis. This chapter will highlight the data collection techniques or instruments that you, as an action researcher, will find most useful when conducting action research.

Primary Data Collection Techniques

Questionnaires

Questionnaires are one of the most common types of data collection instruments (or data sources) used in action research projects. Their ease of use and uncomplicated methods of data analysis make questionnaires an invaluable means of collecting data for an action researcher.

A questionnaire surveys respondents' attitudes toward a particular issue. Educational leaders may distribute questionnaires to assess the attitudes of students, parents, teachers, or even other supervisors about a variety of issues, such as school climate and instructional supervision.

Sometimes, ready-made questionnaires that have been developed by companies are available for use. For example, the National Association of Secondary School Principals (NASSP, 1987) has developed several useful questionnaires surveying school climate as well as teacher, student, and parent attitudes toward school. You can call 1-800-228-0752 for the School Effectiveness Questionnaire, which can be hand tabulated or computer analyzed. In many cases, however, questionnaires may not be available to suit your unique needs. In such cases, you might have to construct your own questionnaire. See discussion below on questionnaire construction.

Two types of questionnaires are most common: close ended and open ended. Open-ended questionnaires include questions that allow respondents to elaborate on a given question. A questionnaire, for instance, composed of questions to ascertain a teacher's attitude toward supervision may include the following open-ended question: "Can you provide an example of a situation or experience in which you have benefited from supervision? Explain."

Note that while questionnaires are usually data collection instruments used in quantitative approaches, the responses to open-ended questions in questionnaires can be seen and interpreted as qualitative data. Very often comments *use open ended more*

generated from open-ended questions can prove very useful and even crucial in determining such things as the value of the program under study. (See Patton, 1990, p. 19, for a situation in which comments made in the open-ended portion of a questionnaire were the basis for a very important decision made by a school board that would not have been made had only the close-ended portion of the questionnaire been analyzed quantitatively.)

Close-ended questionnaires, on the other hand, do not allow respondents to elaborate, but rather structure respondents' answers to predetermined choices. One of the most commonly used closed-ended questionnaires is known as the **Likert scale.** Many of us have taken a Likert scale questionnaire at one time or another. You may recall the choices it gives, such as *strongly agree, agree, disagree,* and *strongly disagree.* A Likert scale is relatively easy to construct and easy to analyze.

Likert Scale Construction: Some Guiding Principles

1. Limit the number of items to as few as possible (ideally 15–20 items). Long surveys are unlikely to be completed by respondents.

2. Avoid ambiguously worded statements. Construct items so that they may be interpreted in the same way by every respondent. Why is the following statement worded ambiguously? "How often do you observe your fifth-grade teachers?" (Rarely, sometimes, often)

    What is meant by *observe?* Is it a casual look; an in-depth, hour-long observation period; or some time in between? Moreover, what do the choices mean? How often is *sometimes?* Once a month, twice a month, or once a year?) Sometimes statements are just phrased ambiguously due to sentence structure problems. Have a colleague or potential respondent proofread your items for ambiguity.

3. Avoid leading questions—that is, don't suggest that one response will be more appropriate than another. For example, avoid using a question like "Don't you agree that peer coaching is marvelous?"

4. Avoid sensitive questions to which respondents may not reply honestly. For example, don't ask "Have you always acted so ethically?"

5. Statements should be concise, not overly lengthy.

6. Develop objectives before you write the items (see examples in sample questionnaire that follows).

7. Questionnaires should include statements that are conceptually related. If you are surveying attitudes of teachers toward bilingual education, then an example of a conceptually unrelated item would be "I get along with my supervisor." This statement has little if anything to do with the major purpose of your questionnaire. One way to ensure that items are conceptually related is to match each item with your objectives. Does each item address one of the stated objectives?

8. Avoid **response sets.** Sometimes respondents will not really read the survey but will merely go down a column circling all the *strongly disagree* choices. To avoid response sets you must word half the items positively and half negatively. Placement of positively and negatively worded statements should be random. Don't intentionally place an item in the order you think is best. As long as about half of the items are positive statements and the other half are negative statements, and the items are randomly distributed, you will have avoided the response set problem. Here is an example of two statements, one positively worded and the other in the negative:

Directions: Circle the response that best indicates the extent to which you agree or disagree with each statement below, where SA = Strongly Agree, A = Agree, D = Disagree, and SD = Strongly Disagree. (a) "Math is my favorite class." (b) "Learning math is a waste of time."

Someone who really enjoys math will circle SA for the first item and SD for the second. If the respondent circles SA for both items, you might have a response set. Too many response sets affect the validity and reliability of your questionnaire.

9. The cover letter should be brief and neat. It should explain the purpose of your study, emphasize its importance, give the respondent a good reason for completing the survey, and ensure the respondent's anonymity.

10. Field-test your survey to ensure consensual validity.

A sample Likert-scale questionnaire below illustrates the objectives that were written prior to developing the items. Note that your objectives would not be shared with respondents.

For more information about questionnaire construction, consult the following excellent references: Fink (1995), Fink and Kosecoff (1998), and Thomas (1999).

On survey validity and reliability see Litwin (1995). For a comprehensive resource containing a collection of many easy-to-use assessment tools, see Bum and Payment (2000). See Appendix C for a sample cover letter and a questionnaire.

Before proceeding with the remainder of the chapter, complete the following exercises to help reinforce some of the ideas expressed above.

SAMPLE QUESTIONNAIRE*

Team Teaching Class

Objectives:

1. Are students' physical needs met in the team teaching classroom?

   _____

   _____

2. How is student achievement affected by team teaching?

   _____

   _____

3. Does having two teachers increase your understanding of this topic?

   _____

   _____

4. Are students finding their teachers more available for help?

   _____

   _____

5. Are students comfortable participating in a team taught (larger) class?

   _____

   _____

6. Does having two teachers help students to stay focused and attentive?

   A Agree   1 2 3   desagree   1 2 3

   B what has help you to stay focused
     and attentive in this class.

*Developed by one of my graduate students, Jamie Horowitz.

Questionnaire:

Milburn High School
Mathematics Department

Place a check in the appropriate space below:

_____ male   _____ female
_____ freshman   _____ sophomore   _____ junior   _____ senior

This scale has been prepared so that you can indicate how you feel about the statements below. Please *circle* one of the letters on the left indicating how you feel about each statement (SA, strongly agree; A, agree; D, disagree; SD, strongly disagree).

SA A D SD   1. I understand explanations given by my teacher(s).

SA A D SD   2. I can see the board and overhead screen clearly.

SA A D SD   3. When something is unclear, I am not comfortable asking a question in class.

SA A D SD   4. Being in a class taught by two teachers helps me to be more attentive.

SA A D SD   5. I am not doing very well in this class.

SA A D SD   6. My teacher is available for extra help.

SA A D SD   7. I am not comfortable participating in this class by responding to teacher questions.

SA A D SD   8. I am confused by explanations given by my teacher(s).

SA A D SD   9. It's hard for me to see the board and overhead screen from where I'm seated.

SA A D SD   10. I am comfortable asking a question in class if I don't understand something.

SA A D SD   11. I find it harder to pay attention in class with two teachers.

SA A D SD   12. I am doing pretty well in this class.

SA A D SD   13. My teacher is not available when I need extra help outside the classroom.

SA A D SD   14. I am comfortable participating in class by responding to teacher questions.

Exercises

1. Explain why response sets might skew results from a questionnaire, How would you avoid a response set?

_____

_____

_____

See discussion above in point 8

2. You are a principal of Hartworth High School, located in an affluent suburb with an enrollment of 2,000 students and an active parent body.
   You are acutely aware that a successful school has the following characteristics:

   A. A commonly held sense of mission or purpose

   B. A strong academic focus

   C. A strong administrative and instructional focus

   D. Collegial relationships and collaborative planning

   E. A positive teaching and learning climate where success is recognized and rewarded.

   F. A well-coordinated and articulated curriculum

   G. High expectations for all (equality of opportunity and excellence)

   H. High standards for all

   I. Frequent monitoring

   J. Parental and community involvement

   You sense that this school may be lacking in many of these areas. You see the need for improvement and would like to undertake a survey (needs assessment) of your school's organizational health."
   Compose a questionnaire to assess the relative health of your school. Be certain to include all the essential ingredients of a good questionnaire (see points explained above). Your questionnaire should include at least 15 items. For example:
   Have participants respond to the following statements by noting strongly agree, mildly agree, mildly disagree, or strongly disagree.

   1. Teachers spend time working with students.

   2. Teachers receive administrative help.

   3. Problems are solved, not ignored.

   4. There is a pessimistic atmosphere in school.

5. Decision making is undemocratic.

6. Teachers enjoy working in this school.

Of course, items will depend on the nature of your objectives.

_____

_____

_____

Answers will vary

3. Principal's Rating Scale

You have been a principal of a school for nearly 2 years. You realize that an effective school is one that has a strong, competent leader. How competent are you? Compose a rating scale to measure your effectiveness as a principal. The rating scale will be distributed to all school personnel, parents, and students. For example:

Have respondents note always, sometimes, or never.

   a.   Your principal is accessible.

   b.   He or she encourages a positive relationship.

   c.   He or she encourages innovative programs.

Discuss how you would utilize the findings of this rating scale to improve your performance. Discuss any shortcomings related to using a rating scale to measure the effectiveness of a principal.

_____

_____

Answers will vary

Observation

A very common way to collect data in action research settings is to observe and record information. In chapter 3 we discussed the difference between systematic and nonsystematic observation and explained that both forms of observation are valuable.

In qualitative research approaches, observation may take place in four ways:

1. *As a participant.* The researcher may conceal his or her role when gathering data. For example, a superintendent may want to study interactions among fellow superintendents at a conference. The researcher is able to observe firsthand social interactions among superintendents. Be-

ing actively engaged in the conference affords the researcher firsthand experience and data. Yet the ethics of concealing one's purpose in interacting with others should first be considered very seriously.

2. *As an observer-participant.* The researcher's purpose is known by all participants. The researcher may record data as they occur. Yet participants may be reluctant to share information if they know that what they say or do will be recorded.

3. *As a participant-observer.* The researcher's observation role is secondary to the participant role. The researcher records data; however, the researcher may not attend to all data.

4. *As an observer.* The researcher observes without participating. Recording data can be accomplished without distractions, yet those being observed may feel uncomfortable with the researcher's sole role as observer.

Regardless of the way you collect data through observation, several key questions should be kept in mind. (Thanks to my colleague Barry Friedman, a principal in the New York City Public Schools and an adjunct professor at the College of Staten Island, CUNY, for suggesting these questions.)

1. What is the purpose of the observation?

2. Which individuals, events, settings, and circumstances are the focus of the investigation?

3. How are students, teachers, parents, and administrators behaving?

4. What activities are occurring?

5. How would you describe the social interaction?

6. How do people talk to each other?

7. What is the impact of my presence as an observer?

8. What instruments am I using to record data (e.g., pencil and paper, camera, video recorder, audio recorder)?

Two ways of collecting data through observation have been particularly useful for me. First, written descriptions are most often employed by educational leaders when collecting data. For instance, a leader who observes a teacher may record information by taking field notes or "thick descriptions." Taking field notes is a convenient and simple way of recording observations. Although field notes are vulnerable to observer bias and subjectivity, recording data anecdotally (without drawing conclusions or making value judgments) is highly recommended. Still, this method of recording data is incomplete in the sense that it is impossible to record all events during a given lesson, for instance. Observations are therefore necessarily limited and should rarely be used as the sole means of collecting data. This is why qualitative researchers, as we discussed, emphasize the importance of triangulating on the basis of various data collection methods.

A second way of collecting data through observation is preparing a checklist of some sort to facilitate observations. A checklist allows you to record instances of a particular behavior or practice.

The checklist technique defines certain behaviors or events that can be checked off as they occur during a lesson, for example. Let's say that you are observing a teacher and want to keep a tally of the number of instances in which the teacher "gave directions," "praised," "criticized," "probed," and "asked questions" during a 15-minute segment of a lesson. Your checklist might look something like the one in Figure 7-1. Checklists such as this one can assist systematic collection of data through observation.

Checklist Observation Technique					
Time	Giving Directions	Praising	Criticizing	Probing	Questions
Minute 1					
Minute 2					
Minute 3					
Minute 4					
Minute 5					
Minute 6					
Minute 7					
Minute 8					
Minute 9					
Minute 10					
Minute 11					
Minute 12					
Minute 13					
Minute 14					

Figure 7-1.

Glickman, Gordon, and Ross-Gordon (1998) review several useful techniques for collecting data through observation. I suggest that you review the quantitative and qualitative techniques described by these authors. Also, consult Willerman, McNeely, and Koffman (1991) for a thorough discussion of observation instruments.

Interviewing

Seidman (1998) stated that interviewing is the most suitable data collection method if we are to understand the experiences of others and the meanings they make of them. *Interviews* enable the researcher to learn the complexities of the participants' experiences from his or her point of view. Following the advice of Mishler (1986), the best interviews are flexible and open-ended, allowing for natural conversation. The goal is to understand each participant's experiences and perceptions related to a given situation in a nonthreatening way, such that "meanings emerge, develop, and are shaped by and in turn shape the discourse."

Interviews are often audio-recorded and subsequently transcribed. Transcription, however, can be laborious and time consuming. Action researchers are unlikely to have the time needed to analyze data in such ways. Still, interviewing is a common and invaluable source of data for action researchers. Here are some guidelines to follow when using the interview technique for data collection:

1. Decide why you want to interview someone and what type of information you hope to glean from the interview.

2. Understand the difference between a structured interview and an informal one. A structured interview is one in which the interviewer has a high degree of control over the interview situation. A structured interview has an **interview protocol** that consists of a predetermined set of questions used by an interviewer. In contrast, an informal interview may occur without such a predetermined set of criteria or questions, but rather may be conducted informally, even casually, when speaking with someone. For those of you lacking interview experience, I recommend a structured format. As you develop confidence and skills, a more informal approach may be used.

3. Avoid the following: interrupting the participant; failing to pick up on a topic that the participant considered important; making inappropriate comments or jokes; asking irrelevant personal questions (e.g., "How many children do you have?" unless it comes up in the normal course of "small talk"); failing to check the tape recorder; asking

leading questions such as "Don't you agree that principals should welcome teacher advice?"; asking multiple questions, such as "Why was the supervisor union against shared decision making, and what do you think about the superintendent who was against merit pay?"; inferring something not said or meant by the participant.

4. Do the following: practice an actual interview with a friend, spouse, relative, or colleague; bring a tape recorder and extra blank tapes; organize your questions in advance; have fun; be a good listener; paraphrase the participant's main points; build rapport, especially at the beginning; probe when necessary; use a small inconspicuous tape recorder because a big one might make the participant self-conscious and consequently uncomfortable; ask questions when you do not understand what the participant meant; include open-ended questions such as "Take me through your day" or "Describe that meeting with the student"; send out thank you cards or letters as soon as you complete interviews. Also, read chapter 6 in Seidman (1998) for more detailed suggestions and information. See also Chirban, 1996.

Note the difference between the way qualitative and quantitative researchers would use interviews. The typical qualitative interview would be unstructured and open-ended. Using a protocol with a predetermined set of questions would generally be avoided. Qualitative interviewers want to encourage a relaxed atmosphere wherein ideas can be exchanged freely and easily. Qualitative interviews are really chats rather than formal procedures. Also, a qualitative interviewer would not necessarily feign objectivity, but may at times interact with the participant in an open, lively dialogue. See Appendix C for a sample of how to write up interviews.

Tests

A **test** is perhaps the most common tool used to collect data by action researchers. Two typical tests are commonly used in data collection.

Criterion-referenced tests are one of two major types of testing instruments that measure minimum levels of student performance. **Teacher-made tests** are one example of a criterion-referenced test. The teacher usually establishes an objective (or criterion) and then measures the extent to which students meet the objective. Criterion-referenced tests are one of many possible data collection sources.

Norm-referenced tests (synonymous with **standardized tests**) are the other major type of testing instruments that measure differences among individuals being tested. Each student's score is compared to the norm group, usually a nationally determined norm. A norm-referenced test, such as a standardized math test, can indicate how a given student, such as 10-year-old Jerry, measures up against other 10-year-olds in the nation. For instance, if Jerry scores in the 65th percentile, this indicates that his score on the test was higher than 65% of 10-year-olds who took the test. Obviously, it also means that 35% scored higher than Jerry. Thus, norm-referenced tests compare students to other students on some preestablished norm or standard. Norm-referenced tests are usually important data collection sources.

Another data collection instrument (or data source) that is a kind of standardized or norm-referenced test is an **achievement test,** a commonly used measure or assessment tool in action research. An achievement test assesses an individual's knowledge or proficiency in a given content area. The Stanford Achievement Test and the Iowa Test of Basic Skills are examples of standardized achievement tests.

An achievement test is one form of data collection that may be used by an educational leader, for instance, to arrive at a decision about levels of student achievement in a particular content area. Analysis of results of these achievement tests may yield valuable information in terms of needed remediation in specific content areas.

Achievement or standardized tests are overused sometimes by supervisors and teachers who consider them the most important pieces of data when trying to arrive at a decision about levels of student achievement. Though an invaluable source of information, achievement tests should be considered part of a portfolio of other assessment tools. No single assessment device should be used in making a decision about a program or practice. This book advocates a multidimensional, triangular approach to data collection.

Another data collection instrument that is a kind of standardized or norm-referenced test is an **aptitude test.** This test is designed to predict someone's ability to perform. The IQ (Intelligence Quotient) test is an example of an aptitude test. The SAT (Scholastic Aptitude Test) taken by precollegiate students is another example of an aptitude test.

School profile sheets, discussed below, may contain many of these test scores. School profile sheets frequently analyze test scores over an extended period of time for various groups of students in different grades. As such, they are an invaluable source of information for an action researcher.

Useful information may also be gleaned from tests that do not provide quantitative outcomes. Writing samples, for instance, are usually marked holistically and can be used as qualitative data. Although no longer as common as they used to be, oral examinations may be yet another kind of test used to collect data. Can you think of any others?

Focus Groups

Focus groups (Krueger, 2000; Vaughn, Schumm, & Sinagub, 1996) are groups of individuals who are selected by a researcher and consent to share their views and opinions on specific topics related to an action research project. As a type of survey, a focus group is not unlike a group interview.

For example, as an assistant principal in an elementary school, I asked my upper-grade teachers to join me for a focus group session at lunchtime, during which I heard their opinions about the new textbook series adopted the previous year. Hearing their various views was an invaluable method of data collection that helped our textbook committee arrive at a decision about continuing or discontinuing the series.

Before proceeding with the remainder of the chapter, complete the following exercises to help reinforce some of the ideas expressed above.

Exercises

1. Develop a set of criteria that can be used to observe your school organization. Use some of the sample questions posed in the "observation" section above. Describe your organization in detail.

    _____

    _____

    _____

    Answers will vary

2. Conduct an observation study for one of the following topics:
    A. Observe a classroom teacher giving a lesson in a major subject area.
    B. Observe a principal conducting a faculty meeting.
    C. Observe an entire school and its basic setup.
    D. Observe a supervisor conducting a workshop or grade/department conference.
    E. Observe a school district office and its basic setup.

    Choose only one of the above and make an extensive observation of the situation. Feel free to incorporate any of the following data collection techniques described in the above sections: interview, test data, and focus groups.

    _____

    _____

    _____

    _____

    _____

    Answers will vary

Secondary Data Collection Techniques

School Profile

School profile data sheets, generally available through the district office or state agencies, provide a wealth of important documentary information. These sheets provide reliable, clear data about a school's resources and students' needs in order to plan effectively for school improvement. These sheets provide achievement and background data over a period of years. Assessing student achievement over a 4-year period, for example, is relatively easy. Data may include standardized reading and math scores by grade level over a 4-year period; a statistical overview of a school's characteristics (e.g., percent utilization, capacity, staff-student ratio, repair orders); demographic backgrounds of faculty, staff, and students; teacher characteristics (e.g., certification or tenure status); student characteristics (e.g., mobility, class size, attendance rates).

Data derived from such profile sheets are easily obtained and interpreted. Such information may prove invaluable for collecting data about a specific program, practice, or procedure.

Have you seen your school's profile sheet lately? Ask your principal to give you one to peruse and see how much information is readily available.

Multimedia

Too often researchers neglect this valuable source for collecting data. Use of multimedia (including audiotape recordings, videotapes, films, photographs, electronic mail surveys, among others) has many advantages over more traditional methods for collecting data. Don't overlook using any of these media when collecting data.

For example, taking pictures of students showing how they feel about their projects is a wonderful qualitative way of communicating information. A picture *is* worth a thousand words. Pictures that show a group of eager, enthusiastic, and smiling kindergarten students holding their "Big Books" indicate the pride they must have felt in creating them. Using videotapes to film students' reading skills in September and videotaping them again in June will provide striking qualitative evidence of reading growth.

Although many researchers indicate that use of videotape and photography may reflect a subjective bias, these forms of media, if incorporated properly and judiciously, can provide unique evidence. As long as you triangulate—that is, incorporate other valid and reliable data collection methods—multimedia use makes sense.

How might you use multimedia to collect data? Do you recall why triangulation is important, based on our discussion in chapter 2?

Portfolios

A **portfolio** is a data collection instrument (or data source) that includes a great deal of information about a particular individual or group of individuals. A portfolio may include a student's achievement test scores, book reports, homework assignments, art projects, in-class tests, oral presentations, self-assessments, and artwork (see Wolf, LeMahiew, & Eresh, 1992). Portfolios are excellent ways of collecting data from a variety of perspectives. Portfolios may later be analyzed qualitatively to arrive at a decision about the achievement level, for example, of a particular student in language arts. Portfolio use is very much consonant with the concept of triangulation. Do you know what the connection is? How might you use portfolios to collect data?

Records

School records, other than formal test data found in school profile sheets, are commonly referred to by educational leaders. Leaders, for example, may collect data by examining cumulative record cards (revealing information about students), teacher files (revealing professional data about teachers, such as record of service), anecdotal records, and diaries, journals, or logs. How might you use records to collect data?

Whereas these data collection techniques are more than sufficient for the practicing educational leader, researchers interested in more in-depth techniques will find these and other data collection methods more fully explained in Anderson, Herr, and Nihlen (1994) and Marshall and Rossman (1999).

Exercise

Can you name the five primary data collection techniques used in action research as discussed in this chapter?

Hint: QOITF.

What about the 4 secondary data collection techniques?

Hint: SMPR.

References

Anderson, G. L., Herr, K., & Nihlen, A. S. (1994). *Studying your own school: An educator's guide to qualitative practitioner research.* Thousand Oaks, CA: Corwin Press.

Bum, B., & Payment, M. (2000). *Assessments A to Z: Collection of 50 questionnaires, instruments, and inventories.* Port Chester, NY: National Professional Resources.

Chirban, J. T. (1996). *Interviewing in depth.* Thousand Oaks, CA: Sage.

Fink, A. (1995). *The survey kit.* Thousand Oaks, CA: Sage.

*Fink, A., & Kosecoff, J. (1998). *How to conduct surveys: A step-by-step guide* (2nd ed.). Thousand Oaks, CA: Sage.

Glickman, C. D., Gordon, S. P., & Ross-Gordon, J. M. (1998). *Supervision of instruction: A developmental approach* (4th ed.). Boston: Allyn & Bacon.

Journal of Action Research. (1995).

Krueger, R. A. (2000). *Focus groups: A practical guide for applied research* (3rd ed.). Thousand Oaks, CA: Sage.

Litwin, M. S. (1995). *How to measure survey reliability and validity.* Thousand Oaks, CA: Sage.

Marshall, C., & Rossman, G. B. (1999). *Designing qualitative research* (3rd ed.). Newbury Park, CA: Sage.

Mishler, E. G. (1986). *Research interviewing: Context and process.* Cambridge, MA: Harvard University Press.

National Association of Secondary School Principals (NASSP). (1987). *Comprehensive assessment of school environments.* Reston, VA: Author.

Patton, M. Q. (1990). *Qualitative evaluation and research methods* (2nd ed.). Thousand Oaks, CA: Sage.

*Seidman, I. E. (1998). *Interviewing as qualitative research: A guide for researchers in education and the social sciences* (2nd ed.). New York: Teachers College Press.

Thomas, S.J. (1999). *Designing surveys that work! A step-by-step guide.* Bloomington, IN: Phi Delta Kappa.

Vaughn, S., Schumm, J. S., & Sinagub, J. M. (1996). *Focus group interviews in education and psychology.* Thousand Oaks, CA: Sage.

Willerman, M., McNeely, S. L., & Koffman, E. C. (1991). *Teachers helping teachers: Peer observation and assistance.* New York: Praeger.

Wolf, R. M., LeMahiew, P. G., & Eresh, J. (1992). Good measure: Assessment as a tool for educational reform. *Educational Leadership, 49* (8), 8–13.

Activity 9.   Data Collection Instruments

This activity allows you to record the types of data collection instruments (or data sources) you intend to use. This activity worksheet is meant to allow you to brainstorm different ideas. Changes in your plan can always be made at a later date. This activity serves as a review of the ideas discussed in this chapter.

1. Given the nature of my action research project, what kind of data do I want or need to collect? (Use additional paper to record your responses if necessary.) _____

   _____

2. Who will be responsible for collecting this data? _____

   _____

3. What administrative or logistical concerns should I attend to? _____

   _____

4. Will I incorporate primary and/or secondary data collection instruments? _____

   _____

5. Check the data collection instruments you are likely to need and record relevant information:

Primary Data Collection Instruments

QUESTIONNAIRES

____open-ended   ____close-ended   ____Likert Scale

What are my objectives? _____

_____

What are some sample statements I may incorporate? _____

_____

OBSERVATION

____ participant   ____observer-participant   ____participant-observer   ____ observer

Will I use systematic and/or nonsystematic methods of observation? _____

What type of observation checklist or form will I use? _____

INTERVIEWING

_____ structured (formal)   _____ informal

What questions will I include in my interview protocol?_____

_____

(Continued on back)

TESTS

_____ criterion-referenced _____ norm-referenced

What specific types will I use? _____

_____

Secondary Data Collection Instruments

SCHOOL PROFILE DATA

Where are the profile sheets? _____

What information do I want to collect? _____

_____

MULTIMEDIA

_____ audiotape recordings _____ videotapes _____ films _____ photographs

_____ electronic mail surveys _____ other

_____

PORTFOLIOS

What items can I collect as part of the portfolio? _____

_____

RECORDS

What kinds of records can I collect? _____

_____

OTHER DATA COLLECTION INSTRUMENTS

_____

_____

How to
Analyze Quantitative
Data Easily

Focus Questions

1. Why do you think that calculating statistics in the 21st century is so easy?

2. Why is data analysis so important?

3. What is the simplest way to quantitatively analyze data gathered from a questionnaire?

4. What would you want to know that would allay your apprehensions about statistics?

Research brings light into darkness. Explications of meanings illuminate. Meanings of results truly matter.

—O. L. Davis, Jr., 1996

Two people went out hiking on a foggy day, when one of them fell over a cliff. The person at the top called down, "Are you all right?" "Yes, I'm all right," came back the answer. "Are you sure you have no broken bones?" his friend inquired. "No broken bones," came the answer through the fog. "Well, then, why don't you climb back up?" said the man at the top. "I can't," came the reply, "I'm still falling."

Moral of the story: Don't make a decision until all the results are in. Too often, many of us rush to conclusions because we "think" we know what the data are telling us, but without careful analysis, we may be shortsighted in our conclusions, arrive too quickly at judgments, and, even worse, make erroneous decisions that don't flow from the data. We should take an "I'm still falling" approach until we have adequately analyzed the data we so assiduously collected, and only then can we begin to offer interpretations of the data and arrive at a conclusion or two.

Data analysis consists of looking for patterns, themes, associations, and interrelationships among the data collected. The process entails organizing and finding meaning in the mass of collected data. The process also involves presenting data in ways that will allow for easy interpretation. Displaying or summarizing data using tables, charts, and figures are useful ways of analysis. As we organize our data by displaying them using charts, for instance, we may look for emerging patterns. As these patterns emerge, explanations or conclusions can be drawn and research questions answered.

Data must be looked at holistically to determine a trend or pattern. Since we have relied on a multidimensional (triangular) approach to data collection, it is incumbent upon us to consider all data results. Some researchers rely on only one instrument before arriving at a conclusion. A significant t-test finding, for example, doesn't necessarily mean that a particular program or practice should be implemented or adopted. Data analysis discussed in this chapter should involve consideration of all sources of data.

The purpose of data analysis is threefold:

1. To describe or summarize data clearly
2. To search for consistent patterns or themes among the data
3. To enable us to answer our research questions and/or hypotheses

As you know, this book has addressed two approaches to research: quantitative and qualitative. Because data derived from quantitative research are usually numerical and data derived from qualitative research are usually verbal, data analysis for each method will vary. Quantitative data are summarized statistically or mathematically, whereas qualitative data are analyzed through a logico-inductive process that includes grouping and comparing findings with research questions. This chapter outlines the ways in which data might be analyzed quantitatively.

Data derived from descriptive, correlational, and/or group comparison research can be analyzed quantitatively. Some sort of statistical analysis is required to analyze quantitative studies.

Statistical Analyses

Sadistic statistics?! Not really. With the advent of computer technology, the use of statistical analysis has become relatively easy. No longer do you have to take out the abacus, calculator, or compute complicated formulas longhand. Computers can conduct statistical analysis faster than you can say, "Hey, that's significant." Computers are readily available at campus computer lab centers and appropriate software packages are menu-driven for easy use.

The only slightly difficult thing to do is to be able to select the correct statistical calculation to match the type of research conducted. Programs exist today to help you do even that. So, as we discuss some statistics, don't fret: The computer can do it all.

Please note, therefore, that longhand calculations will not, for the most part, be described in this chapter. No educational leader would spend the time doing that kind of calculation. Learning how to analyze statistics on a computer is essential and will be part of your training in an action research course or workshop.

Two common types of statistics are descriptive and inferential. **Descriptive statistics** are used to describe and summarize data. See Appendix B for a sample write-up. There are four descriptive statistics that are most useful to action research: mean, standard deviation, percentile, and correlation coefficient.

Mean is synonymous with average score. Mean indicates how a typical person scored on your test or survey. Mean is computed very simply by adding the numbers and dividing by the total number of numbers used. What would be the mean of these numbers: 23, 45, 12, 45, 23? The answer is 29.6. Simply add the five numbers (23 + 45 + 12 + 45 + 23) and divide by 5 (because there are five numbers). Mean (symbolized $\overline{X}$ or M)—a measure of central tendency indicating the arithmetic average.

Standard Deviation indicates how much scores vary from each other. For example, consider the means of these two sets of scores:

Group X = 5 scores	Group Y = 5 scores
50 50 50 50 50	100 50 45 35 20
250 ÷ 5 = 50	250 ÷ 5 = 50

Note that although both groups have the same mean, the scores in group X seem much more homogeneous than the scores in group Y. How do we describe the difference in the variation of the scores in the groups? Standard deviation indicates how the scores in each group vary. It is easily calculated with a calculator or computer. Standard deviation (symbolized *S.D.*)—a measure of dispersion indicating the amount by which scores vary from each other.

Both mean and standard deviation are accurate descriptive statistics since they provide a good picture of a given distribution of scores. Means, of course, tell us the average score. Why do you think it may be important to know the mean of a given group of scores? Knowing the standard deviation tells us how dispersed scores are in a given group. If you find a high S.D., you might want to explore further reasons why scores in this group varied so much from one another. This knowledge may encourage you to examine your treatment and/or design of the study. Also, S.D. helps us draw conclusions about the population from what we know about the sample. How mean and standard deviation can be used is described later in the chapter.

Percentage is also a descriptive statistic in action research projects. Percentage (%) denotes the number (per 100) of individuals who give a particular response or achieve a particular score.

Correlation coefficient (symbolized *r*) is a measure of relationship indicating the degree to which two or more variables are related to each other.

In contrast to descriptive statistics, **inferential statistics** tell us how much confidence we can have in generalizing from a sample to a population. Although action research projects generally do not involve studies that seek generalization, certain useful and common inferential statistics are the following:

> **T-test** determines the significance of a difference between the means of two groups.
>
> **Sign test** determines significance of difference between means of one group.
>
> **Mann-Whitney U-test**—determines if two small groups differ significantly (it works similar to a t-test).
>
> **Chi square analysis** (often symbolized by X^2) determines the relationship between two or more **nominal** (non-quantifiable) **variables.**

The remainder of this chapter will be devoted to more fully explaining some of these descriptive and inferential statistics. An explanation of many other statistical analyses will not be undertaken because they are not usually utilized in action research projects. Note that many statistical operations can be easily calculated today using a computer with a popular and user-friendly statistical software package.

For my action research projects, I find that computerized statistical packages are most desirable. For advanced students of research (usually those completing their doctoral dissertations), Statistical Product and Service Solutions (more commonly known as SPSS) is the most frequently used program. SPSS, in my opinion, is far too complicated and advanced for most statistical analyses needed by students enrolled in action research courses. A number of companies offer more user-friendly statistical packages. The professional educational leader, knowledgeable about applying action research, should become familiar with a statistical computer program.

I find that STATPAK, an acronym for "Statistical Package," is one such user-friendly package, but any similar program will do. STATPAK is available for use with Macintosh and IBM-compatible computers. STATPAK can be obtained from Frisbie (1992) and Gay (1996). Installation procedures and directions on how to use STATPAK are supplied. STATPAK is completely menu driven, is very easy to use, and best of all it's free. STATPAK can be downloaded from my website at www.wagner.edu/~jglanz/.

You can compute the following operations, among others, using STATPAK: mean, standard deviation, correlation coefficient, t-test, Analysis of Variance, and Chi Square. I'm certain that as part of a course on action research you will have opportunities to use some of these computer software programs.

Other comparable statistical packages include the following:

- GB-STAT automatic statistical graphs. Contact Dynamic Microsystems, (301) 384-2754.

- PRO STAT. Poly Software International, (801) 485-0466.

- MYSTAT for Windows published by SYSTAT, Evanston, IL 60201.

Application of Mean, Standard Deviation, and Percentage

In this section, the results of a survey distributed to teachers about their attitudes toward supervision will be analyzed. These results are fictionalized. The purpose of the analysis that follows will be to demonstrate that you, as an action researcher, can easily apply some basic descriptive statistics to analyze survey research. Other forms of descriptive statistics, such as correlational analysis, can easily be carried out with one of the many computer programs.

Other than standardized tests, the most common data collection technique used by action researchers is the questionnaire. Let's illustrate how to apply three very common descriptive statistics: mean, standard deviation, and percentile. Let's apply them to a survey disseminated to teachers in Public School XY. The Likert scale questionnaire was designed to determine teachers' attitudes toward supervision.

The survey was disseminated to a group of 34 teachers. In order to analyze the data, you must develop an answer sheet that indicates favorable responses. The questionnaire is designed to assess attitudes toward supervision. Which choices on the Likert scale questionnaire indicate favorable attitudes toward supervision?

Let's say you develop a 20-item questionnaire that includes the following two items:

1. Your supervisor provides helpful feedback after a formal observation.
2. Your supervisor offers little if any support in student disciplinary matters.

Because you've developed a Likert scale, the choices listed are Strongly Disagree (SD), Disagree (D), Agree (A), and Strongly Agree (SA). Choices are stated as follows:

SD D A SA 1. Your supervisor provides helpful feedback after a formal observation.

SD D A SA 2. Your supervisor offers little if any support in student disciplinary matters.

What response for each question indicates a favorable attitude toward supervision? For the first question, the most favorable response would be SA and the least favorable response would be SD. Because four choices are provided (SD, D, A, SA), you would award 4 points to the most favorable response (SA), 3 points to the next favorable response (A), 2 points to D, and 1 point to SD, the least favorable response.

How might you code the second question? The most favorable response this time is SD, which receives a 4, D receives a 3, and so on. Notice that the value awarded for each response varies depending on the question. You determine favorable responses based on what would be considered to be generally accepted among educators.

If your questionnaire has 10 items, the highest possible favorable score would be 40 (10 items, each receiving a 4 for the most favorable response). The lowest possible score, indicating the least favorable attitudes toward supervision, would be 10 (10 items, each receiving a 1 for the least favorable response).

Mini-exercise: What would be the highest and lowest scores for a questionnaire that has 20 items?

Here's an example of how a researcher coded the following questions indicating favorable attitudes toward supervision (note that the higher the score, the more favorable respondents' attitudes are toward supervision):

1. Supervision facilitates instructional improvement.

SA	A	D	SD
4	3	2	1

2. Supervision is a waste of time.

SA	A	D	SD
1	2	3	4

Now, if 32 individuals completed the questionnaire, you would have a total score for each of them as follows, for example:

$$S1 = 40$$
$$S2 = 34$$
$$S3 = 10$$
$$S4 = 18$$
$$S5 = 26$$
$$S6 = 30$$
$$S7 = 14$$
$$S8 = 20$$
$$S9 = 10$$
$$S10 = 30$$

Obviously, subject 4 (S4) has a more unfavorable attitude toward supervision than subject 1 (S1). Who has the least favorable attitude toward supervision?

How would we apply the three basic descriptive statistics to analyze these data? The results for two questions, shown in Table 8-1, is one common and easy way to indicate results.

Table 8-1. Sample Analysis

Teachers' Attitudes Toward Supervision: Survey Results

1. *Your supervisor provides helpful feedback after a formal observation.*

N = 32

21.9% Strongly Disagree (Raw score = 7)

75.0% Disagree (Raw score = 24)

3.0% Agree (Raw score = 1)

0.00% Strongly Agree (Raw score = 0)

Mean = 1.81

Standard Deviation = .47

Conclusion: An overwhelming percentage of respondents maintain that the supervisor doesn't provide helpful feedback after an observation.

2. *Your supervisor offers little if any support in student disciplinary matters.*

N = 32

0.00% Strongly Disagree (Raw score = 0)

15.6% Disagree (Raw score = 5)

62.5% Agree (Raw score = 20)

21.9% Strongly Agree (Raw score = 7)

Mean = 1.94

Standard Deviation = .62

Conclusion: An overwhelming percentage of respondents maintain that the supervisor offers little, if any, support in student disciplinary matters.

In the example we first note the percentiles. N = 32 for the first question indicates that 32 individuals responded to the first question. Therefore, N signifies the number of respondents. **Raw scores** indicate the number of respondents who filled in a given choice (e.g., seven individuals responded "strongly disagree" to the first question).

Percentages are calculated by dividing the raw score (e.g., 7 in the first question above) N (therefore, 7 ÷ 32 = 21.9%). Calculate the other percentages on your own now.

Many action researchers rely only on percentiles for analyzing data. However, mean and standard deviation are also commonly employed. Mean and standard deviation are easily determined with a calculator or a computer program such as STATPAK.

You enter the STATPAK's main menu and select calculations for mean and standard deviation. You will then be asked to enter a number for the first entry. Note that you will have 32 entries because 32 individuals responded to the first question. To calculate the mean and standard deviation, you need to look back at your key to determine how many points are awarded for a given choice. In the first question above, we awarded 4 points for a "strongly disagree" response because that would be considered the most favorable response to the first question. We also need to note the raw score for each response.

Since a "strongly disagree" response gets 4 points and seven individuals responded "strongly disagree," we would enter the number 4 seven times into the STATPAK program, because seven individuals are awarded 4 points each for the strongly disagree choice.

The next choice, "disagree," is awarded 3 points. How many individuals responded "disagree"? The number is 24, so enter 3 twenty-four times. The next category is "agree." How many respondents chose "agree"? Only 1. Therefore, enter the number 2 (indicating 2 points) only once. No one responded "strongly disagree," so no entry is made for the next choice.

Follow directions on the STATPAK menu and in a few seconds you will see the following page:

Standard Deviation for Samples and Populations

STATISTIC	VALUE
No. of Scores (N)	32
Mean	3.19
Standard Deviation	0.47

Compute the mean and standard deviation for the second question above using a calculator or the STATPAK (or similar) program.

Sometimes, a Likert scale may incorporate other choices, such as Very much, Somewhat, or Not at all. Also, results are often stated simply, using percentages rather than mean and standard deviation. Examine the analysis of results derived from a questionnaire (Table 8-2), which indicates results based on student attitudes toward school:

Table 8-2. Questionnaire Analysis

---

1. *Indicate the degree to which your classes were informative and educational.*

N = 27

61.0% Very Much

28.0% Somewhat

11.0% Not at all

2. *Indicate the degree to which you enjoy your academic studies.*

N = 34

70.0% Very Much

20.0% Somewhat

10.0% Not at all

3. *Counseling has met my expectations.*

N = 35

11.0% Very Well

61.0% Well

28.0% Not at all

Can you figure out how many people responded for each choice above? It's really quite simple. Multiply each percentage by N (the total number of respondents). For example, for the first question, .61 x 27 = 16.47, rounded off to 16 people. That means that 16 people responded "very much" to the first question. Then, .28 x 27 = 7.56, rounded off to 8; and .11 x 27 = 2.97, or 3. Thus, 16 + 8 + 3 = 27 people who responded to the first question.

Whenever you want to determine a raw score, you multiply the percentage by the number (in this case, the number of total respondents). Therefore, for example, if I told you that Jeremy received a 70% on his math test and that there were 20 questions, what would be his raw score (i.e., number of correct responses)? Multiply .70 by 20 for 14 correct responses. Now figure out the number of people who responded for each choice in the second and third questions above (answers can be found in the exercise box).

The examples here analyze results for one group. Sometimes, however, you might want to compare the attitudes of two different groups, such African-

American parents' attitudes toward the school versus attitudes of Hispanic-American parents. To analyze results from two groups, you would follow the same procedures for each group as you did before. You would now, however, have two sets of scores, one for each parent group. Although you could analyze each group using percentages, means, and/or standard deviations as explained above, you might consider another approach, such as the use of correlational analysis or t-test analysis on both groups.

A correlational analysis would indicate the degree of relationship between both sets of group scores. You might conclude, for example, that there is a significant relationship between the way African-American parents feel about the school and the way Hispanic-American parents feel. To ascertain whether there is a significant statistical difference, however, between the two groups, a t-test analysis should be undertaken, as will be explained in the next section.

Before proceeding with the remainder of the chapter, complete the following exercises to help reinforce some of the ideas expressed above.

Exercises

1. You've analyzed the result of an AIDS questionnaire distributed to 70 high school freshmen as follows:

   A. AIDS can reduce the body's ability to fight disease.

SA	A	D	SD
53	14	3	0
75.7%	20%	4.3%	0%

   $\overline{X} = 3.71$
   S.D. $= .54$

   B. AIDS attacks the immune system in the body.

SA	A	D	SD
50	18	2	0
71.4%	25.7%	2.9%	0%

   $\overline{X} = 3.69$
   S.D. $= .53$

C. A person can be infected with the AIDS virus (HIV) but not have the disease AIDS.

SA	A	D	SD
41	20	7	2
58.6%	28.6%	10.0%	2.9%

$\overline{X} = 3.43$
S.D. = .79

Describe how you would compute the percentages, means, and standard deviations. Based on this excerpted data, describe what the survey indicates. What do the means and standard deviations tell us?

_____

_____

_____

Check answers in sections above

2. Develop a 5-item questionnaire, a coded answer sheet, and provide some dummy data. Compute means, standard deviations, and percentages for each item.

_____

_____

_____

Answers will vary. Answers for questions two and three in the previous section are, respectively: 24, 7, and 3 people; and 4, 21, and 10 people.

3. Examine the table below and draw four comparisons between the Cooperative Learning experimental group and the Whole Class control group. This table is culled from a study of a group of secondary school teachers in Israel conducted by Sharan and Shachar, 1988 (reprinted with permission, Springer-Verlag, Inc.)

Effects of Complex Cooperative Learning in a History Course by SES

	Groups			
	Experimental Cooperative Learning		Control Whole Class	
Test	High SES	Low SES	High SES	Low SES
(Pretest)				
M	20.99	14.81	21.73	12.31
S.D.	9.20	7.20	10.53	7.05
(Posttest)				
M	62.60	50.17	42.78	27.03
S.D.	10.85	14.44	14.40	13.73
Mean Gain:	41.61	35.36	21.05	14.92

_____

_____

_____

Answer: Any of the following comparisons can be made: (1) In the pretests the lower-SES students scored significantly lower than the higher-SES students; (2) The lower-SES students taught by cooperative learning achieved over two times higher than those of the lower-SES students taught by whole class instruction; (3) Lower-SES students taught with cooperative learning scored higher than High-SES students taught with whole class instruction; (4) High-SES students scored higher than High-SES students with whole class instruction.

The t-Test

A t-test is a popular and common statistical technique that determines the degree of significance between the means of two groups. In other words, the purpose of a t-test is to determine whether the difference between two means is of **statistical significance**—that is, that the probability of their occurrence by chance is less than 5%.

Let's say you've divided your class into two equivalent groups using the matched pairs technique described in chapter 4. Or let's say you are a middle or high school teacher who wants to compare two equivalent classes (e.g., periods 4 and 6) in science achievement. Both groups or classes would be exposed to a treatment, and then a posttest would be administered. The results of the posttest are indicated in Figure 8-1 for two classes of five students each. A t-test would not ordinarily be used for groups of fewer than 15 participants. I've used five students in each class merely to simplify the explanation of the t-test. For groups of fewer than 15, a Mann-Whitney U-test should be conducted (see discussion in the next section).

Posttest Results for t-Test Computation	
CLASS I	**CLASS II**
S1 = 85	*S1 = 73*
S2 = 82	*S2 = 76*
S3 = 78	*S3 = 80*
S4 = 75	*S4 = 70*
S5 = 72	*S5 = 65*

Figure 8-1.

The numbers in Figure 8-1 represent raw scores or interval data based on posttest results. A score of 85, for instance, in Class I indicates a student's raw score on a science achievement test.

A cursory perusal of the data in Figure 8-1 may lead one to conclude that the students in the first class scored higher posttest scores than students in the second class. In other words, students in the first class have higher achievement in science than the other students. However, we cannot conclude that this difference is statistically significant.

To determine statistical significance requires that some sort of statistical operation be conducted. In this case, a t-test would be the appropriate choice.

Computation of a t-test can be performed using a calculator with a square root function or, more simply, using STATPAK, the computer-based statistical program. It seems to me that no supervisor, teacher, or other practitioner would choose to expend the effort to compute any statistical calculations other than by using a computer-based program. Therefore, an explanation of any long-hand statistical computations will not be undertaken in this text.

To determine whether or not the posttest scores of these classes are significantly different from one another, one would simply input the raw scores in a computer-based program such as STATPAK by pressing a couple of keys. STATPAK is very user-friendly and all you have to do is follow the menu-driven instructions on the screen. (Your professor will certainly demonstrate the ease of computer-based programs, and you will have the opportunity to practice t-test calculations on your own.)

Although some programs actually indicate whether the t-test result is significant, STATPAK does not. To determine significance, you must consult a t-test table that is very easy to interpret.

After inputting the information in Figure 8-1 (using a t-test for non-independent means), you will find that the t value equals 3.00 (ignore the minus sign). The **degrees of freedom** (df), which is always N-1, equals 4. Now all you have to do is consult a t-test table that can be readily found in almost any statistics book. I have, however, included an abbreviated t-test set of values in Table 8-3 for your use in this chapter. You would go down the left column (df) to the number 4 and look across at the values noted. Because your t-value was 3.00, you would look for the value that is less than 3.00. In other words, to be significant,

Table 8-3.

Abbreviated Table of t-Values		
Number of Subjects (df)	.05	.01
4	2.48	5.02
5	2.35	4.54
6	2.13	3.75
7	2.02	3.37
8	1.94	3.14
9	1.90	3.00
10	1.86	2.90
11	1.83	2.82
12	1.81	2.76
13	1.80	2.72
14	1.78	2.68
15	1.77	2.65
16	1.76	2.62
17	1.75	2.60
18	1.75	2.58
19	1.74	2.57
20	1.73	2.55
22	1.73	2.53
24	1.72	2.51
26	1.71	2.49
28	1.71	2.48
30	1.70	2.47
40	1.68	2.42
100	1.65	2.35

Note: t-values for directional hypotheses are presented.

your t-value must be higher than the values noted on the table. In this case, a t-value of 3.00 is higher than the value under the .05 column (2.48) but lower than the value under the .01 column (5.02). Thus there is a statistically significant difference between the posttest results of these two classes at the .05 level. One may, therefore, conclude that the differences between the two classes may be attributed to the treatment and not to a chance error factor. This is called **level of significance.**

In other words, there is a significant difference in achievement between the two groups. If these were posttest scores on attitudes toward science, and not achievement scores, then you could conclude that one group had more favorable attitudes toward science than the other group. The level of significance is indicated in the following statement: $t = 3.00$, $p < .05$.

This statement indicates the obtained t-value (3.00) and the probability (p) that differences between the two groups were due to chance error factors is less than 5%. In other words, you can conclude with 95% certainty that the differences between the two groups were true differences that resulted from the treatment.

Before proceeding with the remainder of the chapter, complete the following exercise to help reinforce some of the ideas expressed above.

Exercise

1. Compare t-test results for the following cases:

	I					**II**		
Class 1		**Class 2**			**Class 1**		**Class 2**	
S1	83	S1	83		S1	10	S1	9
S2	83	S2	83		S2	8	S2	8
S3	80	S3	80		S3	7	S3	10
S4	99	S4	87		S4	7	S4	6
S5	98	S5	77		S5	5	S5	6
S6	76	S6	75		S6	4	S6	3
S7	63	S7	88					
S8	97	S8	75					
S9	79	S9	88					
S10	100	S10	75					
S11	40	S11	84					
S12	83	S12	79					
S13	75	S13	83					
S14	76	S14	84					
S15	77	S15	76					

	III				IV		
Class 1		**Class 2**		**Class 1**		**Class 2**	
S1	90	S1	73	S1	85	S1	73
S2	87	S2	76	S2	82	S2	76
S3	85	S3	80	S3	78	S3	80
S4	80	S4	70	S4	75	S4	70
S5	78	S5	65	S5	72	S5	65

Answers: I, t = 0.20; II. t = 0.00; III, t = 5.50; IV, t = -3.00.
Consult a t-test table to determine whether or not
differences are significant.

The Sign Test

One of the common statistical techniques or procedures used in action research to determine whether the posttest scores are different from the pretest scores in one-group pretest and posttest designs is known as the sign test. Although we cautioned against using one-group pretest and posttest designs because of the inability to control for extraneous factors or variables that might have influenced results on the posttest, this design is still popular in action research and can be utilized if analyzed properly.

Let's say you are working with a teacher who wants to encourage her pupils to read more books and write more book reports (Willerman, McNeely, & Koffman, 1991). The method the teacher has traditionally used is the "stars on the chart" method. You remember that chart, don't you? A chart is displayed on a wall in the classroom with an alphabetical listing of all the names of the students. Stars are placed next to names to indicate the number of books read. As an educational leader, you notice Ms. Smith's use of these charts and you surmise that many students are simply turned off to reading because the competition inherent in this "stars on the chart" approach is too much to bear for some of them. You recommend another approach that you recently read about in *Instructor* magazine: writing and publishing class newspapers that include book reports written by the students. You clip out the article for Ms. Smith and encourage her to try the new method.

Ms. Smith is intrigued by it. She decides to try this approach. Newspapers are to be published weekly and disseminated throughout the school and community. She wonders if this new method for encouraging book reports will significantly increase the number of books read by her students.

She states her hypothesis in null form: "There will be no difference in the number of books read by students whose book reports are rewarded by charting them with stars on the classroom bulletin board and students whose book reports are printed in a classroom newspaper."

Note that there are not two separate groups in this case. One group at a time will be treated with a method for encouraging students to read more books. She now collects her data in the following way:

1. For one month she counts the number of books read by students in her class. This is considered the pretest.

2. During the second month she begins to publish book reports in the classroom newspaper and disseminates them throughout the school. She records the number of books read by students. This is considered the posttest.

3. She charts results by comparing pretest scores (number of books read using the star method) with posttest scores (number of books read using the newspaper technique). A plus sign (+) indicates an increase from pretest to posttest; a minus sign (−) indicates a decrease from pretest to posttest; and a zero (0) indicates no change in scores. See Figure 8-2.

Sign Test Computations			
Student	**Pretest Score**	**Posttest Score**	**Sign**
Mary	6	4	−
Zakia	4	5	+
Juan	6	7	+
Michael	5	6	+
Rochelle	6	4	−
Natasha	3	4	+
Jacob	3	4	+
Jessie	4	6	+
Kevin	6	5	−
Carlos	5	5	0
Mansa	6	7	+
Cynthia	5	6	+
Huan	7	8	+
Linda	5	6	+
Tim	4	7	+
Karim	5	5	0
Rolanda	4	5	+
Joseph	6	7	+

Figure 8-2.

Then she follows the next three steps to carry out the sign test to determine if there is a significant difference between pretest and posttest scores:

1. As noted in the chart, Ms. Smith has 18 students, who are identified as N = 18 (number of students equals 18). She counts the number of scores that were *not* the same, which happens to be 16 (18 – 2). Therefore, N now becomes 16 (N = 16).

2. She counts the number of pluses and minuses and assigns the smaller number the X value. Therefore, there are 13 pluses and 3 minuses; X = 3.

3. Now that you have N = 16 and X = 3, you refer to the "sign table" that can be found in a statistics book. I have, however, included an abbreviated sign test set of values in Table 8-4 for your use in this chapter. Find in the table where the X value and the N value intersect. You'll note that the table shows a probability value of .011.

Table 8-4.

				X values			
N	**0**	**1**	**2**	**3**	**4**	**5**	**6**
5	.031	.188	.500	.812	9.69		
6	.016	.109	.344	.656	.891	.984	
7	.008	.062	.227	.500	.773	.938	.992
8	.004	.035	.145	.363	.637	.855	.965
9	.002	.020	.090	.254	.500	.746	.910
10	.001	.011	.055	.172	.377	.623	.828
11		.006	.033	.113	.274	.500	.726
12		.003	.019	.073	.194	.387	.613
13		.002	.011	.046	.133	.291	.500
14		.001	.006	.029	.090	.212	.395
15			.004	.018	.59	.151	.304
16			.002	.011	.038	.105	.227
17			.001	.006	.025	.072	.166
18				.004	.015	.048	.119
19				.002	.010	.031	.084
20				.001	.006	.021	.058

Abbreviated Table for the Sign Test

How do we interpret this value? We learned earlier that in education the generally accepted level of significance is .05; that is, only a 5 % chance error factor. For the sign test, the minimum level of significance is .10, which means that a less stringent level of significance is used. To find a significant difference between the two sets of scores, the number found on the table must be lower than .10. Since .011 *is* lower than .10, we can therefore reject the null hypothesis that no difference would be found between the pretest and posttest scores. We may conclude, then, that the use of classroom newspapers to encourage students to read more books was a more effective approach than the star method.

As a general rule, one-group pretest and posttest designs use the sign test. The weakness of this design, of course, is that there is no control group. However, the sign test does provide the educational leader with empirical data to help make a good educational decision.

Before proceeding with the remainder of the chapter, complete the following exercise to help reinforce some of the ideas expressed above.

Exercise

1. Describe a situation in which you, as an educational leader, would use the sign test. Create a scenario and provide dummy data. Apply the test and determine whether significant differences are found.

    _____

    _____

    _____

    Answers will vary

The Mann-Whitney U-Test

A second type of statistical test commonly used in action research is known as the Mann-Whitney U-test. The Mann-Whitney U-test can be used to analyze results for small groups of students (under 15 per group) when two groups are formed by (a) dividing one class into two groups using the matched pairs technique described earlier, or (b) comparing two separate groups (e.g., two sections of a math class in high school).

The Mann-Whitney U-test is used for small groups and operates not unlike a t-test. The t-test is preferable for groups larger than 15 students per group.

Let's examine how a Mann-Whitney U-test might work (Willerman et al., 1991):

Let's say you'd like to assist a teacher to assess the effect of computer-assisted instruction on mathematical computation skills among third graders. You would suggest that the teacher follow these steps:

1. Administer a pretest, and with the results divide the class into two groups using matched pairs.

2. One group would be allowed to use computers to assist them in computational work (the experimental group), while the other group would learn computation the traditional way without the use of computer-assisted instruction (the control group). (A null hypothesis could be framed that there will be no difference between the two groups). To avoid **confounding factors**—which cause erroneous conclusions to be drawn—you might want the latter group to have equal access to computers, but do not assist them in mathematical computations. You might allow them to use computer-assisted instruction to enhance vocabulary development, for example.

3. At the end of a given period of time (e.g., 2 months), a posttest is administered to both groups and scores are ranked.

Figure 8-3 indicates that the first group consists of 9 students ($N = 9$) and the second group consists of 12 students ($N = 12$).

Control and Experimental Group Test Scores and Rank Order for a Mann-Whitney U-Test						
Control			**Experimental**		
Student	**Score**	**Rank**	**Student**	**Score**	**Rank**
Fran	87	11.5	Al	98	20
Bob	72	4	Paul	93	15
Tania	65	2	Margie	76	6.5
Jerry	54	1	Stacey	88	13
Ralph	67	3	Allison	96	18
Renaldo	73	5	Melissa	90	14
Ro	78	8.5	Candida	87	11.5
Vivian	82	10	Mark	76	6.5
Sharon	95	17	Cary	94	16
			Helen	99	21
			James	97	19
			Noreen	78	8.5

Figure 8-3.

Considering both groups together, the lowest score achieved regardless of group would receive a 1. The second lowest score receives a 2, and so on. Jerry, with a score of 54, has the lowest score of either group and therefore is awarded a rank of 1. Tania has the second lowest score and thus is awarded the rank of 2.

In the event of a tie, as occurs with Margie and Mark, you would compute their ranks as follows. Since one subject would have received a rank of 6 and the other a 7 if their scores had not been the same, you add 6 plus 7 and divide by 2 (the number of subjects involved). Therefore, $6 + 7 = 13$; $13 + 2 = 6.5$. Margie and Mark are each awarded a rank of 6.5. If three scores were to be tied, then you would add them together and divide by 3 to attain the rank score for each subject.

Try to complete the table by ranking the other scores and check your answers with Figure 8-3.

Now the Mann-Whitney U-test can be calculated as follows.

Step 1. Once scores have been ranked, multiply the number of subjects in the control group by the number of subjects in the experimental group. Thus $9 \times 12 = 108$.

Step 2. Calculate the U1 and U2 with the following formula:

$$U1 = N1\ N2 + \frac{N1\ (N1 + 1)}{2} - R1$$

$$U2 = N1\ N2 + \frac{N2\ (N2 + 1)}{2} - R1$$

Key:
N1 = number of subjects in control group
N2 = number of subjects in experimental group
R1 = sum of ranks for control group
R2 = sum of ranks for experimental group

Try it on your own using a calculator. Now that you have attained U1 and U2 values, you are ready to check the "Table of U-Values." U1 should equal 91 and U2 should equal 17. You should consult a U-value table, which can be found in many statistics books. I have, however, included an abbreviated U-value table in Table 8-5 for your use in this chapter. Select the smaller U-value to estimate the level of significance. If the value of the table is *larger* than the lower U-value, then the groups are statistically significant.

Look where 9 and 12 intersect on the table. You'll notice two points identified on the chart. The 26 is the lower limit and the 82 is the upper limit. Now you notice that our U1, which was 91, falls above the upper limit on the table, whereas the U2, which was 17, falls below the lower limit. Because we are looking at the lower U-value (U2 in this case) and because the values on the

Table 8-5.

	1	2	3	4	5	6	7	8	9	10	11	12	13
1													
2								0/16	0/18	0/20	0/22	1/23	1/25
3					0/15	1/17	1/20	2/22	2/25	3/27	3/30	4/32	4/35
4				0/16	1/19	2/22	3/25	4/28	4/32	5/35	6/38	7/41	8/44
5			0/15	1/19	2/23	3/27	5/30	6/34	7/38	8/42	9/46	11/49	12/53
6			1/17	2/22	3/27	5/31	6/36	8/40	10/64	11/49	13/53	14/58	16/62
7			1/20	3/25	5/30	6/36	8/41	10/46	12/50	14/56	16/61	18/66	20/71
8		0/16	2/22	4/28	6/34	8/40	10/46	12/51	15/57	17/62	19/69	22/74	24/80
9		0/18	2/25	4/32	7/38	10/44	12/51	15/57	17/64	20/70	23/76	26/82	28/89
10		0/20	3/27	5/35	8/42	11/49	14/56	17/63	20/70	23/77	26/84	29/91	32/97

Abbreviated U-Table for the Mann-Whitney U-Test

table (26 and 82) are larger than U2, we conclude that there is a significant difference between the posttest scores of both groups. We therefore reject the null hypothesis and conclude that computer-assisted instruction had a significant effect on pupil achievement in mathematical computational skills.

Before proceeding to the next chapter, complete the following exercise to help reinforce some of the ideas expressed above.

Exercise

1. When would you employ a Mann-Whitney U-Test?

    a. in collaborative planning

    b. assessing posttest results in a quasi-experimental study

    c. assessing posttest results in a single measurement design

    d. when randomization is impossible

Answer: b

The Chi Square and Other
User-Friendly Statistics

A third common statistic, the chi square (pronounced *kiy*-square and represented by X^2) is used for nominal data. Nominal data refer to categories such as gender, ethnicity, and socioeconomic status. Any study that uses nominal data is analyzed using the chi square statistic.

Let's say you are a principal of a high school and want to know if there's a relationship between gender and teacher morale in the school. You would use the X^2 to determine, for instance, whether low morale is more closely associated with male teachers or female teachers.

We will not outline the steps for calculating a chi square but will only mention that such calculations can easily be conducted using statistical programs such as STATPAK. More important is to know when to use each statistic. A summary of relevant and friendly statistics will conclude this section.

Aside from the use of means, standard deviations, sign tests, t-tests, and Mann-Whitney U-tests, which have previously been explained, only four other statistics are likely to be used by action researchers: the Spearman Rho, Pearson r Correlation Coefficient, Analysis of Variance, and Analysis of Covariance.

The Spearman Rho (also known as Rank Correlation) shows the degree of relationship between two sets of scores collected from the same group. According to Willerman et al. (1991), "the Spearman Rho correlation is useful to teachers who do action research because it can be used with groups that have small numbers of subjects and with data that are in either interval or ordinal form" (p. 139).

The Pearson Product Moment Correlation Coefficient (better known as simply the Pearson r) is a common statistic used to correlate two variables. In other words, the Pearson r would be used to determine the degree of relationship between two variables, such as science test scores with math test scores.

Suppose you wanted to correlate (i.e., examine the relationship) between two variables such as teachers' attitudes toward supervision and years of teaching experience. You might have hypothesized that teachers with more years of experience have less favorable views toward supervision. Yet a correlational study or analysis of these two variables might indicate no significant relationship or correlation. If that were so, you might find a .15 correlation coefficient.

Correlation coefficients are expressed from +1.00, which indicates a perfect correlation between two variables, to −1.00, which indicates a perfect negative correlation between two variables. A 1.00 coefficient indicates that as one variable increases, the other increases proportionally. The most common statistic used to calculate correlation is the Pearson r (i.e., coefficients of correlation are also expressed by the symbol *r*). Another statistic, used with ranked data, is the rank order correlation coefficient (called *rho*), but it can be computed through computer analysis.

Correlation is *not* causation. A relationship between two variables does not necessarily mean that a cause-and-effect relationship exists. Research may indicate a strong correlation (i.e., relationship) between teacher use of positive reinforcement and positive pupil behavior in the classroom. Praise, for instance, may be a potent force to mitigate misbehavior; however, one cannot conclude that praising a student will *cause* a positive change in behavior. Any experienced teacher will testify to the fact that effective use of praise doesn't always yield positive student behavior. For some students, praise is ineffective. Yet correlational studies do indicate a strong relationship, which supports the idea that teachers should learn how to effectively and judiciously use praise and other forms of positive reinforcement.

Correlational analyses usually involve one group and two variables (e.g., fourth-grade students' math scores and science achievement scores).

The **Analysis of Variance** (ANOVA, sometimes called the *F test*) is a statistical technique for determining whether significant differences can be found among the means of three or more groups.

Suppose you want to determine possible differences in social studies achievement among three separate groups of eighth graders taught by three different teachers using different methods of instruction. An ANOVA statistical test would be applied to determine whether a statistically significant difference in social studies achievement exists among the three different groups of students. This statistic operates not unlike the t-test. The ANOVA computes statistical differences for three or more groups, whereas the t-test, you may recall, works with only two groups. Though not frequently used in action research, the ANOVA can be effectively used under certain circumstances.

Another statistic, not commonly employed by action researchers, yet nevertheless valuable, is an **Analysis of Covariance** (ANCOVA). The ANCOVA is a statistical technique used in group comparison research when equivalence between the groups (usually only two in action research) cannot be ascertained.

Let's say you are comparing the achievement levels of two groups of seventh graders, one of which is treated with computer-assisted instruction. In group comparison research, posttest scores of both groups are compared to determine which group had higher achievement scores. (We don't measure growth between pretests and posttests, as was explained in chapter 3). Yet without assuring that both groups were initially comparable or equivalent (i.e., had somewhat equivalent achievement levels to begin with), you cannot draw any conclusions from posttest scores.

Why can't comparisons be made? Comparisons cannot be made because one group may have started with higher achievement levels than the other group. How, then, can anyone conclude that the treatment (i.e., computer-assisted instruction) had any effect on achievement? How do you know, for instance, that high achievement levels can be attributed to the treatment as opposed to the fact that the experimental group had higher achievement scores initially? Thus, such comparisons cannot be made.

The ANCOVA statistic can be used when you cannot ascertain group equivalence at the outset of a study. ANCOVA would be conducted with the posttest results of both groups. This statistical procedure takes the pretest scores and adjusts them statistically so that they can be treated identically.

You don't have to understand how this works mathematically or statistically. All you need to understand is that the ANCOVA statistic can be used when noncomparable (nonequivalent) groups are being studied.

The statistics mentioned above can easily be computed using STATPAK or any other computer program. Inputting data and following menu-driven instructions is all you have to do. Your professor or workshop leader will likely demonstrate the ease of using such software.

The following references are very useful in more fully explaining these statistics as well as providing easy-to-follow instructions for computations: Crowl, 1986, 1996; Fitz-Gibbon and Morris, 1987; Willerman et al., 1991. Crowl is especially useful, in that easy-to-follow step-by-step calculations are provided in his appendixes.

Complete the following exercise to help reinforce some of the ideas expressed above.

Exercise

1. Describe a study that you as an educational leader might undertake in which the chi square would be used to analyze data. Set up a scenario and provide dummy data. Apply the test and determine whether significant differences are found.

    _____

    _____

    _____

    Answers will vary

References

Crowl, T. K. (1986). *Fundamentals of research: A practical guide for educators and special educators.* Columbus, OH: Publishing Horizons.

Crowl, T. K. (1996). *Fundamentals of educational research* (2nd ed.). Madison, WI: Brown & Benchmark.

Davis, O. L., Jr. (1996). Some brambles and briars and snares in the paths of research and its reports. *Journal of Curriculum and Supervision, 11,* 295–298.

Fitz-Gibbon, C. T., & Morris, L. L. (1987). *How to analyze data.* Newbury Park, CA: Sage.

Frisbie, L. H. (1992). *STATPAK: Some common educational statistics.* [Computer software]. Columbus, OH: Merrill.

Gay, L. R. (1996). *Educational research: Competencies for analysis and application* (5th ed.). Englewood Cliffs, NJ: Prentice-Hall.

Willerman, M., McNeely, S. L., & Koffman, E. C. (1991). *Teachers helping teachers: Peer observation and assistance.* New York: Praeger.

Activity 10. Quantitative Data Analysis Worksheet

1. What is the purpose of analyzing the data I collected? (Use additional paper to record your responses if necessary.) _____

   _____

2. Will I use both quantitative and qualitative analyses? _____

   _____

3. Which computer program will I use to analyze my data? _____

4. Who will be responsible for analyzing and presenting the data? _____

5. What tables and/or figures might I develop to summarize my data? _____

   _____

6. Statistical and Non-statistical Analyses:

   ## QUANTITATIVE

   ____ Descriptive statistics
   ____ mean   ____ standard deviation   ____ percentage   ____ correlation coefficient

   ____ Inferential statistics
   ____ t-tests   ____ sign tests   ____ Mann-Whitney U-tests   ____ chi square
   ____ Spearman Rho   ____ Pearson r   ____ ANOVA   ____ ANCOVA   ____ other

Cut here

How to
Analyze Qualitative
Data Easily

Focus Questions

1. Why aren't statistics necessary to analyze qualitative data?

2. How do you think results from open-ended questionnaires can best be analyzed?

3. How do you think you might analyze data collected in notation form?

4. Why is qualitative research acceptable today as a form of research?

Analyses of qualitative data differ from analyses of quantitative data. Data analysis, as was explained, is the process of bringing structure and meaning to the mass of data collected. Qualitative research, relying on extensive field notes, yields a bulk of data that is not easily analyzed. Analyzing such data, especially for practicing educators, can be time-consuming and arduous, albeit at times fascinating and creative. Whereas analysis of quantitative data is straightforward, logical, and statistical, analysis of qualitative data is often complex and not readily convertible into standard measurable units.

In addition, whereas quantitative analyses are conducted at the end of a study, qualitative analyses are ongoing; that is, they may occur while data are still being collected. Moreover, qualitative analyses tend to be somewhat eclectic in that there is no one "right way" or preestablished criteria to follow. Data analysis "requires that the researcher be comfortable with developing categories and making comparisons and contrasts" (Creswell, 1994, p. 153). Creswell delineates several guiding principles, however, when undertaking qualitative data analysis.

Simultaneity. In contrast with quantitative data analyses, qualitative data may be analyzed simultaneously with data collection. As you interview various people, for instance, certain phrases or themes may be readily apparent. Making note of these phrases or themes, as you continue data collection, will aid thematic development in subsequent interviews. A summary chart (Activity 11) at the end of this chapter can be used to record such data.

Decontextualization or reduction. These terms refer to the qualitative researcher taking the voluminous data collected and reducing them to patterns, categories, or themes. Reduction is often accomplished by a procedure known as coding. Coding involves attaching meaning to a particular scene, document, or event. For example, in viewing different types of leaders in films, one may categorize the different leaders by style by first coding each leader with a given leadership style.

Content analysis, a process that makes decontextualization or reduction possible, is a method of data analysis in which you analyze the content in a given document according to prescribed categories or criteria while following explicit rules of coding. When you conduct content analysis of any document, categories should emerge naturally based on your analysis rather than using the analysis to verify preexisting categories. As you peruse the data in a document, you would identify key words to create research categories. Krippendorf (1981) reports that content analysis allows for making inferences from the data context using the procedure above.

Let's say you wanted to investigate whether principals are favorably depicted in popular culture (e.g., television and film). You would first obtain several television shows and movies for viewing. You would then identify several categories that would guide your viewing. These categories would depend on the purposes of your research. Let's say you were interested in understanding the different ways principals are depicted in these forms of popular culture. You could identify the following three categories: (a) favorable scenes about principals, (b) unfavorable or unflattering scenes, and (c) neutral scenes. As you watch these shows and movies, you would describe each scene thoroughly and might even transcribe dialogues. You would then classify each scene into one of the aforementioned categories. Frequencies of scenes in each of the three categories are tabulated, and on the basis of content analysis you would arrive at a conclusion about the way principals are depicted in the television shows and films you watched.

Content analysis, then, is a method of analyzing data through a process of categorization. How might you use content analysis to analyze data?

Grounded theory. This refers to the comparison of collected data to extant theory or literature in search of a pattern or theme. Themes emerge as a consequence of collecting data. One should not develop a theme and then look for data to confirm one's expectations (Strauss & Corbin, 1990).

Analytic Procedures

Appendix B provides a sample write-up of qualitative research.

Let's apply the principles explained above by reviewing the main analytic procedures used in qualitative studies. Drawing from the work of Marshall and Rossman (1999), we can see that analytic procedures essentially fall into three categories.

Organizing the Data. Accumulate your data collection types (e.g., observations, interviews, documents, and audiovisual materials) and read and reread all the data. Make notes of anything that strikes you as significant or unusual. You should also make a list of all the main topics you have covered and may begin to cluster together similar topics. Major topics and subtopics may emerge. This stage familiarizes you with all the data you have collected. Computer analysis, as will be described below, may be helpful at this initial stage.

Generating Categories, Themes, and Patterns. This phase of data analysis can be most cumbersome yet interesting. Often simply scanning the data several times will result in some emerging pattern or theme. Feel free to make educated guesses or hunches at this stage.

Developing coding categories occurs at this stage. Our discussion of decontextualization or reduction above comes into play at this phase. Coding systems enable you to see themes emerge from the data. You can choose from a "family of codes" (Anderson, Herr, & Nihlen, 1994; Bogdan & Biklen, 1997). I will introduce four of these codes. Further discussion of these codes can be found in the previous citations.

1. Perspectives codes include codes of ideas or perspectives held by individuals (e.g., liberal or conservative views).

2. Activity codes include codes that demonstrate a regularly occurring behavior (e.g., smoking, cutting class, or attending faculty meetings).

3. Event codes include codes that occur infrequently or only once (e.g., a teacher's strike or a teacher's dismissal).

[handwritten: Class meeting time to]
[handwritten: observe behavi...]

4.0 Strategy codes include codes that refer to methods and techniques that people use to accomplish various things (e.g., behavior management strategies or various instructional strategies).

Working data into codes is an especially laborious process that, to be honest, educational leaders as action researchers are not likely to attempt with as much rigor as someone undertaking a doctoral research project. For more detailed information, consult Wiersma (1999).

[handwritten: understandable to code to present the survey]

Testing Emergent Hypotheses. As categories or themes begin to emerge you will want to initiate the process of framing some sort of hypothesis in order to determine whether or not the theme or category is consistent with the data. What kinds of questions can you pose to verify that the theme you selected is indeed inclusive of most, if not all, of your data?

As themes emerge and are verified, separating each one onto index cards, into folders, or into a data base is a matter left to the discretion of the researcher. Themes, at this point, can be compared to extant theory. Let's say bureaucratic themes have emerged in your study of the way district office supervisors relate to school personnel. That is, a consistent pattern emerges in a particular district in which district office supervisors, by and large, do not relate to teachers in professional, collaborative ways, but rather are officious, aloof, and bureaucratic. You might review the literature to determine whether this observation or theme that has emerged from your data is representative of the way most district office personnel relate to school faculty. In other words, does the literature support your findings? This inductive process of collecting data, developing a theme, and comparing the theme to extant literature is known as *grounded theory.* That is, your findings are "grounded" in real and verifiable data you have collected. You did not develop some theme and then look for data to support it. I should add that, at times, referring to literature as you collect data in an attempt to discover a theme is also an accepted practice in qualitative research.

An application: Imagine that you have collected data on the attitudes of parents and teachers toward inclusion. The qualitative data collection types include observations, interviews, documents (minutes of teacher-parent council meetings), and audiovisual materials (photographs and videotapes of students in inclusive settings). How might you incorporate the data analysis procedures described above?

There are many different and personalized ways to analyze qualitative data. The first step you might take is to separate the written data into three groups: *observation data, interview data,* and *document data.* A fourth group would include the *visual data* from the photographs and videotapes. You would then read and view all the data. As you do so for each group, you would make both mental and written notes highlighting interesting and possibly significant pieces of information or even obvious emerging patterns. This might include underlining key words, phrases, or sentences in text or even color coding different pieces of data. Any logical and workable method can be applied. Whether you use index cards, folders, or a laptop is a matter of personal preference.

Analytic procedures can also be applied during, and not only after, data collection. The purpose of this initial stage in data analysis is to take all the data that have been collected and organize and separate them into workable units. *[handwritten: assign a code.]*

Remember: The goal of analysis is to discover patterns, ideas, explanations, and understandings. *[handwritten: less than + − etc]*

Once you are familiar with the data and have taken preliminary notes that identify key words, phrases, or events that seem relevant, you are ready to generate categories or themes that might emerge from the data. For each group, you would select appropriate codes that highlight appropriate information and better organize the data. Use of codes and subcodes would be in order. For example, from the interview data a major code might be "Friendships," and subcodes might include "with other included students" or "with paraprofessionals." The idea is that a particular interview reveals that included students have developed friendships with other students and paraprofessionals in the inclusive classroom. Each interview might have many different codes and subcodes. If a qualitative researcher has interviewed five individuals, then several pages of coded data might be taken. This procedure would be followed for each data group. How do you think coding might work for videotaped data?

Once a category or theme emerges, such as "teachers' resistance to inclusion," or competing themes emerge, such as "teachers against inclusion, but parents for inclusion," the researcher might review the themes and compare them to extant literature or theory in order to uncover a general theoretical framework that would explain the data—a grounded theory.

A brief word about the credibility of qualitative data analysis is in order. Triangulation enhances the credibility of qualitative data analysis. The use of various data collection instruments and the comparison of emerging themes in one data collection instrument to other instruments greatly contributes to the credibility of the analysis. If the pattern, for example, emerges consistently in the videotaped data as well as in interviews, observations, and documents, then the trustworthiness of the analytic procedures is apparent. Reliability and validity of qualitative data also contribute to its credibility. How do you think reliability and validity of qualitative data is achieved? How does the concept of grounded theory contribute to internal validity?

Computer Applications

Qualitative analyses are enhanced by state-of-the-art computer applications. Software programs are available to sift through qualitative data (e.g., "thick descriptions" from field notes) to locate specified words and phrases, create indexes, attach codes to various parts of the text, and develop categories. The possibilities of computerized data analysis for qualitative research are currently being considered (Fielding & Lee, 1991; Weitzman & Miles, 1995),

General and useful programs include word processors, data base managers, spreadsheets, and text retrievers. Word processors are designed for production and revision of text and are thus useful for taking, writing, and editing field notes. Most of you are already familiar with the advantages of a word processor. How might a word processor help in data analysis of qualitative material? At what phase or phases of data analysis would a word processor come in handy?

A data base program can input text data according to a structured format. Let's say you wanted to use a data base program to keep track of interview data. You could set up a data base that records and keeps files of each interview subdivided into important pieces of information including name of interviewee, date of transcription, time of interview, and other information. Retrieval of various files aids in data analysis.

A spreadsheet program, although established for accounting purposes, can be used to create tables. A spreadsheet allows you to record information in each vertical column and in each horizontal row. Keeping track of your research project will be easier using a spreadsheet. Think of two specific ways a spreadsheet may help in analyzing data.

A text retriever is a sophisticated text search program that allows you to locate all instances of words, phrases, and combinations of phrases in one or more files. How might a text retriever assist in data analysis?

Tables, Graphs, and Charts

Whether you employ quantitative and/or qualitative analyses, using tables and graphs whenever possible to summarize your findings will not only better facilitate data interpretation (see next chapter), it will also serve as a way to display data after analysis, creating as an easy, convenient, and visual way to report your data to others. "A picture [i.e., table or graph] is worth a thousand words." Use your imagination to devise tables and/or figures to summarize your findings. A sample table, graph, and chart are included to demonstrate how data can be displayed visually.

Table 9-1 illustrates how data can be presented in a table. This table indicates that two groups were comparable at the start of the project. How do we know this?

The means and a t-test (t = .19) did not indicate a significant difference. Yet after the administration of the posttest, presumably months later, a significant difference between both groups was apparent (t = 8.69). Therefore, the original hypothesis ("failing sixth-grade math students who participate in the afterschool tutorial programs will have higher math scores than failing math students who do not participate in the afterschool math tutorial programs") was supported.

See Figure 9-1 for a sample graph. Graph your data whenever possible.

Table 9-1.

<table>
<tr><td colspan="4">Means, Standard Deviations, and t-Tests for the Experimental and Control Groups for Reading Comprehension Scores</td></tr>
<tr><td></td><td colspan="3">Group</td></tr>
<tr><td>Test</td><td>Experimental</td><td>Control</td><td>t</td></tr>
<tr><td>*(Pretest)*</td><td></td><td></td><td></td></tr>
<tr><td>*M*</td><td>*24.10*</td><td>*23.90*</td><td>*.19**</td></tr>
<tr><td>*S.D.*</td><td>*2.93*</td><td>*3.59*</td><td></td></tr>
<tr><td>*(Posttest)*</td><td></td><td></td><td></td></tr>
<tr><td>*M*</td><td>*40.90*</td><td>*31.60*</td><td>*8.69**</td></tr>
<tr><td>*S.D.*</td><td>*2.80*</td><td>*3.88*</td><td></td></tr>
<tr><td colspan="4">* $p > .05$ **$p < .05$</td></tr>
</table>

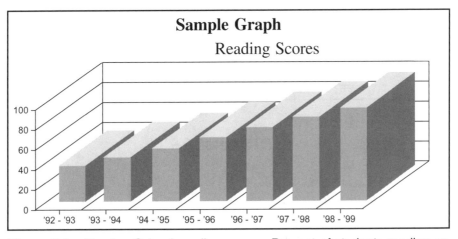

Sample Graph
Reading Scores

Figure 9-1. Bradley School reading scores. Percent of students reading on grade level in the fourth grade from 1993 to 1999.

When analyzing qualitative data, I recommend charting data collection techniques with key findings, shown in Table 9-2.

Table 9-2.

Data collection technique	Key findings
Questionnaire	58% of parents dislike idea of inclusion.
Interview	Teacher X: "I don't think inclusion will work."
School Profile	Test scores indicate...
Multimedia	Videotapes demonstrate...

Before proceeding to the next chapter, complete the following exercise to help reinforce some of the ideas expressed above.

Exercise

1. *What is the purpose of analyzing the data I collected? (Use additional paper to record your response if necessary.)* _____

    _____

2. *Will I use both quantitative and qualitative analyses?* _____

    _____

3. *Which computer program will I use to analyze my data?* _____

4. *Who will be responsible for analyzing and presenting the data?* _____

5. *What tables and/or figures might I develop to summarize my data?* _____

    _____

References

Anderson, G. L., Herr, K., & Nihlen, A. S. (1994). *Studying your own school: An educator's guide to qualitative practitioner research.* Thousand Oaks, CA: Corwin Press.

Bogdan, R. C., & Biklen, S. K. (1997). *Qualitative research for education: An introduction to theory and methods* (3rd ed.). Boston: Allyn & Bacon.

Creswell, J. W. (1994). *Research design: Qualitative and quantitative approaches.* Thousand Oaks, CA: Sage.

Crowl, T. K. (1986). *Fundamentals of research: A practical guide for educators and special educators.* Columbus, OH: Publishing Horizons.

Crowl, T. K. (1996). *Fundamentals of educational research* (2nd ed.). Madison, WI: Brown & Benchmark.

Davis, O. L., Jr. (1996). Some brambles and briars and snares in the paths of research and its reports. *Journal of Curriculum and Supervision, 11,* 295–298.

Fielding, N. G., & Lee, R. M. (1991). *Using computers in qualitative research.* Newbury Park, CA: Sage.

Fink, A. (1995). *How to analyze data.* Thousand Oaks, CA: Sage.

Fitz-Gibbon, C. T., & Morris, L. L. (1987). *How to analyze data.* Newbury Park, CA: Sage.

Frisbie, L. H. (1992). *STATPAK: Some common educational statistics.* [Computer software]. Columbus, OH: Merrill.

Gay, L. R. (1996). *Educational research: Competencies for analysis and application* (5th ed.). Englewood Cliffs, NJ: Prentice Hall.

Kriapp, T. P. (1996). *Learning statistics through playing cards.* Thousand Oaks, CA: Sage.

Krippendorf, K. (1981). *Content analysis: An introduction to its methodology.* Beverly Hills, CA: Sage.

Marshall, C., & Rossman, G. B. (1999). *Designing qualitative research* (3rd ed.). Newbury Park, CA: Sage.

Sharan, S., & Shachar, H. (1988). *Language in the cooperative classroom.* New York: Springer-Verlag.

Strauss, A., & Corbin, J. (1990). *Grounded theory: Basics of qualitative research.* Newbury Park, CA: Sage.

Weitzman, E. A., & Miles, M. B. (1995). *Computer programs for qualitative data analysis.* Thousand Oaks, CA: Sage.

Wiersma, W. (1999). *Research methods in education: An introduction* (7th ed). Boston: Allyn & Bacon.

Willerman, M., McNeely, S. L., & Koffman, E. C. (1991). *Teachers helping teachers: Peer observation and assistance.* New York: Praeger.

Activity 11. Qualitative Data Analysis Worksheet

The following activity worksheet allows you to easily analyze your data. This worksheet is meant to allow you to brainstorm different ideas. Changes in your plan can always be made at a later date. This worksheet serves as a review of the ideas discussed in this chapter.

QUALITATIVE

Organizing the data: _____

_____

_____

Codes for data: _____

_____

_____

Themes that emerge from my data (make certain to note which instrument you are using, e.g., interview, observation, focus group, questionnaire): _____

_____

_____

How do these themes that emerged relate to the extant literature or theory? _____

_____

Computer analyses: _____

_____

_____

Other ideas? _____

_____

_____

Putting It All Together: What Does It Mean?

Focus Questions

1. What is the next important step after you have analyzed data? Explain.

2. How do you best develop conclusions for your study?

3. Under what circumstances would you have to write a formal report of your action research project?

4. What is the best way to most simply report your findings?

Be modest in reporting action research. We live in a time when exaggerated claims for educational accomplishment are almost the norm....Education is not yet a science and may never be, given the differences in individual human behavior: There is very little about education that we can claim with certainty. Action research continues to be promising, but we must be aware of its limitations as well as its possibilities.

—Foshay, 1994

Interpreting Data

Having collected and analyzed your data, you are ready to reach certain conclusions so that you can take some action. The graphs and figures you've accumulated merely present the data in visual form but do not indicate how this data is to be used or interpreted. The fact that you have found, for example, statistically significant results regarding a particular treatment does not necessarily mean that a change in educational programming is inevitable. There is a distinction between statistical significance and educational significance. A .05 statistical difference may not necessarily warrant implementation of a new textbook series, because other factors may need to be considered before investing money and expending additional efforts. What other factors may possibly influence your decision to adopt or discard the new textbook series?

Maybe some data collected qualitatively indicate that teachers find the teacher's editions complicated and not very useful. Perhaps parents complain that the textbook doesn't represent the cultural diversity of the community. Perhaps the cost of the textbook series is prohibitive. Despite statistically significant findings that the experimental group, who used the new textbook series, increased reading comprehension levels, adoption of the series may be precluded by other factors. Obviously, then, the decision to adopt or not adopt the textbook series depends on a variety of factors. Interpretation of data must be viewed as a decision-making process that includes these many possible factors.

How, then, does one decide whether to adopt or discard the new textbook series? In other words, how can we best interpret our data to make informed decisions about the instructional program in our school?

Ultimately, interpreting data must be based on those decisions that are likely to help achieve your goals and objectives. What do you eventually hope to accomplish? Will this program, product, or procedure move you closer to your goals? What evidence exists that this program, product, or procedure is effective? Is this evidence overwhelming, or are there conflicting findings? (One of my mentors once quipped: "If in doubt, do without!"). Reflecting on these and similar questions will assist in appropriately interpreting data from your study.

I have found that establishing a steering committee in charge of interpreting data is quite helpful. The steering committee is provided with relevant data summaries that they can peruse and discuss. After a certain amount of time, the committee makes recommendations for your consideration. In **collaborative action research** projects, the steering committee actually decides on the efficacy of a given program or practice.

Another strategy for interpreting data is to use prespecified standards. You would chart expected results for each data collection instrument employed and note the extent to which the standard is met. Conclusions are then drawn, and final decisions are made based on those conclusions. For an excellent guide to interpreting data, see chapter 5 in Herman and Winters, 1992. Table 10-1 has been adapted from the aforementioned work.

Table 10-1.

Using Prespecified Standards to Interpret Data

Instrument	Standard	Percentage Meeting	Conclusion
Science Aptitude Test	*50% above 50th percentile*	*61% above 50th percentile*	*Above goal; success*
Problem-solving science question	*At least 50% scoring "acceptable" or above*	*37% last year; 52% scored acceptable, but only 20% for girls*	*Met goal overall but examine achievement for girls*
Portfolios	*Average rating: 4 out of 6*	*20% were rated 4 out of 6 or higher*	*Problem here; let's examine*
Parent survey	*At least 80% registered satisfaction with new program*	*90% approval rate*	*Met goal; success*

You'll notice that Table 10-1 displays data and compares results with prespecified standards for an elementary school science program. The table demonstrates various instruments, standards established, percentages met, and appropriate conclusions that can be drawn. Your perusal of the table will allow you to interpret results fairly easily. Multiple indicators should always guide your decision making.

A cautionary, albeit parenthetical, note should be made about the interpretation of test scores. Test scores are still the most frequently used data source in many schools. Misinterpretations of test scores are too common. Although test score interpretation goes beyond the purview of this text, pointing out a few general cautions that apply to the interpretation of any test score is in order (for more detailed information consult, e.g., Gronlund & Linn, 1990).

A test score should be interpreted in terms of the specific test from which it was derived. In other words, look beyond the test title to evaluate a pupil's performance in terms of what the test actually measures. For example, one type of achievement test may measure a pupil's ability to compute mathematical problems, yet another achievement test may measure problem-solving ability. To use, for instance, the former test and then conclude that the pupil needs remedial assistance in mathematics may be an inaccurate generalization. The evidence more accurately indicates that the pupil may need help in computational skills but that his or her ability to problem-solve may, in fact, be satisfactory.

A test score should be interpreted in light of all the pupil's relevant characteristics. In other words, consider such factors as motivational level, physical health, and any disability that may impair performance. Test performance may be affected by these and other factors.

A test score should be interpreted according to the type of decision to be made. Attempting to predict, for example, a pupil's success in college from a criterion-referenced test is not justified when norm-referenced tests more accurately provide such information. Remember to match the test score to the type of decision that needs to be made.

A test score should not be interpreted as a specific value. A grade equivalent score of 5.3, for instance, doesn't indicate that a pupil is exactly one month ahead in reading of a pupil who scores 5.2. These scores, as well as other types of scores, should be considered as merely small differences and not significant in and of themselves. To make a decision about a pupil's performance based on a specific value will lead to erroneous conclusions.

A test score should be considered along with other supplementary evidence. A decision about a pupil's academic performance should involve a variety of data sources. Relying solely on test score information is shortsighted and will lead to erroneous conclusions. Triangulation of data sources is essential for judicious data interpretation.

Using prespecified standards to interpret data may fit nicely with quantitative data, but how do we interpret qualitative data? As with data analysis, interpretation of qualitative research is different than for the quantitative approach. Although generalizations can usually be drawn from quantitative research (but not all quantitative approaches lend themselves to generalization; see chapter 4), no generalizations may be made for qualitative findings, due mainly to the small samples that are used. Conclusions that are drawn from qualitative studies are tentative and speculative and must be viewed within a unique context. In other words, findings from an ethnographic study might be applicable to the particular school under study but may not be applied to all similar schools.

Because a triangulated approach to research has been advocated in this book, findings from both quantitative and qualitative studies should be carefully examined. Overall results from quantitative studies might yield numerical or statistical evidence to support the use, for example, of a particular textbook series, but qualitative findings that present detailed insights into "how" these books are being used on a daily basis might add some important information as well.

It is not a matter of deciding that one approach yields more reliable findings than another. Rather, the cumulative effect of both approaches or methodologies provides the best insight into whether a district or a school should expend thousands of dollars to adopt the textbook series. Sometimes quantitative and qualitative findings support similar conclusions, and sometimes they support different ones. Ultimately you, as the action researcher, will have to decide (perhaps along with your steering committee) what the weight of evidence suggests. The important point is that employing a mixed methodology (both quantitative and qualitative approaches), when feasible, is the best way to conduct research.

Reporting Data

Too often, little attention is paid to reporting data in a clear, cogent manner. This lack of attention to reporting your findings doesn't make sense, considering all the time and energy you have expended. I'm not suggesting that formal written reports are always necessary. In fact, most action research studies will not necessarily need a formal follow-up report. Nevertheless, reporting and documenting findings in some way is highly recommended.

Informal reports may take the form of reviews of findings to parents at local PTA meetings or to faculty at faculty conferences. Informal reports may be distributed to faculty, staff, and parents through a one- or two-page summary of the study, along with findings and recommendations.

At times, however, a formal report may be required. If the superintendent has charged you with the responsibility of evaluating the district's gifted program, you will likely have to submit a formal written report. In my courses, I always require my students to submit a formal summative evaluation report of their action research projects. Such report writing is good practice and also serves to summarize one's project in a disciplined way.

For some useful advice about creating effective reports, see Table 10-2, which has been excerpted from Herman and Winters (1992).

For those of you undertaking a master's degree action research project (thesis), the method of reporting your findings will be prescribed by your professor and/or department. See chapter 11 for my suggested outline. The next several sections provide guidelines for reporting an action research study.

Table 10-2.

Hints for Creating Useful Reports

Both school principals and school board members say that a useful report

- *is brief*

- *contains narrative or explanatory information*

- *presents trends over time in graphic form to support conclusions*

- *has a technical appendix for those interested in more detail*

There are some differences in report content found useful by the two groups:

- *School-level administrators are most interested in the why and how of student outcomes. They seek information clarifying relationships between school policies, curriculum and instruction, and school outcomes.*

- *At the board level, not unexpectedly, the central concern is with the status of school performance and a description of progress rather than the nuts and bolts of planned improvements or reasons for performance.*

- *When you share information with school boards, there is a danger of presenting information at a level of detail and complexity that is not needed.*

Both audiences use and value qualitative information in decision making:

- *Written reports that include summaries of carefully conducted observations, interviews, or attitude surveys will provide powerful information for program improvement.*

- *Teachers, principals, and others form conclusions about school effectiveness and hypotheses about how programs succeed or fail based on impressions and experiences.*

- *A few well-selected anecdotes also can be a powerful device for communicating the meaning of your findings.*

- *Explanations of school results generated during the data interpretation process form yet another source of useful information for school-level decisions.*

- *Qualitative data form an important part of the decision making process; summaries of these data belong in written reports.*

Reprinted with permission, Sage Publications.

Writing the Research Report

The rest of this chapter is devoted to outlining the formal steps for writing a **research report,** the formal document that describes the study's methods, results, and conclusions. No single standard for report writing exists, but the following outline has proven helpful for beginning students to organize their thoughts and data.

Too often, students take courses on research, evaluation, and assessment without actually engaging in a project of some sort. Students who take courses that don't encourage application of research techniques may learn elements of research design and data analysis, but they are unlikely to internalize the lessons they have learned. According to constructivist theory, people learn best when they are given the opportunity to construct meaning on their own. I'm reminded of the story of the fellow who, when taking an undergraduate course in ornithology (the study of birds), was quite surprised by the way in which the professor conducted the course.

Students entered the large lecture hall expecting to learn about birds by visiting nearby forests and outdoor reserves. To their astonishment and dismay, the professor only lectured about the many of species of birds by reading from his notes, rarely looking up at the large, uninterested audience. Jerry, an otherwise studious undergraduate, soon became irritated by the way the professor conducted the class. After about 3 weeks of lecture, the professor began showing slides of birds. Although he was still lecturing, at least the students had some visual stimulation provided by these black and white photographs. Jerry remained silent and dutifully took copious notes.

About 3 weeks before the midterm exam, the professor announced that for the examination he would show them a particular bird and the students would have to identify the species. This infuriated Jerry and many of the other students. Nevertheless, they passively took notes. However, a week before the scheduled exam the professor declared, "I changed my mind. Instead of showing you the whole bird, I'm going to just show you its beak and leg." Then the professor continued his lecture.

Jerry could no longer contain himself. He rose from his seat in the rear of the auditorium and voiced his dissatisfaction: "I can't believe the way you've conducted this class. We entered the course expecting to learn about birds by actually going out into the field and observing. But no, all you do is lecture and show us outdated black-and-white photographs of birds. Then you decide to give us a ridiculous exam. To make matters worse," continued Jerry as his fellow students sat in a mild state of shock, displaying glimpses of delight, "you have the gall to change your mind and show us portions of the bird's anatomy!"

The professor, at this point, was red-faced and boldly retorted, "Young man, stand up and tell me your name, because you just failed this course!"

Jerry rose from his seat, turned sideways, pointed to his nose and, lifting his pants, pointed to his leg and said, "You figure it out!"

I tell my students that, unlike the way this professor conducted his course, I will indeed give them ample opportunity to apply concepts and theories learned in the course. To this end, I require my students to plan and conduct an action research project. I believe that Eleanor Duckworth (1986) said it best: "All people ever have is their own understanding; you can tell them all sorts of things, but you can't make them believe it unless they also construct it for themselves" (p. 495).

As part of their project requirement, the students must write a summative evaluation report. Although action research projects can be conducted without a formal report, sometimes you may have to report your findings to a larger audience (e.g., faculty, superintendent, and school board). Formal reports are often written for program evaluations. Chapter 11 details the steps to be taken in writing a formal paper for an action research project.

Although many acceptable formats exist, I recommend the format below for completing my course requirements. Students have commented that having these steps to follow makes their report writing much easier.

Overview of Steps for Writing Up an Action Research Project

These steps are general guidelines, with the understanding that individual needs may differ. In most circumstances, educational leaders will not have to write a formal report because action research is personal and ongoing. However, sometimes a report of some sort may be relevant to share information with the faculty or to report information to a principal, assistant superintendent, or school board. For a more formal presentation of ideas, see chapter 11. The information contained in this section is also useful for reviewing the steps that go into a successful action research project.

Let's first review the essential elements of an action research cycle and, in doing so, provide some suggestions and ideas for writing the report. Then we'll provide the structured steps to take in writing a report.

Step 1: Reflection

1. Think about your classroom, school, or district. What do you want to know that could help you do a better job?

2. Look around your classroom, school, or district. What activities, programs, or processes need scrutiny or investigation?

3. Talk with key school or district constituents. What are their concerns or the issues they would like addressed?

4. Examine the literature. What ideas emerge as you scan educational databases or literature?

5. Inspect what other schools or districts are up to. What ideas for school improvement can you glean from elsewhere?

When you write this part of the report, simply answer the questions above in any expository format or style that suits you. Be sure to include background information, such as your role in the action research project, the school or district, the members who might have assisted in the project, and any historical information that provides a backdrop to your current study. Remember that this is a "reflection" section, so the ideas you write about are free flowing and inquiry driven. They do not have to follow a prescribed format, as you might have to do when writing a formal report or a master's thesis (see chapter 11).

Step 2: Selection of a Focus

1. Identify a topic. What general topic or area do you want to investigate? (E.g., instructional strategies, school discipline, program assessment)

2. Specify a problem. What major problem or area of concern emerges from this topic that relates to your particular classroom, school, or district? (E.g., overuse of lecture as the primary mode in instructional delivery, lack of an assessment plan of the schoolwide reading program, inadequate use of technology in the classroom or for administrative use)

3. Justify the problem. What evidence exists that this problem is of concern? What strategies for solving the problem exist in the literature or in the world of practice?

4. Develop a purpose statement. How can you phrase the problem you identified into a statement that will guide your action research project? (E.g., "The purpose of this study will be to implement cooperative learning instructional strategies into science teaching in the eighth-grade classes.")

5. Articulate research questions that you want answered as a result of your action research study. Are the questions concise? Do they clearly state what you will examine? Are they measurable? (E.g., "Does the lack of training in instructional technology contribute to teachers' lack of use of technology in the classroom?" "What impact does professional development in technology have on the degree to which teachers incorporate computer technology in their lessons?" "What impact does computer-assisted instruction have on student achievement in reading comprehension at the fifth-grade level?")

When you write this part of the report, divide this step into five subsections: (a) topic, (b) problem, (c) justification, (d) purpose statement, and (e) research questions. Each section is concisely written in outline form.

Step 3: Reviewing the Literature

1. Locate relevant sources. Although action research projects do not involve extensive and comprehensive reviews of the literature as do master's degree projects, action researchers should scan databases and/or Web sites for background information on the topic and problem identified.

2. Select relevant sources. Gather those sources that relate directly to your project. Do they relate similar problems experienced by other educational leaders? Do they offer solutions to the problem?

3. Summarize relevant sources. Organize this literature so that the information can be used later.

Divide your literature review into three basic sections: an introduction (usually one paragraph that provides an overview of what will be included in the literature review); the body (usually divided into subsections, depending on the topic and the number of different ideas included); and the conclusion (usually one paragraph summarizing and drawing a conclusion based on the review of the literature).

Step 4: Developing a Research Action Plan

1. Examine a variety of research designs to determine which is best suited to your interests and situation (see chapters 3, 4, and 5). What sort of experiment can you conduct? What types of approaches to research make the most sense (qualitative and/or quantitative)?

2. Determine your sample. Who will participate in your study? How will they be selected?

3. Specify data collection methods. Will you collect data using a questionnaire or other type of survey? Will you administer some sort of test? What other data collection methods will be used? (See chapter 7.)

4. Outline a plan. Can you develop as detailed an outline as possible to serve as an overview of what you plan to do? Did you include dates, materials, and other items that will serve as guides?

5. Think about data analysis. How do you expect to analyze the data you will collect? (See chapters 8 and 9.)

6. Develop a chart that assists in data interpretation. What does the data say to help answer your research questions and develop a conclusion (i.e., a solution to the problem)?

When you write this part of the report, simply respond to the items above in any organized fashion that makes sense to you. Again, the format is not as important as the inclusion of the ideas.

Step 5: Taking Action and Developing New Questions

Develop an action plan. Based on the results of your study, what action do you plan to take? How can such a plan be most effectively implemented? What new questions arise?

When you write this part of the report, simply answer these questions in an expository fashion.

Elements of the Report

Title Page

Your title should be concise and accurately reflect the variables in your study. Here are five examples of titles for a project. Which ones are satisfactory titles? Which are not? Explain.

Title 1: The Effect of Computer-Assisted Instruction on the Learning of High School Students

Title 2: The Impact of Cooperative Learning on the Attitudes of Elementary School Students With Learning Disabilities in Science

Title 3: Implementing and Evaluating a Literature-Based Reading Series in Grade 7 in a Middle School

Title 4: Discovering New Ways to Teach English to Non-English-Speaking People

Title 5: Action Research Comes Alive in Randolph School District

Title 1 is weak because the word *effect* denotes an experimental study. Experimental studies are rarely used in action research projects. When they are used, the variables under study are clearly identified. Also, the word *learning* is nebulous and not defined.

Titles 2 and 3 are best. They are clearly phrased and specific enough to give the reader a precise idea of the content of the study.

Title 4 doesn't provide sufficient information about the study. Title 5 might be appropriate for the headline of an article in a local newspaper, but it doesn't suffice for the title of an action research study.

Therefore, develop a title that clearly specifies the variables under study and the relationship between them. Also, specify the sample clearly and accurately. Eliminate useless words such as "The Impact..." Just say, "Impact of..."

Brainstorm a title for your project and share it with a colleague for feedback.

Contents

Simply list the five steps of the action research cycle and associate page numbers for each.

Each of the five sections below are included in your report. Simply follow the directions above for completing each section. Brevity is essential. People who read your action research report will want the information presented as concisely as possible. Write in outline form, using bullets to highlight points, and chart your information to assist with readability and usefulness. Don't forget that this report is not meant as a college report or thesis but as a summary of your action research project for practitioners.

Reflection

Refer to discussion above.

Focus

Refer to discussion above.

Literature

Refer to discussion above.

Research Plan

Refer to discussion above.

Action Plan

Refer to discussion above.

References

Duckworth, E. (1986). Teaching as research. *Harvard Educational Review, 56* (4), 481–495.

Foshay, A. W. (1994). Action research: An early history in the United States. *Journal of Curriculum and Supervision, 9,* 317–325.

Gavlan, J. L. (2000). *Writing literature reviews.* Los Angeles: Pyrczak.

Gronlund, N. E., & Linn, R. L. (1990). *Measurement and evaluation in teaching* (6th ed.). New York: Macmillan.

*Herman, J. L., & Winters, L. (1992). *Tracking your school's success: A guide to sensible evaluation.* Newbury Park, CA: Corwin Press.

Activity 12. Reporting Action Research

Feel free to devise your own report based on your needs. Refer to the excerpted suggestions in Table 10-2. The following format is one that I find most useful and practical for action researchers in the field (for guidelines in writing an action research master's thesis, see chapter 11). Use this outline to jot down ideas or take notes as you begin to organize your thoughts and gather information.

TOPIC: _____

TITLE PAGE: _____

REFLECTION _____

_____

_____

_____

FOCUS _____

_____

_____

_____

LITERATURE _____

_____

_____

_____

RESEARCH PLAN _____

_____

_____

_____

ACTION PLAN _____

_____

_____

_____

Cut here

Completing Your
Action Research
Master's Thesis Project

Focus Questions

1. What is an action research master's thesis project?

2. What would you have to know to successfully complete a master's thesis project?

3. What do you think is the most difficult step in completing a master's thesis project?

4. How does a master's thesis project differ from the action research project presented in the last chapter?

Students enrolled in graduate programs for a master's degree are usually required to complete a thesis project of some sort. Action research can easily be incorporated to successfully complete such a project. In some programs, this project represents the culmination of the degree, whereas in others the course may introduce students to the rigors of research. Students usually enroll in a three-credit course in the fall semester. In this course they are expected to complete three basic steps in writing a thesis: (1) identify a topic; (2) write a literature review; and (3) develop a research plan. At the end of the semester they frame their ideas in the form of a research proposal. Students then enroll in a second three-credit course in the spring semester. In this course, they complete the final two steps in a five-step process: (4) carry out the research plan and (5) write up the results.

In some colleges and universities, students complete a research project in only one semester. Under this circumstance they may do one of two things: complete only the first three steps above, or complete all five steps in a curtailed fashion (simulating results).

Regardless of the course format, this chapter will provide readers with simplified suggestions for completing the five steps above, providing concrete examples. A sample project is also provided.

The following general suggestions are recommended:

- Relax. All students confronting the challenges of completing a thesis project experience stress pangs. They are short-lived. Speak to former students and even ask your professor for sample thesis projects.

- Step 1 in the five-step process is the most difficult. After that it's a breeze. Keep this in mind.

- Read the textbook or chapters assigned. Many students feel they can "go it alone." Such an attitude usually gets them in trouble. Therefore, do all assigned readings.

- Develop a study team. Find like-minded students to join to complete literature reviews and survey development together. Brainstorming ideas and working with others in a similar situation will serve to allay your apprehensions.

- Team up with a partner to complete a project. Some professors allow two students to team up to complete a single project. If your professor allows this option, be aware of the advantages and disadvantages of such an undertaking. *Advantages:* (a) Two heads are better than one, (b) you can work problems through together, (c) when one person is unavailable, the other can pick up the slack, and (d) the workload can be divided equally. *Disadvantages:* (a) You are dependent on the promptness and earnestness of someone else, (b) if one person cannot complete his or her phase of the project, you will either have to pick up the slack or just sit it out and wait, and (c) you will get one grade from the professor.

- Develop a time line for completing the project. Certain phases of the project will take longer than others. Know that there may be a lot of "waiting around" time, especially during data collection. Don't get complacent. Remain vigilant and be aware that when the data arrive you must get ready for data analysis and interpretation.

- Rely on your professor for assistance. Most professors remind students that they can submit sections for review prior to the end of the semester. You'd be surprised to know that most students never take up this generous offer. If you do so, you will more successfully complete the project.

Step 1: Identify a Topic

- Don't rush when selecting a topic.
- Choose a topic that is of interest to you, is researchable, and is feasible to carry out.
- Be ready to tolerate initial uncertainty.
- Brainstorm a list of things that you wonder about: your classroom, your school, your profession, or an educational issue.
- Discuss your choices with a colleague or two.
- Select one broad topic, then try to narrow down your area. Develop researchable questions.
- Skim the text.
- Go to the library or scan the Web. Locate articles, books, and journals that interest you. Look for studies on the general topic. Locate dictionaries (e.g., *Dictionary of Education* or *Dictionary of Multicultural Education*), encyclopedias (e.g., *Encyclopedia of Education, International Encyclopedia of Education,* or *Encyclopedia of Educational Research*), handbooks (e.g., *Handbook of Educational Psychology, Handbook of Research on Curriculum, Handbook of Research on School Supervision, Handbook of Reading Research,* or *Handbook of Research on Teaching*).
- Discuss your ideas again with a colleague or two.
- Meet with your professor.
- Voila! You now have a topic.

Here's an example: Reflecting on my classroom, I've read about cooperative learning in journals and magazines and wondered if this strategy might work for me. I think my instructional approach is too lecture and talk oriented. The literature appears to indicate that group work through cooperative learning might yield social and academic results. I am interested in this topic. I know it's researchable because there are many articles on the subject. I know I can easily implement such a strategy in my classroom because my supervisor encourages us to try out new instructional approaches. I teach eighth-grade geography. I can incorporate the approach with my fifth-period class of heterogeneously grouped learners to field-test its use and then expand its use to other classes and ability levels. I want to see what impact cooperative learning has on the social development of my students and their achievement levels in the tests I administer in class.

Step 2: Write a Literature Review

Your literature review does not have to be exhaustive. You don't have to locate every study completed on your topic. The purpose of a literature review is to find out and acknowledge what work has been done on the topic. It merely has to represent accurately what the experts have to say about it.

Include pro *and* con perspectives. Present a balanced, fair review. For instance, if you are reviewing the use of phonics, you should include the work of those who support and oppose its use. You should also review the literature on whole-language instruction to place the subject in proper perspective.

Scan the Web, using key Web sites. Review educational databases (e.g., ERIC) to obtain leads. Copy articles that seem relevant and then read each article. For each article, keep an index card that includes the following: title; author; other publication information necessary to write a reference; a summary of the article, including purpose, methodology, findings, implications, and conclusions. Use your own words and be concise. Number the card and the article so you can refer to it later. If you decide to include quotations on the card, make sure that the quote is accurate and that you include correct page numbers. Label cards by topic (e.g., Pros of Cooperative Learning, Cons, Research Studies at the High School Level).

Divide your literature review as you would any story, into a beginning, a middle, and an end. The beginning includes a one- or two-paragraph introduction that states the purpose of the literature review and what will be included. The middle may include several subsections. Use the various topics you noted on the cards to guide development of the middle section. The end is just a concluding statement summarizing what you found.

Here is an example of a literature review on professional development:

Elements of Staff Development

According to Lieberman (1995), "the conventional view of staff development as a transferable package of knowledge to be distributed to teachers in bite-sized pieces needs radical rethinking" (p. 591). Harrington-Lueker (1996a) noted that Northwest Regional Lab's research shows that for staff development to be effective it must be long-term and ongoing. Therefore, one-time workshops or weekend training sessions will not work (p. 36). Harrington-Lueker (1996b) reinforced her statement in another article, "What Makes a Good Professional Development Program?", in which she stated that according to the National Staff Development Council (NSDC), 20 follow-up sessions might be necessary for a specific teaching strategy to be rooted (p. 35).

Planning Staff Development

Four key questions when planning staff development are detailed by Cifarelli (1998): (1) How can new technologies help the school with teaching, learning, and administration? (2) Who on the staff is qualified and able to teach workshops? (3) How can the staff be motivated to learn new technologies? (4) Does the school have enough hardware and software to teach the teachers? (p. 57).

In addition, staff developers must consider the staff's needs for the training. What is the staff's level of comfort with new technology? What is the staff's level of familiarity with computers? What are the different instructional levels and styles? How many additional sessions will the staff need after instruction? Finally, what are the staff's needs with regard to time, technical support, and instructional resources after the training has occurred? (Cifarelli, 1998, p. 57)

Schools must strategize on how to use their own staff to provide staff development. According to Maddin (1997), the first step is to identify teacher-leaders in the school who are willing to train their peers. This team of leaders should have opportunities to observe teachers in other districts who effectively integrate technology; receive additional training; develop model lessons; and collectively discuss their experiences (p. 56).

Location is another important factor to consider when planning staff development. As Curtin et al. (1994) stated, "for teacher training to be effective it must occur in natural classroom contexts" (p. 77).

Methods of Training

Bradshaw (1997) noted that "implementing technology in particular is, ultimately, a very personal process. Just as teachers must individualize classroom instruction to meet the diverse needs of students, staff development must respond to a wide range of teachers' knowledge, skills, attitudes, and concerns" (p. 90). Tenbusch (1998) suggested the use of individual plans to help teachers with their own personal plan for technology growth. Teachers can set goals that demonstrate computer skills and formalize the teachers' commitment (p. 8). Harrington-Lueker (1996a) also discussed in her article how professional development needs to have a number of different approaches in delivering training, which she calls "multiple entry points" (p. 36). Stager (1995) also reinforced this concept when he stated that "no one approach to staff development works for all teachers" (p. 82). The selection of staff development must engage teachers of different backgrounds and subject areas (p. 81).

Stager (1995) defined staff development as "not meaning pouring information into teachers' heads or training them in a few technical skills. Staff development means helping teachers fearlessly dream, explore, and invent new educational experiences for their students" (p. 79).

In addition, Stager (1995) said that staff development should "immerse" teachers in relevant projects. This will enable teachers to experience constructive uses for computers in their classes. Having teachers work on projects will give them experiences that are "engaging, interdisciplinary, collaborative, and models of constructivist learning" (pp. 78–81). Yocam (1996) reinforced this concept by suggesting that staff development activities should model teaching strategies for the trainees (p. 89).

Nicaise and Barnes (1996) supported the opinions of Stager by suggesting that we need to take the emphasis away from the teacher-centered approach of instruction and bring the emphasis to a discovery learning environment (p. 212). The staff development should model the changed role of a teacher from an "information provider, sequencer of information, and test creator, to guide, scaffolder, and problem or task presenter" (p. 208).

Carter (1996) discussed a teacher-centered approach in which "mentoring relationships between staff members can prove a highly personalized means of increasing proficiency in various areas of technology" (p. 30). Similarly, Cwiklik (1997) noted that some experts believe that a more individualized approach would leverage the skills of the teachers who are "tech-savvy" (p. R8). Ann Lieberman, co-director of the National Center for Restructuring

Education, Schools, and Teaching at Columbia's Teachers College, also supported methods such as mentoring or coaching by stating what she believed to be the two keys to professional development: It is "rooted in a teacher's everyday practice and puts teachers in contact with other professionals" (Harrington-Lueker, 1996b, p. 35).

In addition to modeling different strategies for the trainees, Tenbusch (1998) stated that "teacher technology training should be flexible, yet cover a comprehensible set of skills" (p. 4). Training should meet the teacher where he or she is right now in regard to his or her teaching. Trainers should not make the teacher feel defensive by telling him or her to stop lecturing. Instead, trainers should assess teachers' different teaching styles and identify how that style can be enhanced with technology. (Sulla, 1998, pp. 2–3).

Tenbusch (1998) wrote that teachers should be encouraged to integrate into their daily lessons the programs in which they were trained. Teachers should be given enough information to get started using technology in their classes. Once they begin, students can take over because they are usually more advanced users (pp. 3–6).

Step 3: Develop a Research Plan

A research plan is developed after you have identified a topic and have conducted a literature review. The plan outlines what you intend to do in terms of conducting some research on the topic chosen.

Know what is included in a research plan: statement of the problem, research questions and/or hypothesis, sample, materials, and procedure.

Following is an example of a research plan. The appendixes referred to in this example are found in Appendix C of this book.

Statement of the Problem

The study was conducted to determine whether the professional development program offered in spring 2000 on the use of computers and related technology in the classroom increased the participants' understanding and use of it.

Research Questions

The research questions are "How did the teachers who participated in the professional development program increase their understanding and use of computers and related technology, if at all, from the training?" and "How have the teachers increased their incorporation of computers and related technology in their instruction?"

Sample

The sample for this study was a group of 20 teachers from Silverton High School. There were 7 male and 13 female teachers of various ages and ethnic backgrounds. The teachers were all high school teachers from grades 9–12, and they teach a variety of academic subjects. Nine of the teachers participating in this study were untenured.

The teachers in this study all volunteered to participate in the professional development program that we are evaluating. Each teacher received an hourly wage for the time spent in the training sessions and were paid an additional hour each week in order to practice the skills learned.

Materials

The materials used in this study included two questionnaires and interviews. One of the questionnaires was utilized as a needs assessment for use before the teachers participated in the professional development program in March 2000 (see questionnaire in Appendix A). The other questionnaire was given to the teachers in October 2000, approximately 4 months after the professional development was completed (see questionnaire in Appendix B). Both questionnaires include the same 14 close-ended statements with which the teachers choose to strongly agree, agree, disagree, or strongly disagree. At the bottom of the October 2000 questionnaire there are three open-ended questions to further evaluate the teachers' attitudes. Six teachers were also interviewed using an informal method.

Both of these questionnaires refer to the professional development given to the Silverton High School teachers. The questions in the Computer Software/Hardware Skills and Access section refer to Microsoft Word, Microsoft PowerPoint, and the Internet. These are the topics in which the teachers were trained. This questionnaire could be considered externally reliable if it were replicated by others who are using the same software applications for their professional development.

The questionnaires are internally reliable because we used multiple data sources. In addition to the two questionnaires, the interviewing of six teachers was utilized. The interview questions referred back to the questionnaire, thus strengthening the internal reliability.

The questionnaires could not be considered externally valid because they refer to a small sample of only 20 teachers, all from the same school. This lack of external validity, however, does not in any way diminish the significance of the results from the questionnaire. Given that this study evaluates a program for Silverton High School, a questionnaire used for Silverton High School teachers is still significant.

The internal validity of these questionnaires was threatened by certain factors. Based on the fact that 20 teachers participated in the original professional development program but only 17 responded to the second questionnaire, it produced a 15% rate of mortality. Additionally, we cannot ensure that the responses to the October 2000 questionnaire and interviews were based solely on the professional development. The 4-month gap between training completion and the October 2000 questionnaire and interviews may have left opportunities for the sample to be influenced by other factors. Finally, reactivity to the October 2000 questionnaire and interviews may have been based on an assumption of what the respondent thought we were expecting.

Procedure

This study consisted of the following procedures: (a) a comprehensive review of related literature, (b) the creation of the March 2000 needs assessment questionnaire, (c) the distribution and collection of the March 2000 questionnaire, (d) the implementation of the technology professional development program during March, April, and May 2000, (e) the creation of the October 2000 questionnaire, (f) the distribution and collection of the October 2000 questionnaire, (g) the interviewing of professional development participants, (h) the analysis of data and results, and (i) a report of conclusions and recommendations.

The first step was a review of literature. The literature reviewed consisted of research on staff development and topics related to technology integration. The second step was to create the needs assessment questionnaire for the teachers who volunteered to participate in the professional development program. In March 2000, the needs assessment questionnaire was created and distributed to the 20 teachers who were in the program. In addition, the needs assessment questionnaire was collected from each of the 20 teachers. These same teachers were then trained during the next 2 months.

Using the needs assessment questionnaire from March 2000, the next step was to create another questionnaire, with additional open-ended questions. In October 2000 this questionnaire was created and distributed to the 20 teachers involved in the professional development program. Seventeen teachers completed and returned the questionnaire.

The next step was to interview teachers. Six of the teachers who participated in the program were interviewed. The interviews were informal and were used to enhance the information received from the questionnaires. The interviews were completed during October 2000.

The information collected from the review of literature, both questionnaires, and the interviews were studied for any patterns, ideas, and explanations, which were separated for further investigation. From these items, a grounded theory was established.

The final step was to draw conclusions based on the analysis of the data. These conclusions included the limitations, implications for teaching and supervision, implications for further research, and a discussion of the results.

Step 4: Carry Out the Plan

- At this stage, you are prepared to conduct your study (carry out the procedure as stated above).

- Implement your plan carefully, methodically, and consistently. Collect data and properly file them for later analysis.

- Analyze your data. See chapters 8 and 9.

- Interpret your results. See chapter 10.

Following is an example:

Analysis of Data

In this study there were three data collection methods used to determine how the training program increased the teachers' understanding and use of computers and related technology, and to specifically find out how teachers increased their use of computers and related technology in their instruction. The two questionnaires, one given prior to the training and the other given after the training, included the same Likert-style statements, which were compared to see how the teachers' beliefs changed after the training. The second questionnaire included open-ended questions, which gave teachers further opportunities to express their feelings about the program and its effectiveness. The answers to these questions were analyzed for further insight into the teachers' experiences with the training. Finally, six teachers were interviewed about their participation in the professional development program (see Appendix C). These interviews were also used to gain greater understanding of teachers' experiences and to gather specific information regarding the teachers' use of computers in their personal and professional lives.

Results

A comparison of the Computer Software/Hardware Skills and Access section of the questionnaires from March 2000 and October 2000 yielded the following results:

- Daily access to computers increased from 75% to 88%.

- Regarding knowledge of using Windows 95 or 98, in March 2000 a total of 75% did not think they knew how to use it. In October 2000, that total number dropped to 34%.

- In March 2000, 25% of the teachers strongly believed that they could not use Microsoft Word, but in October 2000 none of the teachers who responded strongly believed that they could not use Microsoft Word.

- 50% of the teachers in March 2000 agreed that they knew how to use Microsoft Word. In October 2000 that number increased to 71%.

- In March 2000, 95% of the teachers agreed that they did not know how to use Microsoft PowerPoint. 55% of the teachers in October 2000 still believed that they did not know how to use Microsoft PowerPoint.

- 20% of the teachers believed that they knew what the Internet was and how to search on it, but in October 2000 that number increased to 53%.

In the Computers in Personal Work section of the March 2000 and October 2000 questionnaires, the following results were found:

- In March 2000, 25% of the teachers strongly agreed that they were afraid to use computers for personal use. In October 2000, none of the teachers responded the same way. Furthermore, the total of teachers who agreed that they were afraid to use computers for personal use decreased in October 2000 to 29% from 65% in March 2000.

- 10% of the teachers in March 2000 strongly felt unafraid to use computers for personal use; this number increased to 20% in October 2000.

- When asking teachers if they used computers often in personal work, 25% of the teachers agreed that they did in March 2000. There was an increase to 47% in October 2000.

When comparing the results from the Computers in Professional Work section of the March 2000 and October 2000 questionnaires, the following results were found:

- The total number of teachers who agreed that computers can help enhance the learning of their students was 85% in March 2000. This number increased to 94% in October 2000.

- In March 2000, 5% of the teachers responded that they often use computers with their students. This number increased to 24% in October 2000.

- 50% of the teachers agreed that they used computers often when preparing materials for their classes. In October 2000, there was an increase of 32% to a total of 82%.

- In October 2000, 59% of the teachers responded that they knew many ways to integrate computers into their content area. This was an increase from the 15% who responded the same way in March 2000.

- In March 2000, 5% of the teachers agreed that they used many different content area software packages. In October 2000, this number increased to 12%.

- 95% of the teachers in March 2000 did not know what to look for when purchasing software for their classes. This number decreased to 83% in October 2000.

- In March 2000, 20% of the teachers who responded agreed that computers were "toys" for students, not tools for good teaching. This response decreased to 12% in October 2000.

The following results from the interviews were found: All of the teachers interviewed were motivated or inspired to use computers at some level, and 50% of those interviewed thought the training was effective if the teachers had prior knowledge of computers. In response to being asked if incorporation of technology in the classroom had increased since training, two of the teachers tried to incorporate technology but had problems, and two of the teachers said they needed more training before using technology in the classroom. One of the teachers increased his incorporation of technology in the classroom. One of the teachers had no interest in using technology at all in her classroom. One teacher said her knowledge of computers was strengthened, but she did not increase her use of computers, and five of the teachers said their use of computers had increased.

Step 5: Write Up the Results

Are you a good writer? See Appendix D of this book.

Title Page

Contents

Chapter 1: Introduction
   Background
   Importance of the Study
   Establishing the Program
   Statement of the Problem
   Hypothesis and/or Research Question(s)
   Definition of Terms

Chapter 2: Review of Literature, Related Research

Chapter 3: Research Design, Methodology
   Sample
   Materials
   Procedure
   Analysis of Data
   Results

Chapter 4: Implications for Teaching, Supervision, and Research
   Limitations of the Study
   Discussion and Conclusions
   Implications for Teaching and Supervision
   Implications for Further Research

References

Appendixes

Chapter 1: Introduction

The introduction provides background in one or two pages and describes the following information:

1. Where the study was conducted

2. The size of the school, the location, the population, and other demographics

3. Performance levels and other relevant instructional information

4. A description of who you are. I require my students to imagine they are a vice principal, a principal, a superintendent, a department chairperson, or any other leadership position in order to undertake the study from a leader's perspective.

5. Any other information that sets the stage for your study.

The importance of the study (one or two paragraphs) describes why you are undertaking this study, why it is significant, and what you hope to ascertain.

Establishing the program (two to four pages) outlines in detail the steps you would take to establish or implement the program in your school or district. Be specific by using the steps outlined in chapter 4. Obviously, if your study doesn't involve program evaluation, then omit this section.

A statement of the problem (one paragraph) states the purpose of the study and should begin as follows: "The purpose of this study was..." Use the past tense throughout to indicate this report was written after completion of the study.

The hypothesis and/or research question(s) should be listed. If you triangulated, then hypothesis *and* research question(s) are likely.

A definition of terms (one or two pages) should define the relevant words, either conceptually or operationally.

Chapter 2: Review of Literature or Related Research

Use the first term for quantitative studies and the latter term for qualitative studies. If you triangulate, either will do.

This chapter, in four to eight pages, reviews the relevant literature pertaining to your topic. What previous research, for instance, informs your study? Professional educational leaders should be aware of relevant and recent literature in the area they are investigating. One easy way of doing so is by consulting the *Education Literature Review,* which is discussed in the annotated reference section later in this book.

In action research, however, such a review of the literature need not be formalized, but for teaching research in graduate courses, students are encouraged to undertake a formal review of the literature.

Chapter 3: Research Design or Methodology

Use the first term for quantitative studies and the latter term for qualitative studies. If you triangulate, either will do.

Describe your sample (one paragraph) in terms of (a) who they are (including gender, ages, grade level data, ability levels, ethnicity, if relevant); (b) where they are from, how many are participating, how they were selected and assigned; and (c) any other information the reader may need to know about the sample.

List and briefly describe (two paragraphs) any relevant materials used in the study. For example, a researcher-developed survey should be described and a sample placed in an appendix. Reference appendix in this section by noting, for example, "See survey in Appendix B."

Also include names and descriptions of any commercial tests, games, computers, children's literature, or other surveys.

Validity and reliability of testing instruments and/or surveys are discussed in this section.

The procedure (one or two pages) describes, step by step, how you conducted your study, including a time line. Anyone reading your report should be able to explain, or at least understand, the steps you took in conducting your study. They should be able to replicate your study from the information provided in this section. Include a description of the treatment and precisely how it was administered.

Briefly explain (one paragraph) how you analyzed your data. See chapter 6 for details.

State and describe the results of your study. Just provide the raw data (one or two pages). Reserve your conclusions and insights for the next chapter. Results should also be presented in table form using graphs, charts, or any other acceptable manner of presenting your findings.

Chapter 4: Implications for Teaching, Supervision, and Research

Every study is limited by factors beyond your control, such as mortality (see internal validity), sample size, and time factor. List and briefly explain each limitation. An example follows:

Limitations of the Study

Sample size. The number of teachers used for this study was limited to those who participated in the professional development program, which was 20 teachers. That is a small number on which to base conclusions and, therefore, results cannot be generalized.

Validity of questionnaires. Content and consensual validity were achieved. 17 of the 20 teachers returned the October 2000 questionnaire. Reactivity to the October 2000 questionnaire and interviews may have threatened the internal validity based on an assumption of what respondents may have thought the researchers were expecting.

External validity of study. Given that the purpose of this study was to evaluate a professional development program for Silverton High School, it may not be considered externally valid. Specific content relating to other schools and districts may differ from the content cited in this study.

Time factor. The internal validity of the October 2000 questionnaire and the interviews due to the fact that there was a 4-month gap between the training completion and the October 2000 interviews may have left opportunities for the sample to be influenced by other factors.

Discussion and conclusions should be summarized in two to four pages. Describe your observations, opinions, and conclusions based on the results reported in your previous chapter. Provide possible explanations and note interesting, significant, and/or curious findings. An example follows.

Discussions and Conclusions

The conclusions of this study were directly related to the research questions. In order to analyze the results of this study, the researchers first looked at how the teachers increased their understanding of computers and related technology, and then considered how the teachers' use of these technologies increased. Finally, the researchers analyzed how the teachers increased the incorporation of computers and related technology in their instruction.

The teachers did increase their understanding of computers and related technology, as indicated by the responses found in the "Computer Software/Hardware Skills and Access" section of the October 2000. Specifically, none of the teachers who responded strongly believed that they could not use Microsoft Word. The increased understanding of computers and related technology is also demonstrated by increased positive responses on the use of Microsoft PowerPoint and the Internet. Although there was a significant amount of time between the completion of the training and the October 2000 questionnaire and the interviews, it can be concluded that the training the teachers received did increase their understanding of these technologies. The interview answers indicate that the training gave the teachers the increased knowledge, or motivated the teachers to learn more. Either way, an increased understanding of computers and related technology that is connected to the professional development program can be considered a positive result of the training.

The use of computers and related technology was found to increase from the training the teachers received. The interview responses are a strong indicator of how the program affected the use of computers and related technology by the teachers who were trained. Five of the six teachers interviewed did state that they increased their use of technology. There was a significant increase in the number of teachers who use computers often for personal work after they received the training. There was also an increase in the number of teachers who use computers when preparing materials for their classes. The interview responses indicate that the levels of these increases were varied, but overall the professional development program can be considered successful in increasing the teachers' use of these technologies in general.

The long-term desired result of any professional development program is to enhance the learning of students. For this professional development program, one of the goals was to increase the teachers' incorporation of computers and related technology in the classroom. The results of the study indicate that a small number of teachers have increased their incorporation of computers in their classroom; specifically, 24% of the teachers in October 2000 agreed that they use computers often with their students. In March 2000, that number was only 5%. Furthermore, two of the teachers interviewed did attempt to use computers in their classes, even though they were unsuccessful. In order for a training program to have success, it must have the support not just of the supervisor but also in the form of resources. One teacher had no computers to use, and another teacher was "devastated" by the limitations of the school's Internet filtering software. Had these teachers been able to succeed with their plans to use computers with their classes, the results may have been even more positive.

In terms of the use of computers to prepare instructional materials, it can be concluded that the training was very successful. In March 2000, 30% of the teachers strongly believed that they did not often use computers to prepare classroom materials. There were no teachers in October 2000 who still agreed that strongly. Although 18% of the teachers did not use computers often for creation of instructional materials, that is a very small percentage of the population trained.

One of the major steps in the incorporation of technology in the classroom is an understanding of how to integrate technology into the content area. The results from October 2000 demonstrate that there was a significant increase in understanding in this area. Only 15% of the teachers in March 2000 positively responded that they knew how to integrate computers into their content area. This number significantly increased to 59% in October 2000.

In responding to the research questions, it can be concluded that the professional development program was successful. Teachers increased their understanding and use of the Internet, Microsoft Word, PowerPoint, and Windows. These were all of the topics in which the teachers were trained. Furthermore, it can be concluded that the majority of teachers have increased their incorporation of computers and related technology in the classroom. The majority of teachers use computers for material preparation, but only a small number use computers in their classrooms. Curiously, there was almost no increase in the use of different content area software packages. This may be due to the fact that the training program did not teach content specific software. Perhaps future workshops may concentrate on this area. The slight increase that did exist may be due to the increased motivation of teachers that was indicated during interviews.

Describe (one or two pages) the implications your study has for instructional improvement. Be specific about the implications for supervision and school improvement. Describe the areas of further investigation that you might recommend others to undertake (three or four paragraphs). Include areas of investigation that you couldn't delve into but that are important nonetheless. An example follows:

Implications for Teaching and Supervision

A professional development program that motivates and educates teachers to use technology in their instruction improves the educational process. Teachers become knowledgeable in different ways to provide instruction through technology and in turn, students of different learning styles have new opportunities for learning. The ability to create a variety of different assessment tools (e.g., tests, rubrics) through the use of technology is yet another way that learning to use technology improves the instructional process.

Once technology is used in classrooms, students become proficient in using it on a day-to-day basis. This comfort level prepares them for their futures out of high school, whether it be college or work.

In order for technology training to truly become part of Silverton High School's instructional program, it is imperative that all assistant principals of supervision, as well as the principal, receive the same training as their teachers in the use of technology in instruction. As the instructional leaders of the school, supervisors must

support their teachers and be a resource for them in the integration of technology. Without their support and knowledge, it is very
difficult for the teacher who was trained to make the connection
from the training to the classroom.

Once teachers have a knowledge of the use of computers, technology can be used as a communication tool in the school. The
school can become "paperless" and allow the quick and efficient
use of e-mail by teachers and supervisors.

The morale of Silverton High School may change if the school
becomes "technology savvy." Students can be proud and motivated to work in their classes, and in turn the staff will feel successful.

Furthermore, after the recommendations for modifying Silverton
High School's professional development program have been implemented, other schools could use this program as a model for implementing technology training.

Implications for Further Research

Further research may be helpful to others before implementing a
similar professional development program. Creating effective
mentoring relationships is an area into which researchers should
delve. One-on-one training may be necessary to assist teachers
in the incorporation of computers and related technology in the
classroom.

Another area for further research would be to investigate alternatives for schools in using computers and related technology in classrooms. Rather than having computer labs with limited access,
mobile computer labs and "rolling" workstations may allow teachers to bring computers to any classroom.

Using distance learning as a professional development tool may
be another area of investigation. As the Internet becomes part of
everyday life for students and teachers, the possibility of training
teachers from their homes becomes feasible. Schools may like
the concept of distance learning to train their teachers because
many teachers can be trained at once. Researchers may want to
find out if distance learning is an effective alternative to training in
a classroom.

Finally, researchers may want to undertake research on the effectiveness of computers and related technology as a learning tool
for students. As computers become a common tool in schools,
investigations should be made on its effectiveness.

Appendixes

APA prefers *appendixes* to *appendices*. Any relevant materials such as copies of surveys, selected curriculum materials, and photos should be placed in separate appendixes and labeled A, B, C, and so forth in order of occurrence in the text.

References

I recommend use of the American Psychological Association's (APA) *Publication Manual*. All documentation throughout the paper should conform to APA style. See brief description of APA in Appendix E. An example follows:

References

Abrahms, S. (1998, August 16). Bringing teachers into the computer age. *Boston Globe,* p. E5.

Adams, S. (1997, March). Learning together: Teachers and students tackle new technologies side by side [On-line]. Available: http:/www.electronic-school.com/1997/03/0397f2.html.

Bartles, L. (2000, September). Gathering statistics [On-line]. Available: http:/www.electronic-school.com/2000/09/0900f5.html.

Beattie, R. M. (2000, September). The truth about tech support [On-line]. Available: http:/www.electronic-school.com/2000/09/0900f3.html.

Bouie, E. (1998, September). Spotlight on...technology integration: Creating an information rich environment. *T.H.E. Journal, 26* (2), 78–79.

Bracey, B. (1996, March). Kick-start technology for teachers. *Education Digest, 61* (7), 42–45.

Bradshaw, L. K. (1997, December). Technology-supported change: A staff development opportunity. *National Association of Secondary School Principals Bulletin, 81* (593), 86–92.

Carter, K. (1996, March). After the plan's approved: Keeping the technology planning process alive and moving. *Technology & Learning, 16* (6), 28–34.

Cifarelli, R. (1998, September). Anytime, anywhere professional development. *T.H.E. Journal, 26* (2), 57–58.

Curtin, P., Cochran, L., Avila, L., Adams, L., Kapser, S., & Wubbena, C. (1994, April). A quiet revolution in teacher training. *Educational Leadership, 15* (7), 77–80.

Cwiklik, R. (1997, November 17). Those who can't...If technology is going to transform our schools, the place to start is with the teachers. *Wall Street Journal,* R8–12.

Daniel, M. (1998, March 1). Schools Seeking Access to Computer Education. *Boston Globe,* 1–4.

Deal, N. (1998, August). Getting teacher educators caught in the web. *T.H.E. Journal, 26* (1), 50–53.

Dockstader, J. (1999, January). Teachers of the 21st century know the what, why, and how of technology integration. *T.H.E. Journal, 26* (6), 73–74.

Garavaglia, P. (1996, March/April). The transfer of training: A comprehensive process model. *Educational Technology, 36* (2), 61–63.

Garcia, R. (1998, September). Hang-ups of introducing computer technology. *T.H.E. Journal, 26* (2), 65–66.

Harrington-Lueker, D. (1996a, September). Coming to grips with staff development. *Electronic Learning, 16* (1), 32–40.

Harrington-Lueker, D. (1996b, September). What makes a good professional development program? *Electronic Learning, 16* (1), 35.

Holzberg, C. S. (1997, March). Teach your teachers well: Successful strategies for staff development. *Technology & Learning, 17* (6), 34–40.

Huntington, F. (1997, October). Easing a reluctant school staff into technology. *Technology & Learning, 18* (2), 58.

Lewis, A. C. (1998, February). Teacher development. *Education Digest, 63* (6), 70–71.

Lieberman, A. (1995, April). Practices that support teacher development. *Phi Delta Kappan, 76* (8), 591–601.

Maddin, E. A. (1997, September/October). The real learning begins back in the classroom: On-the-job training and support for teachers using technology. *Educational Technology, 36* (5), 56–69.

Marshall, G. (1996, September). Teacher tech 101 [On-line]. Available: http://www.electronic-school.com/0996f5.html.

Meltzer, J., & Sherman, T. M. (1997, January). Ten commandments for successful technology integration and staff development. *NASSP Bulletin, 81* (585), 23–32.

Milone, M. (1998, March). Growing together. *Technology & Learning, 18* (7), 48–49.

Moore, P. R., Rieth, H. J., & Ebeling, M. (1994, Fall). An analysis of the impact of computer placement and training on special education teachers' attitudes and perceptions of the role of computers in instruction. *Teacher Education and Special Education, 17* (4), 236–248.

Nicaise, M., & Barnes, D. (1996, May/June). The union of technology constructivism, and teacher education. *Journal of Teacher Education, 47* (3), 205–215.

Redding, J. C., & Kamm, R. M. (1999, February). Just-in-time staff development: One step to the learning organization. *NASSP Bulletin, 83* (604), 28–30.

Schulz, C. (1997, Winter). Today's school library media center—technology is key. *Educational Horizons, 75* (2), 78–82.

Sibley, P.H.R., & Kimball, C., (1998, January 1). Technology planning: The good, the bad and the ugly. *Microsoft in K–12 Education,* pp. 1–8.

Stager, G. S. (1995, October). Laptop schools lead the way in professional development. *Educational Leadership, 53* (2), 78–82.

Sulla, N. (1998, March). Winning teachers over: How you can battle resistance to technology—and win [On-line]. Available: http://www.electronic-school.com/039812.html.

Tenbusch, J. P. (1998, March). Teaching the teachers: Technology staff development that works [On-line]. Available: http://www.electronic-school.com/0398f1.html.

Toroian, D. (1998, September 17). Schools face challenge getting teachers to use computers effectively. *St. Louis Post,* p. B1.

Yocam, K. (1996, November). Teacher-centered staff development for integrating technology into classrooms. *T.H.E. Journal,* 88–91.

See Appendix F of this book for evaluation criteria for the report. Happy report or thesis writing!

Activity 13. Reporting Data for a Master's Degree Project

Feel free to devise your own report based on your needs or your professor's requirements. The following format is one that I find most useful. Use this outline to jot down ideas or take notes as you begin to organize your thoughts and gather information.

TOPIC:

TITLE PAGE:

CHAPTER I: INTRODUCTION
  BACKGROUND
  IMPORTANCE OF THE STUDY
  ESTABLISHING THE PROGRAM
  STATEMENT OF THE PROBLEM
  HYPOTHESIS
  RESEARCH QUESTION(S)
  DEFINITION OF TERMS

CHAPTER 2: REVIEW OF THE LITERATURE OR RELATED RESEARCH

CHAPTER 3: RESEARCH DESIGN OR METHODOLOGY
  SAMPLE
  MATERIALS
  PROCEDURE
  ANALYSIS OF RESULTS
  RESULTS

CHAPTER 4: IMPLICATIONS FOR TEACHING/SUPERVISION AND RESEARCH
  LIMITATIONS OF THE STUDY
  DISCUSSION/CONCLUSIONS
  IMPLICATIONS FOR TEACHING AND SUPERVISION
  IMPLICATIONS FOR FURTHER RESEARCH

APPENDIXES

REFERENCES

OTHER INFORMATION: _____
_____
_____

Action
Research
in Practice

Focus Questions

1. How do you find the time to reflect on your practice as an educational leader?

2. How can you put into action all that you've learned in this book?

3. What else do you need to know to implement an action research project?

4. Describe a time in which you observed action research in action.

Research that produces nothing but books will not suffice.

—Lewin, 1948

The process by which practitioners attempt to study their problems scientifically in order to guide, correct, and evaluate their decisions and actions is what a number of people have called action research.

—Corey, 1953

*We must find a way of bridging the traditional divide
between educational theory and professional practice.*

—Whitehead, cited in McNiff, 1991

*Action research can take place anywhere: in one's office,
in one's mind.*

—Gauthiel, 1992

*Action research is a powerful tool for simultaneously
improving the practice and the health of an organization.*

—Calhoun, 1993

I fail, therefore I research.

—Mellor, 1994

*Think of action research as a huge meteor falling into the
middle of the supervision ocean. As it hits, it causes a
rippling of water....The rippling of water continues to
increase in force until a giant wave gathers and crashes
onto all instructional shores, sweeping away the old sand
of past instructional failures and replacing it with the new
sand of instructional improvement.*

—Glickman, Gordon, & Ross-Gordon, 1998

*Action research is more of a commitment than a set of
techniques—a commitment to exploring—exploring the
meanings of, and hence, the practical possibilities for, our
professional lives.*

—Editors of *Educational Action Research:
An International Journal,* 1996

Action Planning and Implementation

Becoming reflective practitioners through action research is not so easy. Many organizational and individually imposed obstacles exist. Finding the time and support for action research undertakings is a challenge that you are likely to encounter. Finding the time and support for action planning certainly warrants much discussion. Although a complete analysis of this urgent problem goes beyond the scope of this volume, a few words are in order.

Given the current organizational framework of many schools, action research projects are not likely to be encouraged or supported. Too many schools and districts still administer programs, innovations, and interventions by administrative fiat or mandate. Change, however, is in the offing. The literature is replete with new visions and new realities. Schools that are framed as learner-centered communities, where empowerment and collegiality are the norm, are growing in number and quality. These schools, in which action research is possible, are energized with a mission that affirms that "quality learning for all students depends on quality learning for all educators" (Fullan, 1995, p. 5).

If educators are to make a difference in the academic and social lives of students, then educators themselves must be exposed to quality learning. According to Fullan (1995), quality learning depends on the "development of the six interrelated domains of teaching and learning, collegiality, context expertise, continuous learning, change process, and moral purpose" (pp. 5–6). As Figure 12-1 demonstrates, all educators must do the following:

- Understand that teaching is complex and contextual; that teachers are facilitators of learning; that learning occurs when learners construct meaning on their own (Cochran, DeRuiter, & King, 1993).

- Value collegial relationships and participate as active members in a democratic learning community (Glickman, 1998; Goodlad, 1997; Guarasci, Cornwell, & Associates, 1997) .

- Demonstrate a commitment to specific knowledge, understanding, and skills required for relating to and taking account of parents, communities, businesses, and social agencies and, as such, appreciate and consider all aspects of cultural diversity among students and community (Nieto, 2000).

- Develop intellectual and emotional habits of critical reflection and action about one's professional work, and recognize that the mark of a professional is exhibited in a sustained effort of self-improvement (Goodlad, 1998).

- Tolerate ambiguity, remain flexible, and be willing to take risks; realize that in a complex, ever changing world, they must not only cope with unpredictable events and trends but must become agents of change in their own right (Fullan, 1993; Gunter, 1995).

- Believe that they make a difference in the lives of all students; that they are driven by a moral purpose that affirms human dignity and a sense of caring for all people (Noddings, 1992).

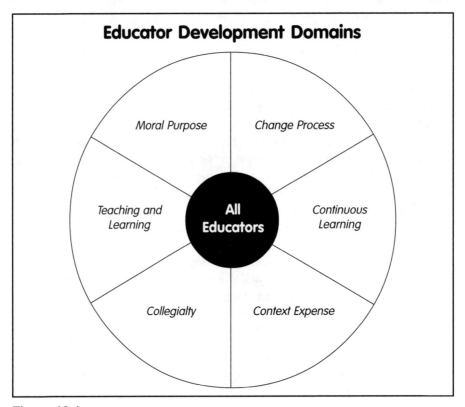

Figure 12-1.

Within such a framework, action research becomes part of a continuous improvement process, whereby leaders "take stock" within their organization (or "learning community") and collect data for the purpose of identifying problems. Also, action research can be used for benchmarking—examining what other organizations are doing and assessing the applicability of certain interventions for their own organization. Therefore, educational leaders might first collect diagnostic or benchmarking data, then act, and then evaluate the results. More important, however, many educational leaders would benefit from a greater understanding of the flexible planning process now recommended for creating meaningful organizational change. If you would like to see how schools (suburban and urban) are implementing these ideas, I highly recommend that you view the *Action Research* video series produced by the Association for Supervision and Curriculum Development (ASCD), and read and use the facilitator's guide (Glickman, 1995).

As educational leaders, you are the change agents to effectuate the kind of milieu in which action research is not only viable but an integral part of a learning community (see Fullan's 1993 discussion of the eight basic lessons of the "new paradigm" of change). The organizational framework of schools and districts was created by people, and it stands to reason that people can change them. Educational leaders can and must create the readiness and willingness for change that our schools need. Educational leaders are in a pivotal position in which to overcome inevitable resistances by articulating a vision of a school that supports a learning community. Vision leads to commitment, and commitment leads to action planning and implementation. I think it was Margaret Mead who once said, "Never doubt that a small group of thoughtful, committed citizens can change the world; indeed, it is the only thing that ever has." Michael Fullan and Andy Hargreaves (1996) stated that we must "fight" for what we think is best for our schools. "It is individuals and small groups of teachers and principals who must create the school and professional culture they want" (p. 107).

What can *you* do tomorrow to make your school or district a learning community? What can *you* do tomorrow to make action research a viable and meaningful tool for school improvement? Can you think of some small steps you can take to make action research a reality in your school?

Finally, some practical guidelines for school improvement, drawn in part from Fullan and Hargreaves (1996), are helpful.

Locate, listen to, and articulate your inner voice. Recall our discussion in chapter 1 of the importance of finding time for reflection-on-action. Review the suggestions offered for finding the time to do so. Know that educational leaders must want to reflect deeply. As Fullan and Hargreaves (1996) underscore:

> Often, when we say we have no time for something, it's an evasion. What we mean is we have more immediate or convenient things to do with that time. Of course, bulletin boards and visual aids are important. But doing them doesn't make you feel personally uncomfortable. It isn't disquieting. It isn't a personal challenge. Listening to our inner voice is. It requires not just time, but courage and commitment too. Having the courage and commitment to reflect means putting other things aside to do it. (pp. 65–66)

Develop a risk-taking mentality. Change (i.e., innovation and improvement) is accompanied by anxiety and stress. Whenever we take steps to change anything, we are undertaking a degree of risk. One concrete way, among many others, to minimize the risk is to start small and take a first step. One of my mentors once quipped, "Change occurs best by degree, not decree." Collect some data for the purpose of identifying any instructional problem you think may exist. Present the data you collected objectively to faculty, perhaps at a grade conference. Facilitate discussion that will include their reactions and suggestions for follow-up. Realize that no initial interest may be generated. "It is all right to fail, as long as you learn from it" (Fullan & Hargreaves, 1996, p. 73). However, continue by listening to your inner voice.

Balance work and the rest of life. Change requires not only commitment but priority-setting. As committed and enthusiastic educators, we sometimes try too hard. "More is not necessarily better," and sometimes "enough" is "too much." Stephen Covey (1989) described the habit of a "highly effective" person as "sharpening the saw." We need to take the time to "sharpen our saws." We must realize that our effectiveness as educational leaders is dependent upon leading a fulfilled social and personal life, not just a professional one. Those who take the time to balance work and other aspects of life and to "sharpen the saw" make the best action researchers.

Believe that you can make a difference. The importance of developing a learning community has been stressed. Commit to continuous improvement and perpetual learning as a foremost goal. Educational leaders must demonstrate the intestinal fortitude, if you will, to "push themselves to create the professional learning environments they want" (Fullan & Hargreaves, 1996, p. 82). More than that, educational leaders must believe that they can make a difference (Denham & Michael, 1981).

Becoming Reflective Practitioners Through Action Research

Carl Glickman (1998) laments the tendency in American education to eschew reflective inquiry in favor of employing quick-fix approaches when addressing rather serious educational and instructional problems:

> Do not act unless you can study what you act. It is irresponsible for a school to mobilize, initiate, and act without any conscious way of determining whether such expenditure of time and energy is having a desirable effect. This sounds obvious, but most schools move from innovation to innovation, expending great amounts of time developing new curricula, learning new practices, and acquiring new materials and equipment. Then, after the initial enthusiasm has passed, they have no sense of whether these efforts helped students. This is the American tendency in regard to education: grab the latest innovation, get on with it as quickly as possible, and drop it just as quickly when a new innovation appears. (pp. 54–55)

As educational leaders, we must think critically about the plethora of instructional challenges that confront us daily. We must first reflect on what needs to be accomplished and then take purposeful actions to enhance school improvement. Action research may be the very means to accomplish these objectives.

Formulating research questions, designing data collection tools, analyzing data, drawing conclusions from data, and considering action plans are part of the new professional repertoire of educators, as action researchers. As explained in chapter 1, action research empowers educational leaders by affording them the opportunity to reflect upon practices, programs, and procedures for instructional improvement.

Educational leaders who are proactive and willing to apply research strategies for instructional improvement know the value of "learning by doing." As John Dewey (1899/1966) said nearly a century ago, there's nothing to compare with learning by doing. Educators are indeed lifelong learners who appreciate new learning experiences and look for opportunities to improve instructional programming. They realize that "learning" involves "doing." They realize that to improve the school's programs, procedures, and practices involves "doing"— taking action by proactively planning a research agenda to accumulate information on ways to improve the school organization. That's what action research is all about: "learning by doing."

Three stages of action research, then, become apparent:

1. Reflection
2. Action
3. Improvement

Every educational leader should keep in mind the premise that "reflection" must lead to "action" in order to "improve" our schools.

As was mentioned in chapter 1, reflection involves time for "reflection-on-action." Problem identification and planning are integral in this initial stage. Action involves observing, gathering data, analyzing and interpreting the data, and making a decision that will lead to some degree of instructional improvement.

Nevertheless, as Figure 12-2 shows, more stages are inevitable.

Action research is indeed a cyclical process. A proactive, reflective practitioner understands that in order to maintain instructional improvement, one must continually reflect and take appropriate, judicious action. School improvement can be accomplished only by sustained efforts at systematic, gradual, and ongoing attempts to find a better way.

This book has not merely advocated reflection that should lead to action but has also provided you with concrete strategies and tools to accomplish instructional improvement through action research. Now it's up to you to apply these principles in your school. Begin slowly, as was mentioned in the previous section, by conducting a small action research study (use the activity sheets at the

REFLECTION ➤ ACTION ➤ REFLECTION ➤ ACTION

Figure 12-2.

end of chapters 4 and 5). Learn from your experiences and build your confidence. In a short time, you will truly realize the efficacy of action research to enhance school improvement. You can and will become the catalyst for developing a learning community in your school or district.

Conclusion

If you are using this book as part of a course on action research, then you are likely to be involved in actually designing an action research project. Such simulated experiences are wonderful opportunities to apply action research skills without any of the possible harmful side effects that we, as educators, inevitably experience as we seek to improve our schools. Instructional improvement involves risk-taking, of course. The rewards, however, far outweigh any possible disadvantages. Negative consequences can be minimized by experiencing simulated activities. This will build your confidence level and raise your self-efficacy (Sullivan, 1996).

Begin by designing an action study on your own by applying these three steps—PIE:

1. Plan

2. Implement

3. Evaluate

The first step is to plan. As educational leaders, you may be interested in conducting studies involving some of the following broad areas of concern:

1. *Classroom environment.* How does the physical and psychological environment affect student learning and attitudes?

2. *School climate.* How does the school climate affect parental involvement and teacher morale?

3. *Instructional materials.* Do the instructional materials reflect issues of diversity and multiculturalism?

4. *Classroom management.* What new behavioral management strategies might be employed to encourage and support appropriate student behavior?

5. *Teaching.* How might supervisors or lead-teachers encourage and support innovative teaching strategies and practices?

6. *Communication.* How can communication linkages between parents and teachers be enhanced?

7. *Supervision.* How might a developmental model of supervision be effectively implemented and evaluated?

8. *Curriculum.* What changes are necessary to realign curricula in the state, district, or school?

9. *Evaluation.* How might a more collaborative and comprehensive plan be developed for evaluating teaching effectiveness?

10. *Public relations.* How might supervisors engender community involvement and support for instructional practices?

11. *Leadership.* Which leadership style is most conducive to encouraging and supporting site-based management?

How might you initiate a research study to answer a question posed in one of the areas noted above? What evaluative measures will be taken to determine the impact of a particular approach?

To assist you in building your confidence levels, the remainder of this chapter presents 11 exercises for you to practice planning, implementing, and evaluating various aspects of instructional improvement.

Exercises

1. Evaluate, Interpret, and Apply Research Findings

    One of the important responsibilities of an educational leader is to read relevant educational research, interpret its findings, and apply them to practical situations in a school.

    Consider that you are an assistant principal in an elementary school of an urban school district. You are responsible for grades 4–6, consisting of approximately 500 students.

    A. Identify one major problem in any of the following areas: teacher training, teacher methods, curriculum, and school-community relations.

    B. Describe the problem in detail. Be creative, realistic, and specific.

    C. Conduct an Internet search for any information that will inform the problem you have highlighted above.

    D. Explain how the findings of the study can be applied to the problem you have identified in your school.

    E. Describe the course of action you would take based on your evaluation of the research findings in order to alleviate the problem. Describe the leadership (including supervisory) strategies you would employ.

    F. Be prepared to discuss your answers.

2. Evaluate a Program

    Situation:

    You are a district office supervisor whose specialty is professional development. The superintendent has informed you that she wants you to evaluate the district's teacher mentor-intern program, which is now completing its first year of operation. It is now April and she wants your completed evaluation report by August 1.

    The district has 15 schools (five elementary, five intermediate, and five high schools) which are involved in the teacher mentor-intern program. each school has two teacher mentors and four interns.

    Question: Assuming you have all the necessary resources at your disposal (the board of education's Office of Assessment has provided sufficient funding), how would you conduct your evaluation of the teacher mentor-intern program? Be specific about research techniques and procedures employed, evaluation criteria, recommendations, etc.

    _____

    _____

    _____

    _____

3. Evaluate a Program

   Develop a written plan for evaluating a specific area of an instructional program with which you are familiar (for example, a K–6 math program, a senior high school Spanish program, or a remedial reading program). Discuss research design(s) utilized. Develop a questionnaire you would employ. Be specific, realistic, and practical.

   _____

   _____

   _____

4. Needs Assessment

   Your school has reorganized into a school-based management team. Committees have been formed and have met many times. Describe what site-based management (SBM) and shared decision-making (SDM) is all about. Why is it so important (if it is)? What are some advantages and disadvantages of this strategy? Develop a questionnaire polling staff members' opinions about the concept, effectiveness, and suggestions. Write a bibliography of 10 books or articles that you as educational leader would distribute to faculty in order to familiarize them with SBM. Describe the program (pros and cons). How would you evaluate its effectiveness?

   _____

   _____

   _____

5. An Example of Action Research

   Consult Glickman, Gordon and Ross-Gordon (1988). See pages 414–415, where an action research project is described: Classroom Research Using the Graphic Organizer in English. An excellent overview of an action research project is provided. Apply the principles of research design, data collection (using both quantitative and qualitative measures), and data analysis and interpretation to the case study. Be as specific as possible and be prepared to share your strategies.

   _____

   _____

   _____

6. Miscellaneous Items

   Consider these questions:

   A. What are some ways that a supervisor or a lead-teacher might get teachers more interested in research?

  B. Explain two ways in which an educator might misuse test results.

  C. Create a self-evaluation instrument for supervisors and lead-teachers.

  D. Create an instrument by which teachers may evaluate supervisors' and lead-teachers' performance.

  E. Interview an educational leader and ask how he or she evaluates the instructional program. Describe and critique.

7. Research Applications: Directions and Case Study 1

 These instructions should be followed for the remaining exercises:

 I. Purpose and Tasks

   The purpose of these exercises is to apply the theories and principles of action research to practical school situations.

 Each group member is to carefully read each case study, noting the circumstances described and relevant information needed to adequately assess the situation. A brief discussion among group members should ensue in order to develop group strategies in dealing with the case study. Sufficient time should be allocated to complete research, analyze, and organize data; answer case-study questions; and prepare for group presentations in class. Format for presentation is at the sole discretion of the group.

 II. Group Size

  A. Three to five people

 III. Determining Factors in Formation of Groups

  A. Diversification

   1. Different levels of schools: Elementary, Middle and High School

   2. Different levels of specialty in administration: Assistant Principal, District Office Supervisor/Coordinator, Principal, Lead-Teacher, and Special Education Supervisor

   3. Compatible personalities

 IV. Guiding Principles

  A. Cooperative group work

  B. Group strategy discussed

  C. Obligations of members defined

  D. Effective use of time

  E. Location of meeting places

  F. Preparation for group presentation

 V. Suggested Strategies for Groups

  A. Throughly read and review case studies

  B. Group discussion of key points and strategies

  C. Assign each member a task or the group works as a unit

D. Pitfalls to avoid
   1. Excessive socializing
   2. Postponing research
   3. Arguing
   4. Holding back information from other group members
E. Rehearse for each oral group presentation
   1. Develop strategies
   2. Individual and group discussions
   3. Techniques to enhance audience participation

Developing a New Program

You are a principal of William Heard Kilpatrick Middle School, which has a population of 1,200 pupils in grades 6 through 8. You are a conscientious administrator concerned about the welfare of the students and the quality of the curriculum. You are also an active participant in the meetings of the PTA, and you encourage parental interest in school affairs. You perform your duties effectively and serve your institution well.

At a recent PTA meeting, several parents complained that the school lacks a "gifted" program. They felt that such a program should be developed in order to meet the needs of a growing population of students in the school. You thanked them for their input and promised to consider the matter. You informed them that you would bring the matter to the attention of the superintendent at your next meeting with her.

Two weeks later, you meet with the superintendent. She is enthusiastic about the possibility of establishing a gifted program at the middle school level. Although there is no program for the gifted in the district, she informs you that a colleague of hers has developed and implemented a districtwide gifted program in a different township. "The program is very popular and successful," she says.

The superintendent encourages you to develop a gifted program for your school, with the intent that the program you establish would serve as a model for other schools in the district. The superintendent requests that you address the following points:

A. Definition of gifted
B. Criteria used in selecting target population
C. A curriculum based on the needs and interests of the identified target group
D. Teacher recruitment and training
E. Activities and approaches unique to the gifted
F. Integration of learning with highly realistic life experiences
G. Administration, supervision, and organization of the program

The superintendent requests that you submit a plan for the gifted program for her consideration.

NOTE: You are not at all knowledgeable about the gifted or talented.

Your group should do the following:

A.   Develop a gifted program for your school

B.   Describe how you would utilize research in developing your program. Be specific.

C.   Discuss steps that you would take to evaluate the program.

NOTE: Be creative in your approach. Assume that you have sufficient resources for materials, personnel, etc. at your disposal. Be certain to consider the seven points the superintendent outlined above.

8.   Research Application Case Study 2

Teacher Evaluation

You are a newly assigned assistant principal (AP) in charge of grades 4, 5, and 6. In your new position, you discover low teacher morale, due in large part to the strict rating and observation methods used by the former AP. In your discussion with teachers, you find that the former AP used to observe teachers without notice and would write lengthy reports criticizing their teaching methods. Teachers did not find this supervisory approach to be worthwhile or constructive. Teachers were also anxious and disturbed about this method of teacher evaluation.

You are sympathetic toward the resentment felt by these teachers, and you would like very much to allay their apprehensions by using alternative means of teacher improvement and evaluation. You were, however, trained to be a supervisor who uses the traditional methods of teacher observation. You have little, if any, knowledge about alternative approaches to supervisory observation.

However, you recently attended a convention for administrators sponsored by the Association for Supervision and Curriculum Development (ASCD), during which you heard about a unique approach to teacher observation. One of the speakers talked about Morris Cogan's Clinical Supervision and Carl Glickman's Developmental Supervision. You were quite interested in these methods and would like to gain more information about Clinical and developmental supervision.

Your group should do the following:

A.   Research these alternative approaches to traditional supervision. Describe these approaches and how you would implement them in your capacity as AP in the situation above. Be specific and be certain to mention the guiding principles or philosophy of the approach, the steps you would take to prepare for the observation, the criteria you would use for evaluating the lesson, and techniques you would employ during the post-observation conference. (See, for example, Morris Cogan, *Clinical Supervision*, 1973, pp. 10–12, for the eight-phase process for implementing clinical supervision. See Robert Goldhammer, *Clinical Supervision*, 1969, pp. 89–90, for 11 suggestions for using clinical supervision. See Glickman's model discussed in Glickman, Gordon, and Ross-Gordon, 1998.)

   B.   Research at least one recent study showing the effects of these approaches to supervision (positive or negative). Present findings and interpret them.

   C.   Discuss how you would evaluate the effectiveness of this new supervisory approach.

9.   Research Application Case Study 3

The Problem of Change in Schools

You are a newly assigned principal in an elementary school of an urban school district. The school population is 900 pupils, with a staff of 35 teachers and 15 paraprofessionals. The former principal, who recently retired, had a reputation for running a "tight ship." He believed that a school should be academically oriented, traditional, teacher-centered, and administered closely.

You, on the other hand, though inexperienced (this is your first assignment as a principal), have a strong commitment to nontraditional education. You believe that alternatives to traditional teaching methods should be developed in order to offer choices not readily available to teachers or schools. Unfortunately, not many teachers in your school have experience or interest in alternatives to traditional education. In your observations of many teachers in the school, you find that instruction relies on the textbook and that many teachers do not even group for instruction in reading. You also observe that science instruction is neglected.

Your long-range goal as principal is to develop an alternative educational model school. Your reasons for interest in alternative education are based on the following assumptions:

   A.   Existing programs are not meeting the needs of pupils, especially in reading and science.

   B.   Advances in science and technology are rapidly changing the organization of instruction and the content of curriculum.

   C.   A whole-child approach is more beneficial than an intellectual aims approach.

   D.   The educational theories of Dewey, Brunner, Trump, Goodlad, Oakes, Dunn, and Gardner are most intriguing.

Your short-range goal is to improve instruction in reading and science schoolwide.

IMMEDIATE STRATEGIES

1. What would you do immediately to remedy weaknesses in reading and science instruction and justify recommendations in terms of benefits to learners?

2. How would you help teachers to handle science equipment and improve their science instruction?

3. Which research design would you use to determine the effectiveness of the changes you incorporate. Describe, in general, the research methodology you would employ.

LONG-TERM STRATEGIES

1. Describe how you would effect the changes you desire in each of the following areas: curriculum, instruction, and teacher attitudes.

2. Describe how you would use research in establishing and evaluating your new program.

In answering these questions, it may be helpful to consider the following points relating to any innovation:

I. Program Definition
   A. Clarify the problems the program is designed to solve.
   B. Identify objectives of the program.
   C. Identify possible alternatives for reaching the objectives.
   D. Establish priorities.
   E. Anticipate criteria and strategies for evaluating the program.

II. Program Initiation
   A. Create a climate of concern and interest in the new program—pupils, faculty, parents, school board members, community.
   B. Planning and decision making

III. Program Implementation
   A. Coordinate all activities needed to implement the program.
      1. Arrange schedules.
      2. Provide for space needed.
      3. Assign staff.
      4. Order and distribute materials.
   B. Provide for necessary supervisory assistance.
      1. Professional development for faculty
      2. Schoolwide pupil activities (fairs, poster contests, trips, assemblies, etc.)
      3. Parent activities

IV. Program Evaluation
  A. Establish criteria.
  B. Select instruments of evaluation.
  C. Involve all participants.
  D. Utilize results to modify the program.

10. Research Application Case Study 4

Test Evaluation in Mathematics and Science

You are one of the lead-teachers of mathematics and science in a high school. The principal is concerned about the lack of clarity and comprehensiveness of the school's testing program in math and science. The principal has asked you to set up a testing program for these two curriculum areas.

Describe, as specifically as you can, what you would do to establish a comprehensive testing program for the following areas:

A. In Relation to Pupils
  1. To determine student progress and achievement in math and science
  2. To assess potential abilities and special aptitudes
  3. To assess student difficulties and recommend remediation
B. In Relation to Teachers and Teaching
  1. To increase teaching effectiveness
  2. To assist teachers in self-evaluation
  3. To determine necessary areas of emphasis in instruction
C. In Relation to Supervision and Administration
  1. To specify responsibilities for planning, scheduling, administering, scoring, and recording test results
  2. To interpret and analyze test results
  3. To utilize test results
D. In Relation to Community
  1. To report progress to parents

Be sure to consider the following:

1. The kinds of tests involved (achieve criterion-reference, diagnostic, intelligence, formal and informal
2. Guidelines for evaluating a test (validity, reliability, scales, norms)
3. Scheduling and dates
4. Professional development (workshops, conferences)
5. Training of students in test-taking skills
6. Arranging for locations, retesting, scoring

7. Statistical procedures for test interpretation
8. Strengths and weaknesses in specific areas
9. Workshop for parents to explore the significance and limits of testing and to interpret test results

_____

_____

_____

11. Research Application Case Study 5

School Improvement

You have been newly appointed as a principal of a prekindergarten through sixth-grade elementary school.

The school plant is 45-years old and is in relatively good condition. Custodial care of the school is considered satisfactory.

The school is located in a community that has a low- to middle-income public housing project, a number of six-story apartment buildings, and a number of two- and three-family brownstone homes. There are several streets in the community that have a number of unoccupied, sealed, apartment buildings.

The school has on register 750 pupils. The ethnic background of the pupils is 45% African-American, 40% Hispanic-American, 10% Asian-American, and 5% others. Forty percent of the pupils are reading on grade level or above.

The school has a full complement of classroom teachers. Sixty-five percent of the teachers have been teaching for less than a decade.

The executive board members of the Parents Association work hard to support programs that will benefit the pupils in the school. There is limited participation in school programs and activities by the parent body, in general.

As the new principal you realize that much remains to be done to make this into an effective school. Your long-range goal is to establish strong instructional leadership, a safe environment, schoolwide excellence in basic skills, and a disciplined student body. You are eager to apply the research findings on effective schooling to your school situation. Describe the steps you would take to improve your new school.

_____

_____

_____

References

Calhoun, E. F. (1993). Action research: Three approaches. *Educational Leadership, 51* (2), 62–65.

Cochran, K. F., DeRuiter, J. A., & King, R. A. (1993). Pedagogical content knowing: An integrative model for teacher preparation. *Journal of Teacher Education, 44* (4), 263–272.

Cogan, M. L. (1973). *Clinical supervision.* Boston: Houghton Mifflin.

*Corey, S. M. (1953). *Action research to improve school practices.* New York: Teachers College Press.

Covey, S. (1989). *The seven habits of highly effective people.* New York: Simon & Schuster.

Denham, C., & Michael, J. (1981). Teacher sense of efficacy: An important factor in school improvement. *Elementary School Journal, 86,* 173–184.

Dewey, J. (1996). *The school and society.* Chicago: University of Chicago Press. (Original work published 1899)

Fullan, M. (1993). *Change forces: Probing the depths of educational reform.* Bristol, PA: Falmer.

Fullan, M. (1995). In M. J. O'Hair & S. J. Odell (Eds.), *Educating teachers for leadership and change* (pp. 1–10). Thousand Oaks, CA: Corwin Press.

Fullan, M., & Hargreaves, A. (1996). *What's worth fighting for in your school.* New York: Teachers College Press.

Gauthier, C. (1992). Between crystal and smoke: Or, how to miss the point in the debate about action research. In W. Pinar & W. Reynolds (Eds.), *Understanding curriculum as phenomenological and deconstructed test* (pp. 184–194). New York: Teachers College Press.

*Glickman, C. D. (1995). Action research: Inquiry, reflection, and decision-making. [Video]. Alexandria, VA: ASCD.

Glickman, C. D. (1998). *Renewing Americas schools: A guide for school-based action.* San Francisco: Jossey-Bass.

Glickman, C. D., Gordon, S. P., & Ross-Gordon, J. M. (1998). *Supervision of instruction: A developmental approach* (4th ed.). Boston: Allyn & Bacon.

Goldhammer, R. (1969). *Clinical supervision: Special methods for the supervision of teachers.* New York: Holt, Rinehart, and Winston.

Goodlad, J. I. (1997). *In praise of education.* New York: Teachers College Press.

Goodlad, J. I. (1998). *Educational renewal.* San Francisco: Jossey-Bass.

Guarasci, R, Cornwell, G. H., & Associates. (1997). *Democratic education in an age of difference.* San Francisco: Jossey-Bass.

Gunter, H. (1995). Jurassic management: Chaos and management development in educational institutions. *Journal of Educational Administration, 33,* 5–20.

Lewin, K. (1948). *Resolving social conflicts.* New York: Harper and Brothers.

*McNiff, J. (1995). *Action research: Principles and practice.* London: Routledge.

Mellor, R (1994). *Action Researcher, 1* (1), 1.

Nieto, S. (2000). *Affirming diversity: The sociopolitical context of multicultural education* (3rd ed.). White Plains, NY: Longman.

Noddings, N. (1992). *The challenge to care in schools: An alternative approach to education.* New York: Teachers College Press.

Sullivan, S. (1996). Creating leaders: Fostering self efficacy in aspiring educational administrators. *Focus on Education, 40,* 24–28.

Seven Suggestions for Action Researchers

Focus Questions

1. What suggestions would you make to your colleagues prior to undertaking action research?

2. What do you think is the first rule of ethics in action research?

3. How does action research lead to school improvement?

4. What three valuable ideas have you learned from this book?

5. How do you plan on implementing your next action research project?

Through action research...changes in educational practice...[are] more likely to occur because teachers, supervisors, and administrators...[are] involved in inquiry and the application of findings.

—Oja & Smulyan, 1989

Congratulations, you have completed *Action Research: An Educational Leader's Guide to School Improvement.* Allow me to offer seven suggestions for educational leaders who are interested in implementing action research to improve schools.

Some of the following stories were culled from *The Executive Speechwriter Newsletter* (802-748-4472) and from Oracle Service Humor Mailing List (jokes@oraclehumor.com).

Expect the Unexpected

Implied in this common-sense admonition is the notion that one must realize that research is a slippery, unpredictable process. This reminds me of a story.

There was once a fellow who worked in an office in New York City and would leave the building for lunch at noon each day. He would pass the pretzel stand on the corner and place a quarter on the cart but would never take a pretzel. This continued every day, week after week. Finally, the elderly woman running the stand spoke up as the fellow put his daily quarter down without, of course, taking a pretzel. "Sir, may I have a word with you?" she asked. The fellow said, "I know what you're going to say. You're going to ask me why I give you a quarter every day and don't take a pretzel." The woman responded, "Not at all, I just wanted to tell you that the price is now 35 cents!"

Learning to expect the unexpected when conducting action research is highly recommended. Action research is not a neat, uncomplicated process of applying "four easy steps." Researchers too often undertake a project with preconceived notions. They sometimes *expect* certain situations to develop. Research is unpredictable. As action researchers who work in school settings, we must be ready for change at any moment. Of course, we cannot foresee everything that may happen, but once we are aware that endless possibilities exist, we're less likely to be surprised and caught off guard. Enjoy the thrill of being engaged in the exciting yet unpredictable experience of action research. Not only will your school benefit by the process, you'll also have lots of fun.

Be Receptive to Both Quantitative and Especially Qualitative Approaches

I cannot overemphasize the importance of a mixed methodology approach to action research. Too often researchers have a latent bias against qualitative research as being "unscientific," especially if a project doesn't incorporate meta-analyses or multivariate statistics. Similarly, many educators are skeptical of traditional research that doesn't have immediate utility. Both views are shortsighted. Action researchers should incorporate both methodologies, when warranted and reasonable.

Making a case, it seems to me, for quantitative research is not very difficult, as it has had a long and cherished tradition in American educational research communities. Qualitative methods, however, are sometimes viewed less favorably. I'm reminded of a wonderful little story about Picasso that the makes the point quite well.

The story is told of a French railroad passenger who, upon hearing that his neighbor in the next seat was Picasso, began to grouse and grumble about modern art, saying that it was not a faithful representation of reality. Picasso demanded to know what was a faithful representation of reality. The man produced a wallet-size photo and said, "There! That's a real picture—that's what my wife really looks like." Picasso looked at it carefully from several angles, turning it up and down and sideways, and said, "She's awfully small. And flat." (Cited in Shagoury-Hubbard & Power, 1993, p. xvi)

Give It Your All

Good advice for life in general, "giving it your all" also has relevance for action research. Certainly, action research requires persistent effort over time. Even though identifying problems, posing critical research questions, collecting and analyzing data, reporting initial results, monitoring progress, and offering research-based solutions are essential elements of action research, they are difficult to accomplish and sustain. Yet, reflective practitioners know that their efforts will pay off, in the long run.

Persistence and hard work are critical, especially for reporting your research findings through written reports. The written final report is an important document for reporting your research findings. The report communicates your results and offers recommendations. Your diligent efforts in conducting the study are worthwhile only to the extent that you've taken the time to write the report carefully and accurately.

I once submitted a report to a superintendent based on an evaluation of the district's gifted program. My written report could have been more thorough and precise. To make a long and unfortunate story more concise, the superintendent wasn't happy. Take my advice, "giving it your all" is especially important in writing final reports. Preparing reports that represent your best work is the point of the following anecdote involving Henry Kissinger.

During the Gulf of Tonkin situation, Henry Kissinger asked an assistant to prepare an analysis. The assistant worked night and day for a week and put the document on Kissinger's desk only to receive it back within an hour. Affixed to the report was a note asking that it be redone. The assistant dutifully redid it; he slept a total of 9 hours in a week. The document again went to Kissinger's desk, and an hour later it was returned with a note asserting that Kissinger expected better and asking that the work be done again. Thus the assistant went back to the drawing board once more. After another week of intense work, the assistant asked if he might present it personally to Kissinger. When he came face to face with Kissinger, he said, "Mr. Kissinger, I've spent another sleepless week. This is the best I can do." Said Kissinger, "In that case, now I'll read it."

Point well taken?

Don't Make a Decision Too Quickly

Action researchers sometimes think that because "action" is required, one must hurry to make a decision. If you've learned anything from reading and studying this book, it's that the purpose of action research is to carefully deliberate prior to making any important decision. Decision making in educational administration and supervision is too often plagued by snap judgments. Not rushing a decision before all the information is in is the point of the next two stories.

One night at sea, a ship's captain saw what looked like the lights of another ship heading toward him. He had his signal man blink to the other ship: "Change your course 10 degrees south." The reply came back: "Change *your* course 10 degrees north." The ship's captain answered: "I am a captain. Change your course south." To this the reply was: "Well, I am a seaman first class. Change your course north." This infuriated the captain, so he signaled back: "Dammit, I say change your course south. I'm a battleship!" To which the reply came back: "And I say change your course north. I'm in a lighthouse."

The next story is told by British actor Jeremy Irons to illustrate the potentially fatal effects of making a decision too quickly.

Recently, a small aircraft was flying over the Nevada Desert carrying three passengers: the president of the United States, a priest, and a California hippie. Engine trouble occurred and the pilot came back into the cabin to break the news to the passengers. "You're going to have to jump," he told them, "and, unfortunately, we have only two parachutes for the three of you, so you must decide among yourselves who will be left behind." The president made a strong case about how he was a possible saviour of the world, the man who singlehandedly is defending democracy on all fronts, and the man who is the figurehead of the free world. There was, therefore, no doubt that he should be allowed to live. The priest and the hippie agreed, and, with that, the president strapped on a backpack and jumped out of the airplane.

Next, the priest began to say how since he was an old man and had little more to give to the world, the last remaining parachute should be taken by the hippie. But the hippie disagreed, saying, "Don't worry, man, the saviour of the world just jumped out wearing my knapsack!"

Certainly make decisions, but do so thoughtfully and only after conducting a well-planned action research project.

Keep Lines of Communication Open and Clear

Throughout an action research project, especially when collecting and analyzing results, clear communication among participants is essential. The value of exact communications to prevent misunderstandings is the point of the next story.

When I was working my way through college, I got a job one summer as a delivery man. I had a small pickup truck, and if anyone had an item they wanted delivered, I did it. One day, I had a very unusual delivery. I was to pick up six penguins and deliver them to the local zoo before closing time. I loaded the penguins into the truck and I was doing fine until I developed a flat tire on a major highway. I pulled over and surveyed the damage. I knew that I could fix the flat, but it was getting late, and I doubted that I could get my cargo to the zoo before it closed. I was wondering what it would be like to spend the night with six penguins when I saw a friend of mine driving down the highway in his own truck. I flagged him down and explained the situation to him.

"Look," I told him, "I have to get these penguins to the zoo before it closes. It's going to take at least a half-hour to fix this flat, so I wonder if you'll do me a favor. I'll give you ten dollars. Will you take them to the zoo?" My friend said that he would, so we transferred the birds to his truck, and he took off down the highway. By the time I had fixed the flat tire, it was rather late. I drove into town and decided that what I needed was a cup of coffee. I parked my truck and went into the local diner. I was sipping my coffee and gazing absentmindedly out the front window of the diner, when all at once, my eyes went wide. There, coming down the main street of the town was my friend, followed by the six penguins, all in a row, looking like a procession of head waiters.

I rushed out of the diner and ran up to my friend. "What is this?" I shouted. "I thought I gave you ten dollars to take them to the zoo!" My friend was puzzled. "I did take them to the zoo," he answered, "and they enjoyed it very much, but that cost only four dollars, so I figured that with what was left I'd take them to the movies."

Appreciate Your Enlightened Eye

Most of us think that we're known as "supervisors" because we are presumed to have *super* vision. The origins of supervision are, unfortunately, based on hierarchical and bureaucratic notions about supervisory practice (Glanz, 1991). Hence, the term *supervision* implies that supervisors are imbued with superior status and, perhaps, even intelligence. No doubt many supervisors of the past relied on these hierarchical, and sometimes patriarchal, sources of authority to accomplish their supervisory tasks. Current thinking and practice about supervision refrain from such outmoded conceptions.

Nevertheless, supervisors do have special knowledge and skills that allow them to influence instruction in positive ways. Supervisors do not gain legitimacy by virtue of their status or position in schools. Rather, their unique training and experience affords them *special* vision—*super,* if you must—regarding, for instance, observing classroom interaction during a lesson. Just as a connoisseur can distinguish tastes from a variety of wines that a novice to wine tasting might overlook, so too educational leaders have special skills that allow them to see things during a lesson that might otherwise be overlooked by the untrained or unenlightened eye.

In *The Enlightened Eye,* Elliot Eisner brilliantly describes the unique contributions that trained supervisors make while observing classroom interaction. Eisner distinguishes between seeing and merely looking. He says, "Seeing, rather than mere looking, requires an enlightened eye" (Eisner, 1997, p. 58). So too, supervisors, while undertaking action research, see things that others miss. Do you see the image in Figure 13-1 on the next page? (There *is* an image; keep trying or ask someone for assistance.) Hint: Turn the figure sideways with the title to the left.

Take Action

There is a story about a geologist who was doing research in Alaska in 1964. That also happened to be the year the great earthquake hit. It seems that the geologist was at home when he felt the floor suddenly sway under him. Then the walls buckled, and finally part of the roof collapsed. With the earthquake in full tilt, so to speak, Joe ran outside to see a street full of people shocked, confused, and helpless. At that point, his neighbor, with a child under each arm, rushed up to him and said, "Joe, you're a geologist! For God's sake, do something!"

Like the geologist in the story, we, as educational leaders, are also being asked to respond to problems and "do something." To take action now and meet the challenges we face is our greatest task. Armed with action research, we are in an optimal position to effect fundamental and positive changes in the school organization.

Do You See the Image?

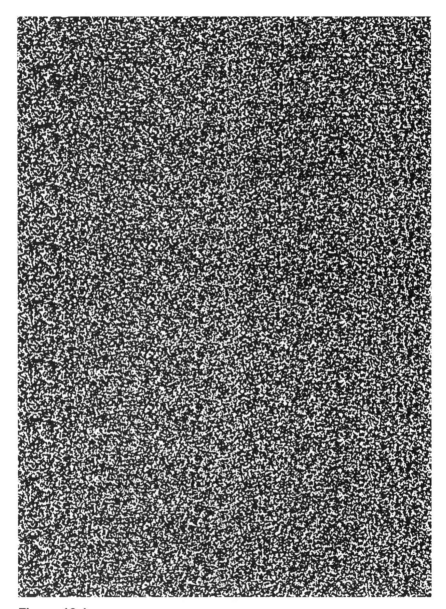

Figure 13-1.

Reprinted with permission, Kodesh, Inc.

The Ethics of Action Research

The first rule of ethics in action research...is "Do no harm."

—McLean, 1995

The study of ethics focuses on moral issues involving right or wrong behaviors and actions. As professionals who utilize action research as a tool to achieve and maintain school improvement, we have a moral responsibility to conduct ourselves honestly and ethically. Conducting research may present us with challenging dilemmas. Do the ends justify the means? If our ultimate concern is school improvement, does that lofty goal allow us to pursue a research agenda that may border on unethical behavior? Should you inform survey respondents, for example, that their anonymity will be assured when, in fact, you have no intention of doing that?

A complete treatment of this important issue is not our primary concern in this section. For a more complete discussion of a range of guiding principles in conducting research, see, for instance, Charles (1997, pp. 8–16) and Drew, Hardman, and Hart (1996). Also, the American Educational Research Association has developed six ethical guiding standards. These have been reproduced by Crowl (1996, pp. 376–382) and warrant your attention. Also, consult Newman and Brown (1996) for ethics in program evaluation. In this section, I'd like to just point out five ethical principles that I consider to be of foremost concern to action researchers:

1. *Accurate Disclosure.* Participants in a study should be informed of the general purpose of the research project and any unusual procedures or tasks in which they will be involved where subjects can be harmed.

2. *Beneficence.* Research will not harm people in any way but is conducted to benefit people educationally.

3. *Confidentiality.* Participants in your study should be assured that the information they share with you will not be made public knowledge and that *their identities will remain anonymous.* If you inform respondents or participants that they will be anonymous, you should do everything to ensure that their identities are concealed.

4. *Honesty.* As an action researcher you are obligated to report your findings in an honest fashion, without embellishment or intentionally erroneous information. Report data exactly the way they were obtained.

5. *Privacy.* Whether you are conducting an interview or distributing a survey, questions of a personal nature should be avoided. Many researchers, for instance, ask for a respondent's ethnicity or gender when these factors have no relevance to the study. Should you wish to report private information such as demographics or opinions about sensitive issues, be certain to obtain *written* consent.

To support some of these principles, I have included Sample Consent Forms (reprinted with permission from Crowl, 1996). See Appendix G. Also, see sample cover letter in Appendix H to introduce your study.

In general, keep in mind the following question, which I have posted on the bulletin board opposite my desk at home: "What ethical concerns should I, as an action researcher, consider when conducting research in order not to violate anyone's individual rights?"

Conclusion

In September 1995, the National Council for the Accreditation of Teacher Education (NCATE) established curriculum guidelines for advanced programs in educational leadership for principals, superintendents, curriculum directors, and supervisors. As part of the first major area of "strategic leadership," NCATE outlined specific guidelines for preparing supervisors in Information Management and Evaluation. Prospective supervisors, according to the guidelines (p. 150), must demonstrate an understanding of, and the capability to do, the following:

1. Conduct needs assessment by collecting information on students; on staff and the school environment; on family and community values, expectations, and priorities; and on national and global conditions affecting schools.

2. Use qualitative and quantitative data to make informed decisions, to plan and assess school programs, to design accountability systems, to plan for school improvement, and to develop and conduct research.

3. Engage staff in an ongoing study of current best practices and relevant research and demographic data, and analyze their implications for school improvement.

4. Analyze and interpret educational data, issues, and trends for boards, committees, and other groups, outlining possible actions and their implications.

Action Research, to a great extent, has addressed these critical areas and guidelines. I have stressed our obligation as educational leaders-as-researchers. Educational leaders are thoughtful, reflective practitioners who question, reflect, and make sense of their situations. They are committed to inquiry and scholarship. They mediate ideas, construct meaning and knowledge, and act upon them (Atwell, 1991). *Action Research* has, I hope, equipped you with the necessary prerequisite knowledge, skills, and values (dispositions) to be easily implemented in your school.

As a former teacher and administrator for 20 years in New York City public schools, I appreciate the complex social, political, and technological challenges confronting practitioners. I truly believe that action research, as described in this volume, can assist you in confronting and solving many problems as you attempt to improve your classrooms and schools. Action research is an invaluable asset that will not only lead to schoolwide instructional improvement but will serve to enhance your professional practice. Continued success to all!

References

Atwell, N. (1991). *Side by side: Essays on teaching to learn.* Portsmouth, NH: Heinemann.

Charles, C. M. (1997). *Introduction to educational research.* New York: Addison-Wesley Longman.

Crowl, T. K. (1996). *Fundamentals of educational research* (2nd ed.). Madison, WI: Brown & Benchmark.

Drew, C. J., Hardman, M. L., & Hart, A. W. (1996). *Designing and conducting research: Inquiry in education and social science.* Boston: Allyn & Bacon.

Eisner, E. W. (1997). *The enlightened eye.* New York: Macmillan.

Glanz, J. (1991). *Bureaucracy and professionalism: The evolution of public school supervision.* Rutherford, NJ: Fairleigh Dickinson University Press.

*McLean, J. E. (1995). *Improving education through action research: A guide for administrators and teachers.* Thousand Oaks, CA: Corwin Press.

National Council for the Accreditation of Teacher Education. (1995). *Guide to folio preparation for advanced programs in educational leadership.* Alexandria, VA: Educational Leadership Constituent Council.

Newman, D. L., & Brown, R. D. (1996). *Applied ethics for program evaluation.* Thousand Oaks, CA: Sage.

Oja, S., & Smulyan, L. (1989). *Collaborative action research: A developmental approach.* London: Palmer Press.

Shagoury-Hubbard, R., & Power, B. M. (1993). *The art of classroom inquiry.* Portsmouth, NH: Heinemann.

Pretest

Part I

Choose the answer that is correct or most nearly correct.

1. You are an assistant principal in an elementary school and you want to raise student attendance rates in grade 5 by fostering school spirit. You initiate a program that fosters school spirit by involving students in schoolwide projects, elections, and competitive academic contests. Which of the following methods of data collection would most accurately allow you to conclude that, indeed, school spirit affects higher rates of student attendance?

   a. descriptive data that includes pretest and posttest attendance rates
   b. attitudinal surveys distributed to students
   c. informal observations
   d. analysis of standardized test scores

2. Janice Barnett, supervisor of curriculum, wanted to evaluate a new reading series that her district was considering. She decided to study fifth graders in a particular school. She selected one class of fifth-grade students who were

introduced to the new reading series. Another comparable fifth-grade class would use the "old" reading series. At the end of the year, Ms. Barnett tested all students in reading comprehension. What type of study is this?

    a. pretest and posttest control group
    b. nonequivalent
    c. case study
    d. historical

3. The major purpose of using an interview protocol is to

    a. offer respondents a way to participate in the interview without having the interviewer present
    b. increase the chances that the respondent will respond honestly
    c. be able to conduct the interview in case the interviewer is not present
    d. provide the interviewer with a set of guidelines for conducting the interview

4. Classify the following study:

Research Hypothesis: Achievement in Spanish is affected by class size. *Procedure:* At the beginning of the school year the students in Highpoint High School are randomly assigned to one of two types of Spanish classes: a class of 20 students or fewer and a class of 40 or more. The two groups are compared at the end of the year in Spanish achievement.

    a. historical
    b. descriptive
    c. correlational
    d. experimental

5. As an educational leader you will have to evaluate many programs in order to ascertain their effectiveness. Let's say you are experimenting with a new supervisory technique known as *clinical supervision.* After 5 months of its implementation, you wish to evaluate its usefulness. You therefore prepare a number of evaluative tools in order to determine whether or not to continue its use. Clinical supervision in this example is known as the

    a. dependent variable

    b. independent variable
    c. treatment
    d. status dependent
    e. coefficient

6. You are a principal in an intermediate school with a population of 750 students. As indicated by recent districtwide tests, student reading achievement has increased. You are interested in discovering how well the students in your school perform in reading compared to students in other schools throughout the country. Which of the following instruments of measurement would you use?

    a. classroom achievement test
    b. observation
    c. examination of school records
    d. questionnaire
    e. standardized test

7. As an assistant principal in an inner-city elementary school with a population of 650 students, you have recently addressed the fifth-grade assembly about their behavior in the lunchroom. You explained a number of behavioral procedures for them to follow. Before you decide to take more drastic measures, which of the following instruments of measurement would you use?

    a. written essay test
    b. questionnaire
    c. interview
    d. examination of records
    e. observation

8. Which of the following is the best example of an "unobtrusive instrument"?

    a. walking into class for an on-the-spot observation
    b. peeking into the window of the classroom without letting the teacher see him or her
    c. determining staff morale by examining the quantity and pattern of staff attendance
    d. interviewing teachers
    e. administering an anonymous questionnaire

9. A quasi-experimental design involving one group that is repeatedly pretested, exposed to an experimental treatment, and repeatedly posttested is known as a

    a. pretest and posttest design
    b. posttest-only design
    c. time-series design
    d. revolving series design
    e. none of the above

10. A sample in which every 10th name is picked from an alphabetical list of students would be an example of which type of sampling?

    a. cluster
    b. stratified
    c. random
    d. systematic
    e. none of the above

11. In qualitative data analysis the goal is to

    a. discover patterns among the data
    b. uncover errors in data interpretation
    c. compare findings to quantitative studies
    d. all of the above

12. A "good" sample is one that is

    a. free of random errors
    b. large
    c. representative
    d. small
    e. systematic

13. You take 50 fourth-grade students, assign 25 randomly to one class and 25 randomly to the other class. Both groups are measured beforehand. Two different treatments are presented, then a follow-up measurement is given. Which type of design is this?

    a. pretest and posttest control group design
    b. pretest and posttest only design
    c. one-shot case study
    d. non-equivalent control group design
    e. one-group pretest and posttest design

14. Mrs. James teaches computers at P.S. 999. She has a new programmed instruction textbook that she wishes to use with her classes. She decides to test the effectiveness of the new textbook. She chooses two classes that rank similarly in ability on a pretest in computer literacy. She gives her programmed text to group A, but with group B she continues her normal instruction. At the end of the semester, she gives a test on computer knowledge and discovers that the class using the new text (A) outperformed the other group (B). She concludes that the new text should be incorporated in all the classes. What research design did Mrs. James use?

    a. nonequivalent
    b. interrupted time series
    c. pretest and posttest
    d. pretest and posttest control group
    e. control group only

15. Mr. Solomon is a supervisor in an elementary school. Mr. Jones, a sixth-grade teacher, complains that one student, Billy, is disruptive and recalcitrant. Mr. Solomon tells the teacher to record Billy's behavior in anecdotal form for 2 weeks before scheduling a conference with the guidance counselor. During the first week, Mr. Jones discovers that Billy acts out 26 times. During the second week, he acts out 22 times. During the third week, Mr. Jones meets with the guidance counselor to work out Billy's problems. The counselor sets up a special reward system for Billy. During the fourth week, Billy acts out 18 times. During the fifth week, the disturbances decrease to only 5 times. Mr. Jones and the counselor conclude that the technique used with Billy is successful. What research design was employed?

    a. pretest and posttest control group
    b. control group only
    c. interrupted time series
    d. single measurement
    e. nonequivalent control group

16. You are an educational leader who wishes to establish a new science program in your school. What is the first step that should generally be taken?
    a. consult with parents
    b. hand out new textbooks and get feedback from teachers
    c. establish summative evaluative criteria
    d. disseminate goals and objectives to all staff
    e. conduct a needs assessment

17. The greatest obstacle that an educational leader faces in undertaking evaluative research is that he or she
    a. is deluged with other administrative and instructional tasks
    b. doesn't really care to go to the trouble of undertaking extensive research
    c. is not knowledgeable about how to conduct research in schools
    d. is not given sufficient leeway from the building principal
    e. has no support from the district office or central board of education

18. The purpose of giving a pretest to both the experimental and the control group is to
    a. ensure equivalence of posttest results
    b. define parameters of sampling techniques
    c. ensure group comparability
    d. develop reliability of assessments
    e. all of the above

19. When would you employ a Mann-Whitney U-test?
    a. in collaborative planning
    b. in assessing posttest results in a quasi-experimental study
    c. in assessing posttest results in a single measurement design
    d. when randomization is impossible

20. A researcher tested the effectiveness of a new reading program compared to an older one. If the difference between the two programs was statistically significant at the $p < .05$ level, this means that

    a. the new program made meaningful changes in the student's reading skills

    b. the results are probably due to the researcher's program and not a chance occurrence

    c. the probability of being incorrect is 95 chances out of 100

    d. the new program should be introduced to all grades

    e. the statistical analysis used was the correct one and the program has educational significance

21. Which is not an accurate statement about the four steps in action research?

    a. Defining a problem can be teacher or supervisor initiated.

    b. Always state the hypothesis, when applicable.

    c. In the research design you must state how the sample was formed and what statistical measures will be employed.

    d. The final stage is to collect and analyze the data.

22. Likert scales usually have half the items worded positively and half negatively in order to

    a. ensure validity

    b. control for intervening variables

    c. avoid response sets

    d. calculate statistical regression

    e. ensure a mathematical balance among the questions

23. A study entitled "pupil attitude toward mainstreaming" would most likely be

    a. historical

    b. descriptive

    c. experimental

    d. correlational

24. To determine if a particular textbook is appropriate for a fifth-grade class, your analysis would entail which type of research?

    a. content analysis
    b. ethnography
    c. case study
    d. naturalism
    e. simulation

25. A test of significance used to determine whether there is a significant difference between two means at a selected probability level is known as

    a. ANOVA
    b. self-report research
    c. chi square
    d. t-test
    e. analysis of covariance

26. The degree to which a test consistently measures something is called

    a. reliability
    b. validity
    c. coefficient
    d. statistical analysis
    e. none of the above

27. An instrument that asks respondents to strongly agree, agree, disagree, or strongly disagree to a particular statement is called the

    a. Likert scale
    b. chi square scale distribution
    c. null hypothesis
    d. Flander's interaction analysis
    e. Eisner's continuum

28. When subjects sense that they are part of an experiment and react in a special way it is known as the

    a. John Henry effect
    b. Norton's Law
    c. Halo effect
    d. Hawthorne effect
    e. Pearson r

29. Which of the following is an identifying characteristic of a well-formulated research hypothesis?

   a. It is stated in question form.
   b. It includes a detailed description of the population under study.
   c. It includes references to educational theory.
   d. It is always short.
   e. It specifies the variables to be studied and the nature of the expected relationship between these variables.

30. "The correlation between the amount of time spent playing video games and scores on a science exam is .12." What does this mean?

   a. There is a strong relationship between the variables, but no causal statements can be made.
   b. There is practically no relationship between the two variables.
   c. There is a strong negative relationship between the variables.
   d. There is a cause-and-effect relationship between the two variables.
   e. Not enough information is given to assess this study.

Answers to Part I: 1. b; 2. b; 3. d; 4. d; 5. c; 6. e; 7. e; 8. c; 9. c; 10. d; 11. a; 12. c; 13. a; 14. a; 15. c; 16. e; 17. c; 18. c; 19. b; 20. b; 21. d; 22. c; 23. b; 24. a; 25. d; 26. a; 27. a; 28. d; 29. e; 30. b.

Part II

Here is a question on the Board of Examiner's principal examination in New York City many years ago when I was getting my license. How would you answer it?

"Assume that one of the teachers assigned to an elementary school of which you are the principal tells you in June that she has seen demonstrated at a recent convention a set of reading materials consisting of packets, each containing a coordinated filmstrip, a long-playing record, and a colorful illustrated book. She says that these materials have not been evaluated as to their usefulness. She is eager to undertake such an evaluation and asks permission to use these packets during the next school year as supplementary reading materials in the second-grade class that she will teach. An evaluation of their usefulness would be undertaken at the end of the school year, she explains, solely by judging through careful observation whether the children have grown a year in reading, more than a year, or less than a year.

"Of the five second-grade classes scheduled for the coming school year, her class is to be the middle one in ability. The children programmed for it have reading grade levels, at present, ranging from reading readiness to 1.5.

"*Question:* Evaluate, justifying each of your conclusions, the research plan proposed by the teacher referred to above. Be certain, in your answer, to cover each of the important considerations that should go into the construction of a meaningful and useful research design."

Sample Write-Up of Quantitative and Qualitative Methods and Results*

Methods

Both qualitative and quantitative methods were used in this study. Quantitative assessment included the creation and validation of a survey assessing the knowledge and implementation of the Teacher Performance Review (TPR). The survey consisted of two parts. Part I asked for some basic demographic information. Part II was directed at personal knowledge of the performance review agreement. Content validity was established by distributing the survey to educators and administrators for review and comments. Quantitative analysis utilized descriptive statistics to report the findings.

We used a stratified sample of seven schools representing elementary, middle, and high schools in the New York City public school system. This sample included two elementary schools, three intermediate schools, and two high schools from the boroughs of Brooklyn and Staten Island, serving a total of 10,108 students. A total of 696 staff members from these seven schools received the surveys in their school mailboxes. Attached to each survey was a stamped envelope with a return address. We received responses from 158 faculty members (23%).

---

*Extracted with permission from Sullivan, S., Shulman, V., & Glanz, J. (2002). Good intentions, questionable results: Implications for the professional development of teachers. *Education and Urban Society, 34* (4): 451–476.

In order to address the process of implementation of the professional development initiative, qualitative data was collected by conducting interviews with staff from the seven schools. Two formats were used: (a) focus-group interviews of teachers and administrators, and (b) individual interviews of teachers, administrators and union representatives. Dialogues and interviews focused on the following:

- Documentation of professional development policies
- Analysis of what worked, what didn't work, and why
- Staff development practices
- Support services

The following questions were used to begin the discussions, with follow-up questions as needed:

1. What do you know about the TPR and its implementation in your school?
2. What do you think impeded the implementation of the TPR Initiative?
3. What do you think facilitated the implementation of this item of the contract agreement?
4. How could the TPR have been implemented more effectively? What suggestions would you have for future teacher development initiatives?
5. What professional practices do you consider effective in your building?
6. What professional practices haven't worked, and why?
7. What impact has the TPR had on the professional development of teachers?
8. What is the TPR's value versus traditional teacher evaluation?
9. What specific alternatives have teachers selected?
10. What criteria have principals used to assess the effectiveness of these alternative approaches?

The research team synthesized the data in written narratives. A modified form of grounded theory was implemented in order to reveal patterns and to analyze the data. Clear, consistent patterns emerged from the constant comparison of the results of the survey and the interviews. The comparative analysis of these results led to the findings, conclusions, and implications.

Results

Analysis of Responses to the Survey

A total of 158 people responded to the survey. Part I of the questionnaire referred to the background characteristics of the respondents. The overwhelming majority (85%) of respondents were teachers. The remaining 15% of the sample included UFT representatives, assistant principals, counselors, deans, and project coordinators.

The majority of respondents (78%) indicated that they had tenure status. However, approximately 50% of those surveyed reported that they had 2 years or less of teaching experience, whereas 50% reported having more than 3 years of teaching experience. Approximately 17% of the respondents reported having more than 6 years of teaching experience.

Table B-1 represents the frequencies and percentages of responses to Part II of the survey regarding personal knowledge of the performance review agreement.

Table B-1. Personal Knowledge of the Teacher Performance Review

Question	Yes	No	Missing	Total N
1. I have read the Performance Review Resource Handbook that explains the Teacher Performance Review Initiative.	27 17%	127 80.4%	3 1.8%	154
2. My principal or assistant principal discussed the Performance Review Resource Handbook or the Initiative guidelines with the staff.	37 23.4%	119 75.3%	2 1.3%	156
3. The UFT representative discussed the handbook or guidelines with the staff.	34 21.5%	120 76%	4 2.5%	154
4. I attended a boroughwide conference to acquaint staff with the new Teacher Performance Review model.	4 2.5%	154 97.5%	4 2.5%	154
5.* I attended district workshops to acquaint staff with the new Teacher Performance Review model.	10 6.3%	147 93%	1 .6%	157

(Continued on next page)

Table B-1.   Personal Knowledge of the Teacher Performance Review (*Cont.*)

Question	Yes	No	Missing	Total N
6. Teachers and administrators in my school have received on-site training on performance review procedures.	24 15.2%	116 73.4%	18 11.3%	140
7. Parents in my school received a brochure describing the new citywide Characteristics of Good Teaching and new Teacher Performance Review procedures.	9 5.7%	114 72.2%	35 22.1%	123
8. The faculty voted on the adoption of the guidelines as a school-based option during the first 3 years of the union contract.	20 12.5%	113 71.5%	25 16%	133
9. I have the opportunity to select either component A or B.	47 29.7%	52 32.9%	59 37.4%	99
10. I selected Component A (annual performance options) for my performance review in the Spring of 1999.	14 8.9%	62 39.1%	82 52%	76
11. I selected Component B (the traditional classroom observation) for my performance review in the spring of 1999.	48 30.4%	35 22.2%	75 47.4%	83

*Only 10 of the 158 respondents reported attending workshops. Of this group, 4 reported attending one workshop, 4 reported attending two or more workshops, and the remaining 2 respondents did not report how many they attended.

Table B-1 clearly demonstrates that most teachers did not get information about the TPR option. Of those who were informed about the option, less than 9 percent selected the annual performance option for their performance review, and only three teachers (1.8%) provided information concerning the activities they selected as part of that option.

Of the 20 respondents who indicated that faculty had adopted the guidelines as a school-based option (see question 8), no one indicated the performance option that the school utilized. When asked to indicate activities utilized in the implementation of the performance option, one person indicated classroom visits, one indicated portfolios, and one indicated "other." There were no other responses to this question.

Analysis of Surveys: Qualitative

Respondents were asked to provide additional comments on the TPR Initiative. Of those who provided comments, the majority (70%) of respondents indicated a lack of information regarding the TPR. Several teachers indicated that they were not given forms on which to record a choice for the initiatives. Comments from teachers included the following:

> "What is the Teacher Performance Review?"

> "Parts of this initiative may be in place in my school, but initiatives were not presented as such in any training or communications within the school."

> "As a new teacher, I should have been observed more often....This is the first time I am hearing of the Teacher Performance Review model."

> "I don't think anyone does it here."

Several respondents who were aware of the initiative mentioned that implementation of the TPR was impeded because they had received little or no training, as evident in the following remarks:

> "At the time it was introduced at my school, little information was provided."

> "It [TPR] has not been widely publicized at our school site."

Some teachers' responses indicated that they had felt pressured by the school administration to select component B (observation). The following response indicates evidence of strong encouragement on the part of supervisors to select the observation over component B:

> "At the time it was introduced in my school, little information was provided, and my direct supervisor encouraged the use of component B."

Both teachers and supervisors thought that traditional observations were less time-consuming, as supported by the following comments:

> "I found it less time-consuming to just be observed."

> "No one wanted to be bothered...it's too involved."

Two respondents reported being afraid that selecting component A would be viewed as hostile by their supervisors. They therefore selected component B in order to avoid future harassment.

> "Although I and some other colleagues wanted to select A, we decided to stick with B....We thought that if we chose A (TPR), it would be viewed as hostile by our supervisors and they would harass us in the future."

One of the factors that impeded selection of option A was the fact that teachers did not feel invested in a new performance review option. Some teachers indicated that the TPR (option A) was not a better choice than being observed (option B). In fact, 20% of the respondents indicated that being observed by a supervisor was preferable to option B. These teachers did not believe that option A was better in any way than traditional observation. Some teachers indicated that the descriptions of the TPR options were unclear and they were therefore better off with the traditional observation.

> "I think it's easier to be observed."

> "Option A [TPR] was considered to be vague and could be interpreted by ourselves and supervisors in different ways...which could lead to conflict."

Clearly, both teachers and administrators did not feel that the new TPR would be more beneficial than the traditional observation.

Analysis of Interviews

Representatives from four New York City schools were interviewed regarding the implementation of the TPR. In each of the four schools, the principal, the union leader, and at least one teacher were interviewed, totaling 10 people. In one of these schools an "alternative assessment" model has been implemented, in which teachers select a project to complete instead of being observed. However, school personnel have not developed criteria to assess the effectiveness of selected projects. Participants who were interviewed from the remaining three schools indicated that traditional observations were the mode of assessment.

Findings Regarding Knowledge and Implementation of the TPR Option

Principals from two schools had to be reminded about the details of the TPR. Except for one school, where school personnel described the implementation of the alternative assessment model as successful, the TPR option was not being implemented and was not viewed as having any impact on the professional development of teachers.

One of the researchers held a small focus group with principals about the TPR. Her findings are summarized below.

She met with a small group of principals to ascertain what they knew about the guidelines for and implementation of the TPR. The group was composed of three active principals and one principal who had retired the previous year (1998). Two of the principals were from Brooklyn, one from Manhattan, and the fourth from Staten Island. All are middle school principals; one runs a school for grades 6–12.

All but one Brooklyn principal seemed familiar with the guidelines publication. "It looks familiar." "I think I received it a couple of years ago." One didn't remember it at all. Only one principal had been involved in any professional development related to the guidelines. She mentioned that a couple of principals in her district were officially implementing the program. She had attended one workshop (LIFE) that an arm of the Council of Supervisors and Administrators (CSA) had offered in her district. Her next comment was that some teachers in her school were unofficially involved in that type of professional development: "They're doing it without realizing that they are." She had not pursued the official program herself.

When asked how the program had been implemented, only one principal spoke clearly about a process. She said, "The UFT representative could present it to the staff in the fall, and individual teachers could request to participate." Although it had not been officially presented in her school, one of the authors was involved in providing peer coaching workshops for a minischool in her building. The researcher mentioned that the superintendent in her district had commented that it hadn't taken hold in the district because, during the first 3 years of implementation, the union contract stipulated that it had to be voted as a school-based option (the previously mentioned official staff vote, with 75% of the faculty voting for the proposal). The principal responded, "So many initiatives are presented and demands made that the superintendents can't keep track of them." None of the principals was aware of any other staff development opportunities related to the initiative.

Views on the Impediments to the Implementation of the TPR Option

The overwhelming response on impediments to implementation was a lack of sufficient training. In the words of one principal whom we interviewed:

> "There isn't sufficient training so that supervisors [can] feel comfortable approving requests....Training was not well organized or meaningful. People don't remember, it's not something you do once and not repeat. You need to revisit it regularly."

Both teachers and administrators viewed option A (TPR) as vague in terms of how to set up professional goals. Teachers and administrators in the New York City schools are products of a bureaucratic culture that, until recently, prescribed what teaching and leading were. The researchers have seen many instances of bewildered staff members who have difficulty reflecting and creating without defined parameters, thereby resulting in a fear of changes that provide choices. A teacher and dean of students explained his feelings in the following conversation:

> "[It is] difficult to determine how to approach goals...[it is] difficult to know what goals are important and what type of professional development [is needed] to address goals....No one is saying how to do this."

Part of the problem with instituting the TPR option is the outlook of both teachers and administrators that option B (observation) is preferred, as it allows administrators to see the classroom. Several principals who were interviewed believed that teacher observation was critical:

> "The traditional observation is a lot more concrete and immediate in assessing performance."

> "The observation shows me the teacher's instructional ability. I think observations are critical."

It is clear from these responses that many administrators don't look at performance review as a means to further teacher development. Instead it is seen as solely an evaluative experience; a tool for an administrator to use to gauge the performance of his or her staff. Observations are therefore clearly a necessary part of the TPR. From the perspective of teachers, the impediment to a novel type of performance review was shown to be the investment of time and energy into something new whose value as a means of teacher growth as opposed to its use as an evaluation tool has not been clearly demonstrated. Teachers clearly preferred a performance review that was a known phenomenon and easy to implement:

> "No one wanted to be bothered. It's too involved."

> "People wanted to do the observation and get the process over with. The other is too involved."

The view that teachers as a group don't like or want change is evident in the following remarks made by a principal: "Teachers as a group are routinized in what they've done. They are frightened of change."

Finally, both teachers and principals view competition with other reforms (such as assessments and curricular changes) as impediments to the implementation of the TPR.

Appendix
C

Sample
Appendixes

Appendix A: Likert Questionnaire

Silverton High School

Technology Professional Development Program

Congratulations! You have been selected to participate in Silverton High School's new technology professional development program. This program has been developed to give teachers the opportunity to learn how to use computers and related technology. There will be a focus on how to integrate these technologies into your instruction.

In order to prepare a professional development program that is challenging, useful, and effective, we must gather information on what your needs are in the area of instructional technology. Please answer the questions below and return to Barbara Cammalleri by March 29.

Thank you for your help and for volunteering to be part of this new program. We look forward to working with you. If you have any questions, please call Christine Drucker at extension 331.

Sincerely,

The Technology Team

Read each statement below and check off how much you agree or disagree with it.

	Strongly Disagree	Disagree	Agree	Strongly Agree
Computer Software/Hardware Skills and Access				
I have daily access to a computer.				
I know how to use Windows 95 or 98.				
I know how to use Microsoft Word.				
I know how to use Microsoft PowerPoint.				
I know what the Internet is and how to search on it.				
Computers in Personal Work				
I am afraid to use a computer for personal work.				
I use a computer often for personal work.				
Computers in Professional Work				
I believe that computers can help to enhance the learning of my students.				
I often use a computer with my students.				
I often use a computer when preparing materials for my classes.				
I know many ways that computers can be integrated in my content area.				
I have used many different content area software packages (e.g., Mighty Math, Inspiration)				
I know what to look for when purchasing software for my classes.				
I believe computers are "toys" for students, not a tool for good teaching.				

In addition, please list any special needs or interests you would like to investigate during our sessions together (e.g., *I'd like to learn how to use a scanner*).

Appendix B: Open-ended Questionnaire

Silverton High School

Technology Professional Development Program

Welcome Back! As a continuation of Silverton High School's technology professional development program, it is necessary to evaluate the effectiveness of the computer and related technology training you received during spring 2000 on learning how to use Microsoft Word, PowerPoint, and the Internet.

It would be appreciated if you could fill out the questionnaire below and return to Barbara Cammalleri by Oct. 10.

Thank you for your help and for volunteering to be part of the program this past spring. We hope to be able to expand and enhance the program during the 2000–2001 school year. If you have any questions, call Christine Drucker at extension 331.

Sincerely,

The Technology Team

List any uses of computers and related technology that you started *after* receiving the computer training.

_____

_____

Looking back at the training you received during the spring, do you feel it was helpful? Why or why not?

_____

_____

Would you like to participate in computer training this year? What would you like to learn?

_____

_____

Appendix C: Interview Summaries

Interviews of Teachers Who Participated in
Professional Development Program

Teacher A (Social Studies)

Initially Teacher A was asked about his knowledge of computers prior to the professional development program. He stated that he used "computers at times, but not often." In the classroom, he used the computers for students to write essays in Microsoft Word and search on-line encyclopedias, like Encarta. He went on to state that after the program, he went "computer crazy," using it at home and at school a great deal. Specifically, he now uses e-mail to interact with students in his class. He also used Internet research for his classes in the fall term, having students research the Israeli-Palestinian conflict and the presidential campaign. His classes use Microsoft PowerPoint for oral presentations on the topics they research and he learned Microsoft Excel over the summer, which he uses to keep track of his grades.

Teacher A was asked to what extent his increased interest in using computers was due to his participation in the professional development program. He responded that "this training allowed me to gain confidence in using computers and to really see how it [sic] can be used in the classroom. I would say that the training had a significant impact on my computer use."

Teacher A was questioned about what changes, if any, he would make to future professional development programs of this type. He initially stated that "this program was wonderful for me, because I was already a supporter of computer use in schools" and because he already was familiar with computer technology. However, he believed that for teachers with no computer background, the program may have been too "overwhelming and not basic enough."

Teacher B (Language Arts)

When Teacher B was asked about her knowledge of computers prior to the professional development program, she commented that she "knew how to use America On-Line to get e-mail and that's about it." After taking the professional development program, she felt more comfortable using computers and "will use computers at home and work." Specifically, she stated that all of her tests since May have been created in Microsoft Word, which has made her much more productive. She stated that she "probably won't use computers in her classroom lessons until she has further training." The training she thinks she still needs includes how to fix computers when there are problems, how to integrate software into the curriculum, and how to use e-mail to communicate with students and parents.

According to Teacher B, the professional development program did increase her interest in computers and allowed her to reach a comfort level with Microsoft Word so that she can use it to help create tests and activity sheets. If the program was offered again, she feels that more time should be spent on the basics such as Microsoft Windows and Word. She would rather learn more about how to use computers for personal work before spending so much time on how to use them in the classroom, since that is "so difficult."

Teacher C (Math)

The computer knowledge that Teacher C had before the professional development program included using e-mail and the word processing and spreadsheet programs in Microsoft Works. She has had four computers in the back of her classroom for the past 2 years but has used them only twice, when students needed to use Microsoft Word. She never used them in her instruction and feels "guilty" that she's "wasted the school's money."

Teacher C stated that her participation in the professional development program "inspired" her to use computers in her instruction. In June she created a lesson in which her students would research on the Internet different careers in mathematics. It ended up as a "disaster," with her feeling "incompetent" and unable to use computers comfortably in her class. The students were unfocused and were downloading obscene and irrelevant information. She thought that the students "were protected" from Web sites with inappropriate content and was "devastated" when she realized how quickly the students "went nuts."

Due to this experience, Teacher C believes that much more training is necessary before she will ever try using computers in her classroom again. She wants to know how to manage a classroom when using four computers, how to keep students from entering inappropriate Web sites, how to keep students focused on assigned activities, and how to keep track of students' work on the computers. Despite the problems she faced, Teacher C has increased her use of computers for personal work and to create instructional materials, especially using Microsoft Word and searching the Internet. She uses computers almost on a daily basis now, whereas she used computers a few times a month prior to the training.

Teacher D (Science)

Teacher D's computer knowledge prior to participating in the professional development program was how to "push the power button." In the spring, the training inspired him to buy a computer for home and use it several times a week. He purchased the book *Computers for Dummies* and feels confident in using the Internet, e-mail, and Microsoft Word. Over the summer Teacher D took a UFT computer course, which reinforced what he learned in the professional development program offered at Silverton. He came to school in the fall "excited and ready" to bring his classes "into the 21st century."

For his biology classes, Teacher D prepared an activity in which students would dissect a frog on the Internet. He contacted the technology coordinator to set up a date to use the computer lab for each of his five classes, only to find out that the computer lab was no longer available for subject classes to use. Overcrowding required that the lab to be used as a regular classroom. Teacher D was "angry and frustrated" that Silverton High School would take time and money to train teachers only to let them "hang out to dry in the end." There are no computers in his classroom, and his assistant principal does not see the need to purchase computers for Teacher D's use. This experience has left Teacher D feeling "unmotivated, unappreciated, and useless to the students."

Teacher D would not attend any further training sessions if they were offered. If he can't use the knowledge he has now, "why bother learning more?" However, he does suggest that if the program is offered again, it should highlight the use of the Internet in content areas.

Teacher E (Social Studies)

Teacher E started the professional development program knowing how to use Microsoft Word to type letters and other simple documents. She "was excited" about the prospect of learning more about computers and related technology. After attending two or three sessions, she realized that the class was "moving too fast" and she wasn't "retaining" the information she was given. However, "being a professional," she stayed with the program and practiced with her son's computer. Her son has helped her to create tests and activity sheets, but it is impossible to "imagine" allowing her "students to use the computers during class time." In addition to not feeling comfortable with computers, given the new standards in global history and government, she states that "there is no way to teach students what they need to pass the Regents and play with computers at the same time." Teacher E acknowledges that computers can enhance the learning of students, but she does not have the knowledge or the ability to do it herself. She would welcome more training and/or having someone work with her one-on-one in using computers to teach social studies.

Regarding the professional development program, Teacher E thinks that more training is necessary in organizing the classroom for computer use and developing lessons that use computers effectively. She enjoyed the program and said that it strengthened her knowledge of the basics, motivated her to learn more, and gave her "quality time" with her son. Her use of computers has increased in that she now knows how to create more complicated documents, such as tests and activity sheets. Teacher E usually "works on the computer two to three times a week," which is much more than she used computers before. She recommends this program to other teachers, if they already have basic computer knowledge.

Teacher F (Mathematics)

Teacher F initially signed up for the professional development program "to get the per session money." However, she found it interesting and possibly worthwhile for some of the teachers. For her purposes, "computers really aren't necessary" to increase the learning of her students. She has been "teaching for 20 years" and has excellent results from her students. To take time away from her "effective lessons" and incorporate a "time-consuming computer project would hurt the students."

Teacher F mentioned that she has always used Microsoft Word in the past to create word problems for her students, and she has also used the computer in the math office to search the Internet. The professional development program allowed Teacher F to become a more confident computer user by "making searching the Internet much quicker and using Word much easier," but she "will never" use computers in the classroom.

Regarding the professional development program as a whole, Teacher F believed that it was "comprehensive and useful for some of the teachers." She saw that many teachers were enthusiastic and highly motivated about bringing computers into their classrooms. She has no recommendations for further workshops.

Appendix
D

Are You a Good Writer?

Good writing is an art and a craft. You can achieve clear communication by presenting ideas in an orderly manner and by expressing yourself smoothly and precisely. Are you a good writer?

Good writing takes practice. Three approaches to achieving effective communication are: (1) compose an outline and write without regard to style, punctuation, and grammar; (2) put aside the first draft, then reread it after a delay; and (3) ask a colleague to critique the draft for you.

I suggest you consult some of the many excellent publications available on writing style (see below). Some of you might benefit from taking a course on writing style as well. I suggest you carefully assess your writing ability and take the necessary steps for improvement. Good writing skills are necessary for continued success in your professional endeavors. Good luck *and* good writing!

Note: These questions refer to writing for research purposes, not necessarily for general writing.

Circle the correct, acceptable, or better sentence for each of the following pairs of examples.

1. a. Glanz (2000) designed the experiment.
    b. The experiment was designed by Glanz (2000).

2. a. Participants sat in comfortable chairs equipped with speakers that delivered the tone stimuli.
    b. The participants were sitting in comfortable chairs equipped with speakers that delivered the tone stimuli.

3. a. Glanz (2001) presented the same results.
    b. Glanz (2001) presents the same results.

4. a. Since that time investigators from several studies have used this method.
    b. Since that time investigators from several studies used this method.

5. a. The data are complete.
    b. The data is complete.

6. a. The percentage of correct responses, as well as the speed of the responses, increases with practice.
    b. The percentage of correct responses, as well as the speed of the responses, increase with practice.

7. a. The phenomena occur every 100 years.
    b. The phenomena occurs every 100 years.

8. a. Neither the participant nor the confederate was in the room.
    b. Neither the participant nor the confederate were in the room.

9. a. The positions in the sequence were changed, and the test was rerun.
    b. The positions in the sequence were changed, and the test rerun.

10. a. The group improved its scores 30 percent.
    b. The group improved their scores 30 percent.

11. a. The rats that completed the task successfully were re-warded.
    b. The rats who completed the task successfully were re-warded.

12. a. Name the participant who you found scored above the median.
    b. Name the participant whom you found scored above the median.

13. a. We had nothing to do with their being the winners.
    b. We had nothing to do with them being the winners.

14. a. Using this procedure, the investigator tested the subjects.
    b. The investigator tested the subjects using this procedure.

15. a. I hope this is not the case.
    b. Hopefully, this is not the case.

16. a. Brag (1999) found that participants performed well, whereas Bohr (2000) found that participants did poorly.
    b. Brag (1999) found that participants performed well, while Bohr (2000) found that participants did poorly.

17. a. The names were difficult both to pronounce and to spell.
    b. The names were difficult both to pronounce and spell.

18. a. In regard to this matter,…
    b. In regards to this matter,…

19. a. Charles's friend
    b. Charles' friend

20. a. None of us is perfect.
    b. None of us are perfect.

Answers: choice "a" for all questions

Suggested book list:

1. Consult the classic—Strunk, W., Jr., & White, E. B. (2000). *The elements of style* (4th ed.). New York: Macmillan.

2. Bates, J. D. (2000). *Writing with precision: How to write so that you cannot be misunderstood* (4th ed.). Washington, DC: Acropolis Books.

3. Consult the latest edition of the American Psychological Association (APA) manual for other relevant books.

Appendix

E

Brief Description of APA

The *Publication Manual* of the American Psychological Association (APA) (2001) is the accepted manual of style for writing reports in the social sciences. I recommend that my students adhere to this manual of style for several reasons:

1. It is relatively easy to learn and use.
2. It is widely used and known.
3. It enhances the professional appearance of reports.

Although you may have to refer to the *Publication Manual* for details about specific guidelines for documenting sources, here are some basic rules and sample references that should get you started.

APA uses no footnotes. All references are placed in the main body of the text as follows: "Jones (2000) stated that…"

To find the Jones reference you would consult the list of references placed at the end of the report that lists alphabetically, by author's last name, all works referred to in the report. In this example, you merely paraphrase what Jones stated, rather than quoting directly from the source. When paraphrasing is used, no mention of page numbers is necessary.

If you quote an author in the text of your report without mentioning his or her name, you might reference the work as follows: "It is maintained that cooperative learning is an effective means of...(Johnson & Johnson, 1990)." Note the use of the ampersand (&). The ampersand is always used instead of *and* when referenced with parentheses (for more explanation, see below). To find the reference in which "cooperative learning" is explained, consult the list of references placed at the end of the report. Note that paraphrasing is again employed, so no mention of page numbers is necessary.

A direct quote within the text is referenced as follows: "Moreover, Tanner and Tanner (1987) were correct when they stated that 'the development of public education and the field of supervision are so completely intertwined that they defy separation, even for purposes of analysis' (p. 4)."

Here a page number is cited because a direct quote is used. Page is abbreviated as "p." Notice the placement of the period after the closing parenthesis. Also, notice that *and* is used in "Tanner and Tanner" because you mention the names of the authors in the text instead of in parentheses.

Offset a lengthy quote as follows. Spears (1953) stated:

> Thirty or forty years ago, when supervision was first settling down in the organizational scheme of things as a service to the classroom teacher, a supervisor was a supervisor. Today, when supervision is attaching itself to almost anything that has to do with furthering learning, a supervisor masquerades under a miscellaneous array of titles. Supervision today often travels incognito. (p. 84)

Note that the page number is placed at the end of the quote with parentheses but without a period after it.

In general, APA recommends the use of the past tense when reporting research findings: Smith (2001) *reported,* not *reports.*

Use of *and* or *&.* In the reference list at the end of the report, always use &. In text, the & is used within parentheses, but when noting authors in the text, without the use of parentheses, the *and* is used. For example, in text you write "Welfel and Ingersoll (2001) reported that..."

Document a book in the references as follows: Glanz, J. (1991). *Bureaucracy and professionalism: The evolution of public school supervision.* Rutherford, NJ: Fairleigh Dickinson University Press.

Note several unique aspects of APA when referencing a book:

- The title of a book is italicized.
- Always use initials for the author's first and middle names.
- Only the first letter of the first word in a title is capitalized, as well as the first letter of a word appearing after a colon. Always capitalize the first letter of proper nouns.
- The year is placed in parentheses, followed by a period.

Document an article in the references as follows: Glanz, J. (1994). Dilemmas of assistant principals in their supervisory role: Reflections of an assistant principal. *Journal of School Leadership, 4,* 577–593.

Note several unique aspects of APA when referencing an article:

- The title of a journal name is italicized, as is the volume number.

- Always use initials for the author's first and middle names.

- Only the first letter of the first word in the title of an article is capitalized, as well as the first letter of a word appearing after a colon. Always capitalize the first letter of proper nouns. The year is placed in parentheses, followed by a period.

- The volume number is referenced by simply placing the number after the name of the journal, preceded by a comma. Sometimes an issue number is referenced as follows: "*76* (3)." This refers to volume 76, number 3. An issue number is referenced only for journals that begin a new pagination with each issue. For example, the *NASSP Bulletin* begins each issue with page 1. Therefore, referencing any article published in this journal would include an issue number: Glanz, J. (1994). Where did the assistant principalship begin? Where is it headed? *NASSP Bulletin, 78* (564), 35–41.

Notice that only the volume is italicized along with the journal name. The number is not, and it is always placed in parentheses.

Page numbers follow without designations of *p.* or *pp.* Write out numbers in full. Note the comma before the page numbers, to separate this from the volume and number.

Document a chapter or an article in an edited volume as follows: Garman, N. B. (1996). Is clinical supervision a viable model for use in the public schools? No. In J. Glanz & R. F. Neville (Eds.), *Educational supervision: Perspectives, issues, and controversies* (pp. 143–178). Norwood, MA: Christopher-Gordon.

Note several unique aspects of APA when referencing a chapter or an article in an edited volume:

- The title of a book is italicized.

- Always use initials for the author's first and middle names.

- Only the first letter of the first word in the title is capitalized, as well as the first letter of a word appearing after a colon. Always capitalize the first letter of proper nouns.

- The year is placed in parentheses, followed by a period.

- Names of editors (first initials, then last names). Editors' names are separated by an ampersand. When there are only two editors, no comma is used between the names. For three or more editors, a comma is placed before the ampersand.

- Page numbers of the chapter or the article appear in parentheses, as noted.

Document a newspaper article as follows: Schwartz, J. (1993, September 30). Obesity affects economic, social status. *Washington Post,* pp. A1, A4. The same documentation is used as with a magazine article, except for the abbreviation *pp.* for pages. "A1, A4" indicates that the article appears on discontinuous pages.

Document an edited book as follows: Glanz, J., & Neville, R. F. (Eds.). (1996). *Educational supervision: perspectives, issues, and controversies.* Norwood, MA: Christopher-Gordon. The same documentation is used as with a regular book, except the abbreviation *Eds.* is used to note the "editors."

Document an electronic source as follows: Glanz, J. (1997). Supervision news [On-line]. Available: http:// www.wagner.edu/~jglanz/.

Document a citation as follows. In text: (Rodriguez, 2000, as cited in Mullen, 2001). In other words, you consulted Mullen's work to obtain Rodriguez's quotation. You did not locate Rodriguez's work directly.

To obtain more information on electronic sources for APA citations, consult *Publication Manual of the American Psychological Association,* 5th edition, 2001.

Sample Portion of a Paper in APA Style

The study of history is a struggle to understand the "unending dialogue between the present and the past" (Carr & Smith, 1961, p. 8). As such, the notion of temporality is relevant to understanding the flow of historical events. People and events cannot be explained only in terms of the present but must be understood in terms of a past and a future as well. The past, present, and future, according to Cassirer, form an "undifferentiated unity and an indiscriminate whole" (Cassirer, 1953, p. 219). Kummel and Barnes (1966) explained this notion of temporality as a historical process "in which the past never assumes a final shape nor the future ever [sic] shuts its doors. Their essential interdependence also means, however, that there can be no progress without a retreat into the past in search of a deeper foundation" (p. 50).

The experience of reflective consciousness through historical inquiry implies an awareness of the past and its interconnectedness to present conditions and future possibilities. History, then, can be understood as an attempt to study the events and ideas of the past that have shaped human experience over time in order to inform current practice as well as to make more intelligent decisions for the future (Marsak, 1970).

History is more than simply recording all past experiences and events. Historians are interested in those aspects of the past that have historical significance. Since what may be historically significant to one may be irrelevant to another, the reconstruction of the past must be undertaken from different perspectives by different people. Moreover, significance is granted only when a sufficient amount of time has lapsed in order to ensure that contemporary demands alone do not dictate what is considered historically important (see, e.g., Davis, 1992). Seen in this way, history is the retelling and interpretation of significant events of the past (Kliebard, 1995; Stephens, 1974).

The value of history is its concreteness, its placing of events, people, and theories within context (see, e.g., Goodson, 1985; Kliebard, 1987). History supplies the context with which to view current proposals. More fundamentally, understanding how the field has come to take the shape it has is a compelling reason to undertake historical inquiry of supervision. History can also explore antecedents of current innovations or theories. Thus, having a supervision history will deepen and strengthen identity as a field of scholarship and provide a collective consciousness (Garrett, 1994).

References

Carr, E. H., & Smith, J. (1961). *What is history?* New York: Knopf.

Cassirer, E. (1953). *An essay on man: An introduction to a philosophy of human culture.* New York: Doubleday.

Davis, O. L., Jr. (1992). Memory, our educational practice, and history. *Educational Forum, 56,* 375–379.

Garrett, A. W. (1994). Curriculum history's connections to the present: Necessary lessons for informed practice and theory. *Journal of Curriculum and Supervision, 9,* 390–395.

Goodson, F. (1985). History, context, and qualitative methods in the study of the curriculum. In R. G. Burgess (Ed.), *Strategies of educational research: Qualitative methods* (pp. 121–152). London: Falmer Press.

Kliebard, H. M. (1987). *The struggle for the American curriculum: 1893–1958.* New York: Routledge & Kegan Paul.

Kliebard, H. M. (1995). Why history of education? *Journal of Educational Research, 88,* 194–199.

Kummel, F., & Barnes, M. N. (1966). Time as succession and the problem of duration. In J. T. Fraser (Ed.), *The voices of time* (pp. 31–55). New York: Braziller.

Marsak, L. M. (1970). *The nature of historical inquiry.* New York: Holt, Rinehart, and Winston.

Stephens, L. D. (1974). *Probing the past: A guide to the study and teaching of history.* Boston: Allyn & Bacon.

Note two additional items. In the text, when two or more references are noted within one set of parentheses, alphabetize according to the authors' last names. For example: (see, e.g., Goodson, 1985; Kliebard, 1987). Note that *e.g.* is the abbreviation for "for example." In the references list, if one author has two or more works cited, the earlier one is referenced first:

Kliebard, H. M. (1987). *The struggle for the American curriculum: 1893–1958.* New York: Routledge & Kegan Paul.

Kliebard, H. M. (1995). Why history of education? *Journal of Educational Research, 88,* 194–199.

A Final Word

You will notice that the format for APA is a bit awkward, with its use of capitalization, no mentioning of author's first name, and so forth. You should consult the APA manual in order to accurately apply other rules for documentation. My purpose is only to introduce the style briefly and to indicate its importance. Investment in the *Publication Manual* is suggested. Knowledge of APA will serve you well in other courses and in writing any reports during your professional career. Happy referencing.

Reference

American Psychological Association. (2001). *Publication manual of the American Psychological Association* (5th ed.). Washington, DC: Author. Visit www.apastyle.org.

Evaluation
Criteria
for Report

Students need to be informed in advance how their projects will be evaluated. Below is a list of criteria students have found useful.

The research project will be graded based on the following criteria (serious deficiency in any one of these criteria can affect your grade):

1. *Content:* Does your paper reflect a knowledge and understanding of the content, topic, or problem? Is the problem stated clearly and precisely? Is the author aware of critical issues that relate to the problem?

   Comments: _____

   _____

   _____

2. *Citations:* Are appropriate and sufficient authorities cited? Does the research include at least six articles and one book (seven references)? Are the references timely (within the last 5 years)?

   Comments: _____

   _____

   _____

3. *Coherence:* Is the paper well organized so that ideas "hang together"? Are ideas developed clearly? Are all sections of the research project included?

   Comments: _____

   _____

   _____

4. *Clarity:* Is the paper clear and easy to read? Is it aesthetically pleasing?

   Comments: _____

   _____

   _____

5. *Control:* Does the writing reflect good "technical control," such as, complete sentences, accurate spelling, correct punctuation and grammar, and paragraph development?

   Comments: _____

   _____

   _____

Appendix

G

Sample
Consent Forms

Reprinted with permission, Brown and Benchmark Publishers.

Example of a Research
Participant Consent Form

I, _____ [printed name of participant], agree to participate in the research project [title of project], being carried out by [name of researcher(s)]. I have been informed by the researchers of the general nature of the project and of any foreseeable potential risks.

I understand that I may withdraw from this project at any time, and that even if I do not withdraw, I have the right to withhold permission from the researcher(s) to use any data based on my participation.

I also understand that upon my request, the researcher(s) will provide me with a written summary of the project's findings.

_____

(Participant's signature) (Date)

Example of a Parental Consent Form

I, _____ [printed name of parent or guardian], agree to permit _____ [printed name of child] to partici-pate in the research project [title of project], being carried out by [name of researcher(s)]. I have been informed by the researchers of the general nature of the project and of any foreseeable potential risks. I understand the following:

1. My child may withdraw from this project at any time.

2. I may withdraw permission for my child to participate in the project at any time.

3. Even if my child completes the project, I have the right to withhold permission from the researcher(s) to use any data based on my child's participation.

4. Upon my request, the researcher(s) will provide me with a written summary of the project's findings.

_____

(Signature of parent or guardian)

_____

(Date)

_____

(Relationship to child)

Sample
Cover Letter

Below is a sample cover letter you can use as a model to draft your own when distributing a questionnaire.

Recommended Format for a Cover Letter:

Date

Dear _____ (Parent, Faculty, Staff, Student, Colleague, Participant, etc.):

I am a graduate student in the Masters in _____ Program at _____ University. I am conducting a research study and have attached a questionnaire that asks you to _____ (state its purpose in one sentence). The results of this study will be used to _____ (tell the respondent what the survey will be used for in one sentence).

I know you are very busy but I hope you can assist me. Please take a few minutes to complete and return the questionnaire. It will take approximately _____ minutes to complete. Please use the self-addressed stamped envelope and mail the survey back to me no later than _____ (date).

Thank you for your assistance and cooperation.

Sincerely,

Sign
Your full name

Glossary

A-B; **A-B-A**; or **A-B-A-B research designs**   Types of single subject designs.

Achievement test   A commonly used measure or assessment tool in action research; a kind of standardized test in which an individual's knowledge or proficiency in a given content area is assessed. The Stanford Achievement Test and the Iowa Test of Basic Skills are examples of standardized achievement tests.

Analysis of covariance (ANCOVA)   A statistical technique used in group comparison research when equivalence between the groups (usually only two in action research) cannot be ascertained. To compute an analysis of covariance, you would use a computer program such as STATPAK.

Analysis of variance (**ANOVA,** sometimes called the *F test*)   A statistical technique for determining whether significant differences can be found among the means of three or more groups. To compute an analysis of variance, you would use a computer program such as STATPAK.

Aptitude test   A kind of standardized test used as a data collection instrument (or data source) designed to predict someone's ability to perform. IQ tests are an example of an aptitude test. The SAT, taken by precollegiate students, is another example of an aptitude test.

Assessment   A process of interpreting information to aid decision making. Assessments include all the information an educator collects to help make an informed, thoughtful decision. Thus, assessment is a general term for interpreting the data that is collected. As an educational leader, you may collect data (by various measurements, interviews, observations, portfolios, and surveys) about teachers in your school. Assessment occurs when you interpret the meaning of these data. Your interpretation of the data may lead you to conclude that a particular teacher is having trouble dealing with disruptive students. Your assessment leads you to believe, in other words, that this teacher needs classroom management training.

Because the terms *assessment, measurement,* and *evaluation* are often used synonymously, an attempt to clarify differences is in order. Measurement refers to the process of gathering information and is often expressed numerically. In the case above, for instance, the number of times this teacher refers students to the dean or vice principal is one form of measurement. Ordinarily, scores on tests are considered measurements. However, a measurement really refers to any way of collecting data, including questionnaires, aptitude tests, and other surveys.

Assessment is a broader term that includes measurements, but it also includes interpreting measurements in order to make some sort of decision. Concluding that a student is reading on the sixth-grade level or that a teacher is suffering from burnout is derived though assessment; that is, interpreting various measurements.

Evaluation, in contrast, refers to the process of making a decision based on the assessment process. For example, referring a burnt-out teacher to counseling might be a decision made as a result of interpreting the collected data. Placing a student in a remedial class is an evaluative measure taken after having interpreted or assessed various measurements or data collected.

Every competent leader is continually taking measurements, assessing them, and then taking a course of action by making some decision or evaluation.

Baseline   A graphic record of measurements taken prior to introducing an intervention or treatment in a single subject research design such as a time series design.

Case study   One of three methods of qualitative research discussed in this book. Case studies involve in-depth investigations of an individual or a group of individuals. Findings are stated verbally, not numerically. Case studies are reported by describing in detail observations made of individuals, groups, or school settings.

Chi square analysis (X^2)   A statistical technique for assessing the relationship between two or more nominal variables. (*Chi* is pronounced with a K and long I sound). To compute a chi square, you would use a computer program such as STATPAK.

Close-ended questionnaire   A questionnaire that limits possible responses by providing specific choices or options (e.g., *yes, no, uncertain*) to a respondent. Likert scales are an example of a close-ended questionnaire.

Collaborative action research   A form of action research in which parents, teachers, and principals might be involved in an ongoing program of assessment and improvement. Each group member shares in the planning, implementation, and analysis of the research. A premise underlying this book is that educational leaders should develop their skills in *individual* action research projects before involving others in the process. However, if your school is interested in developing collaborative action research teams, consult the Institute for Responsive Education (see Annotated References) and other works that discuss collaborative and schoolwide action research.

Conceptual definition   One of two ways to define terms in a research study. A conceptual definition is a typical dictionary definition of a term or concept. Sources for conceptual definitions are usually authorities in the field. The following is an example of a conceptual definition: Cooperative learning "involves positive interdependence among students, face to face interaction, individual accountability for mastery of material and the development of personal and small group skills" (Johnson & Johnson, 1985).

Confounding factor   Something that causes erroneous conclusions to be drawn from a study. In group comparison studies, for example, changes in the dependent variable may not be caused by the treatment under study but may in fact be influenced by some other intended or unforeseen factors. Two such confounding factors are the Hawthorne and John Henry Effects.

The Hawthorne Effect occurs when members in the experimental group know they are receiving "special" treatment, and thus they will improve no matter what treatment they are receiving. Members of such experimental groups consider themselves special or privileged. The original Hawthorne Effect studies were conducted by Elton Mayo and his associates in the late 1920s and early 1930s at the Hawthorne Plant of Western Electric near Chicago.

The John Henry Effect, the opposite of the Hawthorne Effect, occurs when subjects in the control group know that they are, in a sense, competing with some other group (experimental) and consequently expend extra effort to perform better than the experimental group.

The Hawthorne and John Henry Effects may cause erroneous conclusions to be drawn from your study and are thus called confounding factors. Obviously, every effort to make each group feel special would avert problems with the Hawthorne Effect. In group comparison research (e.g., assessing the effect of computer-assisted instruction on computational skills between two groups), both groups should be exposed to some special treatment (computers, in this case) without letting the participants know what you are measuring. For example, the control group may use computers to enhance writing skills while using traditional methods to learn computational skills. The experimental group is exposed to computers to enhance its mathematical computational skill development. Participants in this study do not know what you are measuring, and thus the Hawthorne Effect is minimized.

A discussion of other confounding factors should be included in the "limitations" section of your report. Although your study may be limited by several factors, confounding factors refer only to those factors or situations that may cause erroneous conclusions to be drawn.

Content analysis   A method of data analysis in which you analyze the content in a given document according to prescribed categories or criteria while following explicit rules of coding.

Control group (sometimes called *comparison group*)   The term used in group comparison studies to identify the group, sometimes assigned randomly, that remains untreated or receives a treatment other than the one received by the experimental group. Data collected from individuals in a control group are compared with data collected from members of an experimental group. These groups then serve as comparisons or controls for subjects who are receiving special treatments.

Converted score   A raw score that is converted into a grade equivalent, percentile, stanine, or other form. Raw scores that are converted are more easily understood, compared, and interpreted.

Correlation (synonymous with the word *relationship*)   A statistical technique for evaluating the degree to which two variables relate to one another. Correlational analyses are most easily computed using STATPAK or any similar program.

Correlation coefficient (or coefficient of correlation)   A statistic (r) that indicates the degree of relationship between two or more variables.

Correlational research   One of three methods of research that assume a quantitative approach in studying a given educational issue or problem.

Criterion-referenced test   One of two major types of testing instruments that measure minimum levels of student performance. Teacher-made tests are one example of a criterion-referenced test.

Data collection   The process of collecting information to answer one's research questions and/or confirm or reject a hypothesis. One of the major steps of the scientific method, data collection should be comprehensive and multiple.

Degree of freedom (usually abbreviated as *df*)   A term used in statistical inference to connote the amount of choice a researcher has in selecting a given sample for one's study. Degree of freedom is one of the more difficult statistical terms to fully understand. All you have to know is that *df* always = N – 1; that is, the number of subjects in your sample minus one.

Let's say I asked you to choose any five numbers you like, as long as the mean is 10. You would have, theoretically, four degrees of freedom to choose any four numbers you wish. Try this: choose any number. Say you choose 5. Now choose another number; say you choose 9. Then choose a third number, 7, and still another number, 10. You have now selected four numbers (5, 9, 7, 10). You have had complete freedom to choose any four numbers you wished. The mean of these four numbers, however, is 7.75. However, I said the mean must be 10. Thus, in selecting a fifth number, you have no freedom. You must select the number 19. Add, 5, 9, 7, 10, and 19 and divide by 5 to get a mean of 10. Therefore, *df* always equals N – 1; in this case, 5 – 1.

This concept of degree of freedom will come into play when you interpret statistical significance.

Dependent variable   The term used for the outcome variable in group comparison research. In such research, the experimenter manipulates one variable (the independent variable) to measure its effect on a second variable, which is known as the dependent variable. It is the variable that *depends* on the other variable (the independent one). In order to easily remember which variable is dependent, know that the dependent variable is synonymous with the word *outcome*.

Consider this research question: How is math achievement affected by computer-assisted instruction? The desired outcome in this research question is math achievement. Thus math achievement is the dependent variable.

Descriptive research   One of three methods of research that assumes a quantitative approach in studying a given educational issue or problem. Surveys and observational reports are types of descriptive research. It may use statistics or numbers (usually percentages) to describe data.

Descriptive statistics   One category or type of statistics used in descriptive research to describe and summarize data. Two of the most common ways to describe data statistically are mean and standard deviation.

Design   *See* Research design.

Empirical research   A method of investigation based on observation. Any study you conduct that involves investigation by observation is considered empirical research. Action research may be thought of as a form of empirical research, although it encompasses many other methods of investigation as well.

Ethnography   One of three methods of qualitative research discussed in this book. It is used to observe individuals or groups of individuals in natural settings. The ethnographic researcher takes many notes describing what was observed.

Evaluation   An ongoing decision-making process about the quality of a program, product, or procedure. Evaluation takes place only after measurements have been taken and assessment (interpretive) procedures completed. Once data are collected and interpreted, an educational leader can make a better decision or judgment. Evaluations may occur informally or formally.

Evaluation research   The most common use of action research. Evaluation research is not a separate research method, like ethnographic or correlational research. Rather, evaluation research is a common use of action research that may incorporate quantitative and/or qualitative approaches.

Experimental group   A group, assigned randomly in experimental research, that receives a special treatment. Data are then collected to determine the effect that this treatment has on the experimental group. The experimental group is contrasted with data collected from a control group.

Experimental research   One of the three types of group comparison research that utilizes quantitative approaches. Experimental studies assign individuals to either experimental or control conditions. Randomization occurs in experimental studies.

Ex post facto research   One of the three types of group comparison research that utilizes quantitative approaches. Ex post facto studies involve intact classes that are assigned to either experimental or control conditions. No randomization occurs in these studies. Ex post facto research studies involve groups already formed, such as classes in periods 2 and 4 in a high school. The study is carried out after the fact (ex post facto), after the classes or groups have already been formed. You as the researcher have no control over the fact that these students are part of periods 2 and 4. A study involving self-concepts of mainstream and nonmainstream students is an example of ex post facto research because mainstream and nonmainstream groups already exist, with various degrees of self-concept. You are merely using these preexisting or intact classes as part of your study to compare self-concept. Therefore, the major difference between ex post facto research and experimental studies is that in the former, neither groups nor individuals are randomized to form comparison groups. Comparisons are thus made with intact or preexisting classes.

External validity   A form of validity that is synonymous with generalizability—the degree to which results can be generalized to other populations. Action research studies are rarely generalizable and therefore have weak external validity. The lack of external validity does not in any way diminish the significance of action research.

Focus group   A group of individuals who are selected by a researcher and consent voluntarily to share their views and opinions on specific topics related to an action research project. As a type of survey, a focus group is not unlike a group interview.

Generalizability   The degree to which findings derived from one context or under one set of conditions may be assumed to apply to other settings or conditions. Action research studies do not generally yield findings that are generalizable. Studies with large numbers of subjects or participants are more likely generalizable than action research studies, which involve a small group of individuals.

General semantics   The study of the relationship among language, thought, and behavior. It helps us to use language more scientifically and accurately. Often errors occur when we begin to interpret collected data. To avoid possible errors and misinterpretations, the study of general semantics cautions us to incorporate multiple sources of data when undertaking any research project. Using a variety of approaches lessens the chance that we might reach an unwarranted conclusion. Relying on the weight of many sources of information is far better than making some sort of decision based on only one or two pieces of evidence.

Grade equivalent   A converted score that reports how well or poorly a student has done on a standardized test. Raw scores on standardized tests are converted into grade equivalents by indicating grade levels and months. A grade equivalent of 5.3 in reading, for example, indicates that a student is reading at a fifth-grade level in the eighth month. Grade equivalents are usually reported in school profiles. Although more revealing than raw scores, grade equivalents are not as accurate as stanines or percentiles.

Group comparison research   One of three methods of quantitative research that can be used by action researchers. In these studies, the researcher administers different treatments to groups and then compares the groups on a dependent variable.

Historical inquiry   One of three methods of qualitative research discussed in this book.

Hypothesis   A researcher's educated or informed guess about the relationship between two or more variables. A hypothesis is a statement of prediction, an anticipated outcome. Hypotheses are utilized only in quantitative studies. There are three major types of hypotheses: directional, nondirectional, and null.

Directional hypotheses indicate an influence between the variables under study, as in the following example: "Teachers supervised by clinical supervision will have more favorable attitudes towards their supervisors than teachers supervised by traditional forms of supervision." This hypothesis indicates that one group will demonstrate more favorable attitudes, thus indicating that a particular variable will influence, or direct, the other.

Nondirectional hypotheses, in contrast, indicate that there will be a difference between teachers who are observed, but they do not specify a direction between the two variables. "There will be a difference between self-concept levels between mainstream and non-mainstream students" is an example of a nondirectional hypothesis.

Null hypotheses indicate that no relationship or difference between the two groups or variables is likely. "There will be no difference in self concept levels between mainstream and nonmainstream students" is an example of a null hypothesis. As was indicated in Chapter 4, null hypotheses are usually employed when statistical analyses are calculated.

In traditional educational research, hypotheses are generated only after an extensive review of the literature on a given topic. Since a literature review is not extensively employed in action research, I advise my students to always frame their hypotheses in the null form, especially when some statistical work will be done.

Independent variable   The variable manipulated by the experimenter in group comparison research to determine its effect or influence on another variable (the dependent variable). Let's say you're interested in researching the following question: How is teacher satisfaction (morale) influenced by the leadership style of the principal? Leadership style is the independent variable that is manipulated by the researcher to determine its impact on the dependent variable—in this case, teacher morale. The independent variable is considered manipulated because the researcher could have chosen any variable in order to study its effect on teacher morale. Also, it's manipulated in the sense that various leadership styles may be studied in a given context or situation. For example, democratic leaders may influence morale differently than autocratic styles, under various circumstances.

Dependent variables always signify outcomes, whereas independent variables can be manipulated.

Consider this research question: How is math achievement affected by computer-assisted instruction? The desired outcome in this research question is math achievement. Math achievement is therefore the dependent variable. The other variable is independent, because you could have selected any variable to study its influence on math achievement. It's also independent because you can independently assign one group to computer-assisted instruction while another group is exposed to some other treatment.

Inferential statistics   One category or type of statistics that tells us how much confidence we can have in generalizing from a sample to a population. Action research is not very concerned with inferential statistics.

Instrument   Any device used to collect data, such as a test, questionnaire, or portfolio. The word *techniques* should be considered synonymous with the term *instrument*. Although the terms are interchangeable, I prefer the word *techniques,* at times, because it conveys action.

Internal validity   A form of validity that assesses the degree to which the data you collect are unbiased and undistorted. The following two measures increase internal validity: (a) longer periods of data collection, and (b) more subjects (e.g., more respondents to a survey).

   Four factors are threats to internal validity: (a) *Mortality,* a situation in which respondents or subjects of a study drop out for some reason. A poor rate of return of a questionnaire is an example of the concept of mortality. Fewer returns of the questionnaire reduces the number of participants in your study and thus becomes a threat to internal validity. (b) *Maturation,* in which students do well because of physical or mental growth over time and not necessarily because of the treatment. (c) *History,* a situation unrelated to the study that may influence a change in behavior or achievement levels. Let's say you wanted to assess a particular workshop on teacher morale in your district. If at the time of this study or in the recent past, a budget crisis loomed that froze teacher wages, the results of your study might be influenced by this budgetary situation and not be caused by the series of workshops offered. (d) *Reactivity,* the likelihood that a pretest will affect posttest results. Respondents to a questionnaire, for example, may figure out what you are looking for and respond accordingly on the posttest.

Interrupted time series design   *See* Single subject design.

Intervention   *See* Treatment.

Interview   One method of collecting data based on surveying the views of an individual or group of individuals. Although face-to-face interviews are the most common type, phone interviews are frequently employed in action research projects.

Interview protocol   A predetermined set of questions used by an interviewer to conduct an interview. If you were to interview your superintendent, you might want to prepare a set of questions ahead of time. These questions are known as the interview protocol. An interview protocol, especially for an inexperienced interviewer, will lessen anxiety and structure the interview positively. Sometimes the protocol may be shared with the interviewee to allow him or her to see the range of questions that may be asked.

Level of significance   A term used in quantitative studies to refer to the probability that the difference between the variables studied occurred by chance and not because of your treatment. In most educational studies, the desired level of significance is 5% (.05). For some action research studies the level is less stringent (10%, or .10). In other words, there's only a 5% or 10% chance that differences between the experimental and control groups could have occurred by pure chance without any treatment.

Levels of significance are represented by the *p* level or *alpha* level. You are likely to see a level of significance reported as follows: $p < .05$, meaning that the probability that differences between both groups were due to chance factors are less than 5 chances in 100, or 5%.

Likert scale   A type of questionnaire, developed by Rensis Likert, that utilizes the following categories of possible responses: strongly disagree, disagree, agree, and strongly agree.

Mann-Whitney U-test   A statistical technique used to determine whether or not two small groups differ significantly from one another. This test is often used for static-group comparison designs. This test operates like a t-test.

Matched pairs   A technique for equating groups on one or more variables, resulting in each member of one group having a direct counterpart in another group. Matched pairing is used to form equivalent or comparable groups when randomization is not possible. A teacher, for instance, may divide an intact class into two comparable groups for the purpose of conducting a group comparison study. Matched pairs is a very useful technique used by action researchers.

Mean   The arithmetic average of a group of scores. The mean is calculated by the sum of the scores divided by the number of scores.

Multiordinality   A concept from the study of general semantics that implies that language often inadequately describes what we see. What we all call a chair, for example, is a chair only because we have agreed that the object should be called a chair. There is nothing inherent in the object itself that necessitates that we call it by that name. Moreover, similar words may have multiple meanings, or multiordinality. For example, the word *bridge* may have multiple meanings depending on the context in which it is used. The bridge of your nose is very different from the bridge that you cross in your car. Multiordinality refers to the fact that misunderstanding in language is all too common. Therefore, as researchers we must be aware that when we examine a given phenomenon, limitations exist in our ability to accurately describe what is really happening.

Nonequivalent control group design   A research design used in ex post facto studies that involves at least two groups. Both groups are pretested, and one group receives a treatment. Both groups are then posttested. Individuals are not randomly assigned to groups.

Norm-referenced test (synonymous with *standardized tests*) One of two major types of testing instruments that measures differences among individuals being tested. Norm-referenced tests are usually used as important data collection sources.

Observation A data collection strategy involving watching behavior within a social setting. Observer can watch without actually participating or may watch in a detached manner.

One-group pretest and posttest design A research design, sometimes called a preexperimental research design, that involves one group that is pretested, exposed to a treatment, and posttested. This design is considered weak because no comparison group is utilized. Yet one-group pretest and posttest designs are commonly employed by educational leaders as part of action research projects (a) because often only one group is available, and (b) because of its relative ease at administering and analyzing. Although such a design is not usually one's first choice, one-group pretest and posttest designs can be used effectively by employing the sign test for analysis.

Operational definition One of two ways to define terms in a research study. Operational definitions involve observable, measurable, and quantifiable descriptions of key terms in a research study. Science achievement, for example, can be operationally defined as a passing score of 70% on a teacher-made science test. A supervisor-made questionnaire could also be defined operationally by stating the nature of the survey (e.g., Likert), the design (e.g., designed by researcher, as opposed to using some commercially developed instrument), and how the questionnaire will be measured (e.g., a favorable attitudinal score would be 25 and above). Operational definitions do not merely define the terms conceptually but also describe them and state how they will be measured.

Percentage The number per 100 of individuals who gave a particular response or achieved a particular score. Percentages are often used to describe and analyze data in action research projects.

Percentile The percentage of individuals who scored above or below a given score. For instance, if a third grader scored at the 76th percentile, her score exceeded 76% of the third graders who took that same test. Percentiles are converted scores.

Performance-based assessment A type of measurement in which an individual is asked to perform a specific skill (e.g., write an essay on the causes of the Civil War, or perform a series of ballet movements). Student performance is assessed against established criteria. Gymnastic performances at the Olympics are an example of performance-based assessment.

Population   The large or total group from which a sample is derived. For example, all male college students, all principals in New Jersey, or all graduates under age 25 are considered populations. As a researcher, I want to draw a sample from a given population. Members of a sample are called subjects (Ss), or participants.

Portfolio   A data collection instrument (or data source) that includes a great deal of information about a particular individual or group of individuals. Portfolios may include a student's achievement test scores, book reports, homework assignments, art projects, class tests, oral presentations, self-assessments, or artwork. Portfolios are excellent ways of collecting data from a variety of perspectives.

Posttest-only control group design   A research design used in experimental research that involves at least two randomly formed groups in which one group receives a treatment and then both groups are posttested for comparison.

Pretest and posttest control group design   A research design used in experimental research that involves at least two randomly formed groups in which one group receives a treatment and then both groups are pretested and posttested.

Program evaluation   A very common type of evaluation research used by educational leaders who undertake action research projects.

Qualitative research   An approach to examining questions that can best be answered by verbally describing how participants in a study perceive and interpret various aspects of their environment.

Quantitative research   An approach to examining questions that can best be answered by collecting and statistically analyzing numerical data.

Quasi-experimental research   One of the three types of group comparison research that utilizes quantitative approaches. Quasi-experimental studies assign groups, not individuals, to either experimental or control conditions. No randomization occurs. Quasi-experimental studies are the most commonly used in education because teachers and supervisors rarely have the opportunity to truly randomize subjects into groups. Intact classes or groups are most common. For example, let's say you wanted to compare method A to method B. As a high school teacher you might have two equivalent or comparable groups of 10th graders during periods 4 and 7. These are intact classes, because you didn't randomly assign them to these classes. You can, however, randomly assign the *methods*. Period 4 may be assigned method B, and period 7 may be assigned method A. In other words, quasi-experimental studies randomly assign intact groups to different methods rather than randomly assigning individuals. Quasi-experimental research, as used in this volume, also refers to studies that do not use control groups.

Questionnaire   A type of survey that is distributed to a sample to ascertain attitudes about a particular issue or concern. Although a questionnaire is a type of survey, the two terms are not necessarily synonymous.

Randomization   *See* Sampling.

Raw score   The number of correct responses. Raw scores are frequently converted into percentiles so that comparisons can be made with individual test or questionnaire scores. A raw score of 32 does not indicate how well or poorly a certain individual performed on a test. Once the raw score is converted into a percentile (e.g., 89%), one might then ascertain how this particular individual performed in relation to the other test takers. In this case, we may conclude that the individual scored higher than 89% of the test takers.

Reliability   The degree to which an instrument yields consistent results under repeated administrations. When you hear the term *reliability,* you should immediately think of *consistency.* Usually, if you want to know if a particular instrument is reliable, you would consult the test maker's manual. Reliability, whether reported by a manual or computed on one's own, is reported in terms of a correlation coefficient. The closer the coefficient of correlation (which is expressed in hundredths) comes to +1.00, the higher the reliability factor. Thus, for instance, a reliability coefficient of .80 would indicate that the instrument (e.g., a test) is reliable. Remember that no test is ever 100% reliable.

   In qualitative approaches to research, two kinds of reliability are common: (a) *External reliability* refers to the degree to which your study can be replicated by others. In other words, if someone followed your procedures and methods, they would report similar findings. Yet the nature of qualitative research is so personal that external reliability is difficult to attain. In a study I recently completed, I wanted to ascertain the kinds of images of principals that were depicted in film and television. After previewing dozens of sitcoms and movies, I identified, through content analysis, three categories of images. External reliability was confirmed, in this case, by having independent researchers view the same episodes to confirm my categories. (b) *Internal reliability,* which is synonymous with *interrater reliability.* Common reliability tests include the following:

1.   The *test-retest method,* in which the same test is repeated over a period of time. Two test administrations are required. Correlations are taken between the two sets of test results. The resulting correlation coefficient is the index of reliability. Note that correlations can be inflated if the time interval between the tests is short.

2.   The *parallel* (or *equivalent*) *forms method,* similar to the previous method, in which you retest the same group with an equivalent form of the test. This method requires two administrations (form A of the

test is administered in September, for instance, and then form B is administered to the same group in March). The two sets of scores are correlated, as in the test-retest method.

3. The *split-half method,* in which the test is split into two parts (or halves), such as odd-numbered items and even-numbered items. The test is administered to the same group. Two sets of scores are obtained for each person: a score based on the odd-numbered items and a score based on the even-numbered items. These two sets of scores are correlated to obtain a reliability coefficient. Note that the longer the test, the more reliable it will be. Note also that a split-half reliability quotient may be calculated by referring to T. K. Crowl's 1986 book *Fundamentals of Research: A Practical Guide for Educators and Special Educators* (Columbus, OH: Publishing Horizons). Easy-to-follow, step-by-step procedures are provided in the appendixes.

4. The *Kuder-Richardson Formula (KR-21),* used to measure the consistency of an instrument in which all items have the same characteristic or degree of difficulty. Tests that include diverse items or various levels of difficulty should be subjected to split-half reliability assessments. KR-21 may be calculated by referring to Crowl's work, cited above.

5. *Interrater reliability,* used in qualitative research and single subject research designs, involves comparing ratings or rankings given by independent observers. The more similar the rankings, the higher the reliability. Interrater reliability, therefore, refers to the percentage of agreement among independent observers. Teachers use this form of reliability in grading standardized writing tests. Three teachers rate a given essay separately, and an average score is then computed. In this way, no single rating is given preference.

Reliability is enhanced by the use of multiple data sources, and the reliability of qualitative studies is enhanced through the use of multiple observers.

Research design   Sometimes called methodology, this is the overall plan for conducting a systematic inquiry. Usually, four components are included: sample, materials, procedure, and analysis of results.

Research question   The question posed by action researchers as they undertake qualitative studies. Research questions guide the research and are answered as a result of conducting the study. One researcher tells a story of his 2-year-old daughter, who, when asked by her older brother "What is 14 minus 7?", immediately responds, "7." When asked, "What is 88 minus 79?", she responds, "9," and when asked the cube root of 125, she confidently answers, "5." Someone listening to this 2-year-old apparent genius would be amazed. Actually, she has only learned a trick—that when she is asked those particular questions, she should always respond by repeating the last number she heard. When asked "What's three plus zero?" she would incorrectly respond zero. Slavin explains that the message of the story is that "it's not only the answers you get but the questions you ask that determine the value of a study" (p. 1). Research is about finding answers to questions worth asking. Developing research questions is necessary in order to select an appropriate research design.

Simply ask yourself, "What do I want to learn from this investigation?" You might pose this question, for example: "What factors seem to account for differences between boys and girls in math and science achievement in my high school?" Your research would attempt to discover the critical factors that account for such presumed differences.

Research report   A formal document that describes how a study was conducted, including results and conclusions. The format for a research report will vary depending on the school district or agency.

Response set   The tendency to respond in a particular way to the content of a questionnaire.

Sample   The group of subjects or participants chosen from a larger group, known as the population.

Sampling   A technique used to select participants for a study. Sampling involves a process by which members in the population have an equal chance of being selected. Note that as a general rule, the larger the sample, the greater the likelihood for obtaining significant results. There are four types of sampling:

1. *Random sampling* involves each member of the population having an equal chance of being selected. The Table of Random Numbers, which can be found in any book on statistics, can be used for studies involving many subjects. For smaller studies, simply shuffling cards with names of all the members of a population and then selecting a certain number of cards from the top of the deck (like pulling names out of a hat) could also be used, as long as all members of the population have an equal chance of being selected.

2. *Stratified sampling* involves identifying two or more subsets (e.g., gender, ethnicity, geographic location) in a population and taking a random sampling of each subset. Identifying subsets in advance of obtaining a sample reduces the possibility that an important group is left out of the sample. Let's say you wanted a representative number of elementary, middle, and high school teachers for a survey you are conducting throughout a district on attitudes toward supervision. You

would identify the numbers of elementary, middle, and high school teachers and then take a random sampling from each category, thus ensuring representation from all three groups of teachers.

3. *Systematic sampling* involves using a specific method to select a fraction of the population, such as choosing every tenth name on a list.

4. *Cluster sampling* involves identifying a site (e.g., a school, district, or class) and then taking a random sample from it.

Qualitative sampling procedures may be quite different from techniques previously described. Obtaining a representative sample is less important in qualitative research studies because generalization is not a concern. Often, samples are chosen for qualitative studies based on convenience, individual preference, or happenstance.

Scale of measurement   A method by which to determine what type of statistical analysis is appropriate. There are four scales of measurement:

1. *Nominal* (categorical) is the lowest scale of measurement. Nominal categories are not quantifiable; they are nonnumerical, such as gender, ethnicity, and religious affiliation. An easy way to remember nominal variables is to know that nominal means naming. That is, a nominal variable just names things. For instance, gender (male or female), names of states (Texas, California), socioeconomic status (upper, middle, lower), and political party affiliations (Republican, Democratic) are nominal. Nominal variables have no order (from high to low), and one category is not better than another.

2. *Ordinal* (order) ranks subjects from high to low, but it does not indicate how much higher or lower one subject is in relation to another. An example of an ordinal variable is ranking height from tallest to shortest (e.g., Mary, 1; Sue, 2; Fran, 3; Bill, 4) or ranking three brands of cereal by consumer preference. Note that Likert scales are really ordinal, but in education they are treated statistically as interval.

3. *Interval* tells us how much subjects differ from one another. For example, raw scores are interval scales. Subject 1 (S1), with a raw score of 100 (out of 100) has 50 points more than subject 2 (S2), with a score of 50. Although we can say that S1 scored 50 points higher than S2, we can't say that S1 is twice as smart as S2 because interval scales have no absolute zero point (as do ratio scales). Interval data differences are considered real; for example, raw scores of 4 and 2 have the same difference as raw scores of 6 and 8.

4. *Ratio* is the highest and most precise scale, or level, of measurement. The ratio scale is the same as the interval scale, except for the fact that it has an absolute zero point. Weight, for example, is based on a ratio scale. Someone who weighs 140 pounds is twice as heavy as someone who weighs 70 pounds.

Here's a mnemonic to help you recall the 4 scales of measurement: No One Is Ready (N = nominal; O = ordinal; I = interval; R = ratio). Here is a summary:

N = Shaquille O'Neal is tall, and I am short.

O = Shaquille O'Neal is taller than I.

I = Shaquille O'Neal is 7 feet tall, and I am 5 feet tall.

R = Shaquille O'Neal is $^7/_5$, or $1^2/_5$, as tall as I am.

School profile   A document that summarizes quantitative data about a given school. Usually published annually by the district office or board of education, a school profile includes demographic data and detailed summaries of student achievement levels. A school profile summarizes important data from a variety of instruments and, as such, is an invaluable means of data collection. Obtain a recent profile of your school to see the kinds of useful data provided.

Scientific method   A four-step approach to disciplined inquiry that is most usually applied to quantitative studies. As an educational leader who wishes to examine the impact of a new literature series on reading comprehension achievement of two equivalent groups of students, you would apply the scientific method as follows:

1. *Define the problem.* Let's say you wanted to determine the impact of invented spelling on kindergartners' ability to spell. The first step would be to express the problem as specifically as possible. A problem must be expressed behaviorally. A problem that is not defined precisely cannot be investigated scientifically. To ask "Is invented spelling good for kindergarten students?" is imprecise because of our inability to measure *good.* Defining the problem more precisely, one might ask: "What is the impact of invented spelling on kindergartners' ability to spell?"

2. *State the hypothesis.* Action research does not require an extensive review of the literature. Rather, one makes an educated guess about a specific situation. In the case above, one might hypothesize as follows: "Kindergarten students who are taught spelling by invented spelling will score significantly higher on a spelling test than students who are taught by another method." When some statistical work

will be done, the hypothesis should be framed in the null form: "There will be no difference in spelling achievement between kindergarten students taught by invented spelling and students taught by another method."

3. *Collect and analyze the data.* We collect data in order to test our hypothesis. In order to determine the impact of invented spelling on kindergartners' ability to spell, we might administer a spelling test. This would be our primary means of collecting data. We might also collect data by noting the number of words spelled correctly during classwork. We then analyze the data statistically to confirm or reject our hypothesis.

4. *Accept or reject the hypothesis.* Analysis of the collected data will provide evidence for either rejecting or accepting the hypothesis. If the evidence supports the hypothesis, then the hypothesis is accepted. If the evidence is contrary to the hypothesis, then the hypothesis is rejected. Students often think that a rejected hypothesis means a less worthy study. Such a conclusion could not be further from the truth. As long as you have applied the steps of the scientific method properly, your study is valid even when its findings are contrary to the existing literature in the field.

Sign test   A simple statistical technique or test to determine if the posttest scores are different from the pretest scores in one-group pretest and posttest designs.

Single measurement design   A research design that uses one means of assessment for a given treatment.

Single subject design   A research design used in quasi-experimental research that involves one individual or a few individuals with respect to a given variable (e.g., changes in behavior). Subjects are exposed to a treatment, and then multiple measurements are taken over time. The objective of this sort of research is to determine if the treatment had any effect on the behavior of the subject(s). This design is frequently used in special education. Its applicability for action researchers is significant as well.

Standard deviation   A descriptive statistic that measures the variability of a group of scores. The higher the value of the standard deviation, the wider the spread of scores.

Standardized test   *See* Norm-referenced test.

Stanine   A converted score that is frequently reported in a school profile. Stanines convert individual scores into nine bands of scores; hence, the term is derived from *standard nine*. A student scoring in the first stanine scores the lowest, whereas a band of nine represents the highest score. The average, or mean, score is found in the fifth band. Although test results are usually reported in more easily understood ways (e.g., grade equivalents or percentiles), a basic understanding of stanines may come in handy to show the relative position within which all scores are distributed.

Static-group comparison design   A research design used in quasi-experimental research involving two groups in which only one group, the experimental group, receives a treatment. Although a posttest is administered to both groups (experimental and control), no pretest is administered. Individuals are not randomly assigned to groups.

Statistical significance   A term used in quantitative research to refer to results when the probability of their occurrence by chance is less than .05 in educational research in general and less than .10 in action research projects. Significant findings do *not* mean that your study is necessarily important or meaningful. Significant findings mean that the probability that your research findings would have occurred by chance, without the treatment, is low.

Let's say you were conducting a study by comparing two groups (e.g., period 4 and period 7 classes) in their achievement levels in science. You set up a nonequivalent control group design, and after a period of 4 months you posttest both groups on science achievement. You employ a statistical technique (e.g., the t-test) to determine whether one group (class) scored significantly higher than the other group. Let's say the t-test analysis indicates the following finding: $p < .01$. This means that the probability (p) that the difference in achievement levels occurred by mere chance is less than 1% (less than one chance in a hundred), which is a statistically significant finding.

How do you know that this finding is statistically significant? Recall that in order to assert a statistically significant finding you must achieve a p (probability factor) of less than .05 in educational research in general and less than .10 in action research projects. Because $p < .01$, your findings are statistically significant. Many people think that arriving at a statistically significant finding is, by itself, sufficient to incorporate a particular practice or program. This may not be necessarily true.

Subject (*Ss*)   An individual who has been selected or has volunteered to participate in a study. Sometimes researchers like to refer to people who participate in their study as *participants* because *subjects* seems too manipulative. In survey research, the subject is often called the *respondent*.

Survey   A general term for any instrument used to assess attitudes or views of respondents. Questionnaires, interviews, and focus groups are types of surveys. Surveys are perhaps the most common methods of data collection used in action research.

T-test   A popular and common statistical technique that determines the degree of significance between the means of two groups. The purpose of a t-test is to determine if the difference between two means is statistically significant.

Teacher-made test   A testing or assessment procedure created by a classroom teacher for the purpose of measuring growth in a particular content area. Three types of teacher-made tests are common: norm-referenced, criterion-referenced, and performance-based. In action research projects, teacher-made tests are quite commonly used.

Test   Any form of measurement that yields clear, consistent, meaningful data about a person's knowledge, aptitudes, intelligence, or other traits. Standardized and norm-referenced tests are examples.

Theory   A statement of interrelated sets of assumptions and propositions that help us to explain our world. Theories are like mental road maps, guiding the way we perceive the world. Action research contributes very little, if anything, to theory development. Nevertheless, one may conduct an action research project to assess a particular theory.

Treatment (synonymous with *intervention*)   Any specific instructional practice, program, or procedure that is implemented by a researcher in order to investigate its effect on the behavior or achievement of an individual or a group. Examples of treatments are behavioral management strategies, various textbook series, different methods of teaching, and use of instructional technology. As an educational leader, you'll need to evaluate such treatments in order to decide whether they should be retained, modified, or discarded.

Triangulation   Multiple research approaches, data sources, data collection procedures, and analytic procedures. Triangulation strengthens the credibility of data collection and analysis as well as findings. Action researchers should appreciate that the inclusion of both qualitative and quantitative methods is desirable. Triangulation can also be used within each approach to research, especially in qualitative studies. Qualitative researchers emphasize the importance of triangulating on the basis of data sources, data collection methods, researcher perspectives, and theoretical frameworks. To the extent to which you can triangulate, you will make more effective decisions.

Unobtrusive measure   A data collection method that is obtained without directly involving subjects or participants. An educational leader who determines, for example, staff morale by examining the quantity and pattern of staff attendance by collecting written reports and documents utilizes an unobtrusive measure in the sense that data can be obtained without conferring with the staff directly.

Validity The extent to which a test, survey, or some other instrument measures what it is intended to measure. At the outset of *Action Research* you were asked to complete a pretest (Appendix A) on your knowledge of some aspects of research. If the pretest was composed of mathematical questions only, then the test would not be valid, as it measured not your knowledge of research but only your ability to compute and solve mathematical problems. There are four general types of validity: *concurrent, construct, content,* and *predictive.* For action research projects you will not need to use any of these four types of validity. The only exception might be use of content validity, to some extent. In the previous example, a content analysis of the curriculum or knowledge base of action research would be undertaken, and then the test items on the pretest would be compared to the content base to ascertain that the questions on the pretest reflect the content.

Have you ever taken a test in which you said, "We never covered this stuff?!" If you were to administer, for example, a test to a group of 12th graders based on chapter 12 in their social studies textbook, you would check for content validity after writing the test to see if the answers to each question can be found in the chapter. If each question is, in fact, derived from the content of chapter 12, then your test may be said to have content validity. Determining content validity for standardized tests involves more sophisticated procedures.

Two other types of validity, though not thought of highly by many experts in the field, are useful for action research purposes: consensual and face validity. *Consensual validity* would be ascertained by asking people who will not be administered the test or survey (e.g., a colleague or a student in another class) whether the questions selected for inclusion are appropriate, given the purpose of the assessment. *Face validity* would be ascertained by asking participants or subjects to share their views about how valid a test or survey appears. Have you ever taken an examination that was fair because it accurately reflected the content of the course? Such an exam might have high face validity. The converse could, of course, also be true, if the content of the course didn't match the questions on the exam.

Know that, like reliability, the coefficient of validity is determined. The validity coefficient is likewise expressed in hundredths, and the closer the coefficient comes to +1.00, the more valid the instrument is considered.

Variable Any factor that has two or more values or distinguishably different properties or characteristics. Two examples of variables are sex, or gender (two distinct properties are maleness and femaleness) and mathematics achievement (multiple properties are represented by different student test scores). There are two types of variables: dependent and independent.

A dependent variable is one that represents a desired instructional outcome, such as student achievement or high school attendance.

An independent variable is one whose relationship to the dependent variable is being investigated, In a study that attempts to correlate gender and science achievement, gender is the independent variable and reading achievement is the desired outcome or dependent variable.

Some independent variables cannot be manipulated by the researcher to determine their effect on a particular dependent variable. For example, if you were to investigate the years of experience of a group of teachers on morale levels, the independent variable in this case (the number of years of experience) cannot be manipulated because you have no control over a teacher's experience. In other words, years of experience is a characteristic of a particular teacher that you, as researcher, cannot manipulate or control. You can't say, for instance, "For purposes of my study subject 1 (S1) will be assigned 10 years of experience." In this case, the independent variable is non-manipulable.

Examples of manipulable variables are: type of textbook series, exposure to computer-assisted instruction, or a particular method of teaching (e.g., cooperative learning).

Annotated
References

The literature on action research pertaining to teachers as researchers is extensive. For an annotated list of selected sources related to teachers, consult *Teaching Education,* Volume 8, Number 1, Spring/Summer 1996.

   The selected titles below represent a small portion of the literature in the field of action research. No attempt has been made to annotate every reference on the topic. I've selected some of the excellent works that should be part of your reference library.

Arhar, J. M., & Holly, M. L. (2000). *Action research for teachers: Traveling the yellow brick road.* Englewood Cliffs, NJ: Prentice-Hall.

   A practical guide to conducting action research, this easy-to-use book offers step-by-step guidance through the action research cycle. The book effectively combines theoretical background and plenty of real-life examples. Although this work is geared to teachers, it is a useful resource for all classroom educators.

Corey, S. M. (1953). *Action research to improve school practices.* New York: Teachers College Press.

   The classic work in the field, this book represents the first systematic attempt to apply action research in education. Corey, a professor at Teachers College, Columbia University, encourages teachers and supervisors to use action research to improve their own practice. Corey, a man ahead of his time, believed that fundamental change could not occur without the direct involvement of teachers *and* supervisors. Not a "how-to" volume, Corey's work lays the groundwork for systematic inquiry into practical problems in schools. His advocacy for supervisors to play an active role in action research makes this book unique.

Elliott, J. (1991). *Action research for educational change.* Bristol, PA: Open University Press.

   Providing case study analyses to demonstrate the impact that action research can have on educational reform, this volume presents various collaborative research projects. Case studies focus on a variety of issues, such as curriculum reform for average and below-average students, the Ford Teachers Project, and Teacher Student Interaction and Quality of Learning Project. Elliott, a well-known authority in the field of action research, provides concrete examples of direct applications of action research. Emphasizing the role of teachers, this well-organized and clearly written book indicates the benefits that action research has on teaching and learning. Elliott's book has also been published in Spanish, under the title *El cambio educativo, desde fa investigacionaccion,* 1993.

Fink, A., & Kosecoff, J. (1998). *How to conduct surveys: A step-by-step guide.* Newbury Park, CA: Sage.

   This book is one of the most useful of the texts that discuss survey construction and design. Any action researcher will benefit from this well-organized, easy-to-read guide to survey construction. Various types of surveys are discussed, and many practical examples are provided.

Glickman, C. D. (1995). *Action research: Inquiry, reflection, and decision-making.* [Video]. Alexandria, VA: ASCD.

   This video series describes the basic steps of action research. Three case studies are presented, showing how action research has guided an elementary school, a junior high school, and an entire school district. Interviews with Carl Glickman and Emily Calhoun explain why action research ensures sound decision making: decisions are developed from concrete data rather than from snap judgments. Teachers and administrators also relate how action research helps them to pinpoint problems and develop solutions that work. The video includes a five-step approach to action research: selecting a focus, collecting data, organizing data, analyzing and interpreting data, and taking action.

Herman, J. L., & Winters, L. (1992). *Tracking your school's success; A guide to sensible evaluation.* Newbury Park, CA: Corwin Press.

A highly readable and informative guide to evaluation, this book enumerates practical evaluation strategies to match your school's needs, priorities, and goals to action research projects. The steps included in this text were used as a basis for discussing evaluation research in this book. Highly recommended!

McLean, J. E. (1995). *Improving education through action research: A guide for administrators and teachers.* Thousand Oaks, CA: Corwin Press.

One of the few works (if not the only one) written on action research for administrators, this brief handbook provides a cogent rationale for using action research to enhance school improvement. One of the book's contributions is to illustrate how computer applications can easily be used by practitioners to conduct action research.

McNiff, J. (1995). *Action research: Principles and practice.* London: Routledge.

Advocating that educational research be taken out of the confines of academia, McNiff makes an impassioned plea for action research by practitioners. She provides a cogent rationale and reviews some of the major philosophical tenets of action research. She also provides some practical strategies for starting an action research project and gives interesting case studies of attempts at applying action research. This work is an important contribution to the literature in the field and serves as an introduction to action research.

Mills, G.E. (2000). *Action research: A guide for the teacher researcher.* Upper Saddle River, NJ: Merrill.

An outstanding step-by-step guide (with companion Web site) for beginning and experienced action researchers. Includes a chapter on online action research resources, with all key Web addresses and screen captures. Provides a comprehensive coverage of qualitative data collection techniques applied to teacher research. Includes chapter vignettes and a chapter-length case study to illustrate the action research process.

Sagor, R. (1992). *How to conduct collaborative action research.* Alexandria, VA: Association for Supervision and Curriculum Development.

A brief book that describes how teachers can use collaborative action research to improve teaching. After defining and providing a rationale for collaborative action research, this booklet presents a practical five-step approach and includes a particularly useful chapter on data collection.

Sanders, J. R. (2000). *Evaluating school programs: An educators guide.* Newbury Park, CA: Corwin Press.

This work is a practical general guide to help you plan and conduct evaluations of any school program. The five-step approach adopted by the author is easy to follow and one that I have personally used to evaluate many programs. Highly recommended!

Seidman, I. E. (1998). *Interviewing as qualitative research: A guide for researchers in education and the social sciences.* New York: Teachers College Press.

In my estimation, this book is the most useful guide to in-depth interviewing as a research approach. This work demonstrates that interviewing, as a qualitative approach, is applicable to a wide variety of educational situations. Practical methods for conducting interview research are discussed, and guidelines are provided for easy adoption. The steps to follow when conducting an interview are outlined clearly.

Stringer, E. T. (1999). *Action research: A handbook for practitioners.* Thousand Oaks, CA: Sage.

Introducing the teacher practitioner to some basics of research, this volume describes a community-based action research model. Framing a "look, think, act" rationale or methodology for action research, this well-organized book provides a convincing rationale for the legitimacy of action research.

Other
Resources

Resources on the Web

1. Simple and complex directories:

       http://www.yahoo.com
       http://www.infoseek.com
       http://www.altavista.com
       http://www.webcrawler.com
       http://www.lycos.com
       http://www.excite.com
       http://www.dogpile.com, and my favorite
       http://www.google.com

2. Educational Resources Information Center
   (800) LET-ERIC (800-538-3742)
   e-mail address: askeric@ericir.syr.edu

   You can simply e-mail your request for a series of references on a specific topic, and within 48 hours one of the
   ERIC researchers will e-mail you back the citations (not

the actual articles) you requested. For instance, if I wanted to know what articles ERIC has for Howard Gardner, I would simply write to the address above and request this information.

Web: http://www.edrs.com

This Web address links you with ERIC directly. Browse ERIC as you would have had you gone to your local college or university library and used the ERIC CD-ROM.

Web: http://www.ericsp.org

This Web address links you with the ERIC Clearinghouse on Teaching and Teacher Education.

Web: http://ericir.syr.edu/

This Web address links you with the ERIC Clearinghouse on Assessment and Evaluation and provides you with sample attitude scales and much more.

3. Surf the Internet (or Web) to locate other valuable educational resources. Here are some of the many resources I have personally found useful:

> http://www.education-world.com
> http://www.ed.gov
> http://www.ascd.org/
> http://aera.net/
> http://www.eval.org/
> http://www.aspensys.com/eric
> http://www.nctm.org
> http://www.ncss.org
> http://www.nsta.org
> http://beta.open.k12.or.us/arowhelp

4. A wonderful reference list for Web resources can be found in the fine resource titled *The Best Web Sites for Teachers* by Sharp, Levine and Sharp, 2002, published by the International Society for Technology in Education, Eugene, Oregon.

5. Education Literature Review
   (877) 953-5400
   www.edlitrev.com

   Demands made on supervisors and teachers are tremendous. Consequently, many educational leaders who would love to "keep up with the educational literature" simply can't find the time. The *Education Literature Review* summarizes articles in 10 selected journals, including *Educational Leadership, Phi Delta Kappan, Harvard Educational Review, American School Board Journal Principal,* and *NASSP Bulletin.* This resource will keep you abreast of the latest research in the field.

About the Author

Jeffrey Glanz serves as dean of Graduate Studies and Education at Wagner College in Staten Island, New York. He holds faculty status as a professor in the Department of Education. Dr. Glanz was executive assistant to the president at Kean University and was named Graduate Teacher of the Year in 1999 by the Student Graduate Association. He was also the recipient of the Presidential Award for Outstanding Scholarship in the same year. Dr. Glanz has authored nine previous books on various educational topics, including three books with Christopher-Gordon Publishers: *Educational Supervision: Perspectives, Issues, and Controversies* (co-edited), *Relax for Success: An Educator's Guide for Stress* *Management,* and, of course, the first edition of *Action Research: An Educational Leader's Guide to School Improvement.*

Index